W9-BKA-128

Mean Markets and Lizard Brains

HOW TO PROFIT FROM THE NEW SCIENCE OF IRRATIONALITY

Terry Burnham

WILEY

John Wiley & Sons, Inc.

Published by John Wiley & Sons, Inc., Hoboken, New Jersey
Published simultaneously in Canada

For general information about our other products and services, please contact our Customer Care Department within the United States at 800-762-2974, outside the United States at 317-572-3993 or fax 317-572-4002.

Wiley also publishes its books in a variety of electronic formats. Some content that appears in print may not be available in electronic books. For more information about Wiley products, visit our web site at www.wiley.com.

ISBN 0-471-60245-0

Printed in the United States of America

10 9 8 7 6 5 4 3 2 1

Contents

Preface   *vii*

Acknowledgments   *ix*

Chapter One *Introduction:* Mean Markets and Lizard Brains   1

Part One: The New Science of Irrationality   9

Chapter Two *Crazy People:* Lizard Brains and the New Science
        of Irrationality   11
                cognitive confusion • split-brains • superstitious pigeons •
                neuroeconomics • winning

Chapter Three *Crazy World:* Mean Markets and the New Science
        of Irrationality   35
                stampedes • invisible hands • efficient markets •
                financial blind spots • opportunity

Part Two: The Old Art of Macroeconomics   63

Chapter Four *U.S. Economic Snapshot:* America the Talented Debtor   65
                profligacy & productivity • Keynes' grandchildren •
                Darwin's elephants • prosperity

Chapter Five *Inflation:* Rising Prices and Shrinking Dollars   85
         kidney barter • rice dollars • seashell arbitrage • jubilee •
         Yogi Berra's diet • protection

Chapter Six *Deficits and Dollars:* Uncle Sam the International Beggar   115
         loan sharks • a golden brain squandered • limp loonies
         and plummeting pesos • escape

**Part Three: Applying Science and Art to Bonds, Stocks,
         and Real Estate   137**

Chapter Seven *Bonds:* Are They Only for Wimps?   139
         Reagan bonds • the mother of all deficits • social security
         lockbox • squirrel savings • profit

Chapter Eight *Stocks:* For the Long Run or for Losers?   159
         time travel • Michael Jordan • stock speed limits •
         tears and a journey • stock picks

Chapter Nine *Real Estate:* Live in Your Home; Make Your Money
         at Work   193
         Tiger Woods • Godzilla • Groucho Marx • risky ARMs •
         housing bubble • advice

Part Four: Profiting from the New Science of Irrationality   227

Chapter Ten *Timeless Advice:* How to Shackle the Lizard Brain   229
         Isiah Thomas • humans in zoos • lizard logic • mast-strapping •
         beware the red zone • 8 timeless tips

Chapter Eleven *Timely Advice:* Investing in the Meanest of Markets   265
         a golden generation • lizard brain kryptonite • B.F. Skinner •
         returns without risk

Notes   *289*

Index   *299*

Preface

Mean Markets and Lizard Brains applies a new science of irrationality to personal finance. Conventional financial advice is based on the assumption that both people and markets are rational. New research is uncovering the reasons that real people and actual markets are often crazy. This new work leads to novel insights into how and where to invest.

This book combines two of my passions: financial markets and the scientific study of human nature. I had my first taste of speculation back in the early 1980s. Because of asbestos litigation, the price of Johns Manville Corporation's stock approached zero. I thought the low price was irrational so I bought some shares. The stock went up over 20% the day after I bought it; I sold my shares and pocketed several weeks' worth of my salary.

This trade had two effects. First, I acquired a taste for financial markets. I have been actively involved for more than 20 years, and have broadened my scope beyond buying stocks to include options, bonds, gold, currencies, and more. Second, I was puzzled by a market that produced opportunities like Manville almost for free (Warren Buffett also recognized the value and eventually bought the firm).[1]

Years later, while I was getting my Ph.D. in the Harvard economics department, I found an intellectual home in the study of human nature. For more than a decade now, first as a graduate student and then as a

Harvard economics professor, I have studied one central question: Why do people have problems in so many areas, ranging from food to sex to money? My search for an answer has taken interesting turns, including studying negotiators' testosterone levels and living at a research station in Africa to learn from the behavior of wild chimpanzees.

An important source of our problems, I have become convinced, is that we are built to solve the problems faced by our ancestors. Because modern industrialized society differs systematically from the world of our ancestors, we tend to get into trouble. In my first book, *Mean Genes,* Jay Phelan and I investigate how the human brain—shaped in the Pleistocene—contributes to obesity, drug addiction, and poverty.

Mean Markets and Lizard Brains is a much more detailed look at one of the topics from *Mean Genes.* What mistakes do people tend to make in financial markets, and what can investors do to improve performance? Both book titles start with "mean" because each addresses areas of our lives where our instincts push us towards failure. It is a central feature of industrialized life that our passions conflict with our goals. Because of this, the world can sometimes seem mean.

Markets can be mean to investors who buy when excited and sell when afraid. Because we are built for a very different world, our instincts tend to be out of sync with financial opportunity. Consequently, making money requires understanding and shackling that part of our brain that pushes us to make costly investing decisions. This "lizard brain," which we all have lurking underneath the more cognitive parts of our brains, is great for finding food and shelter, but terrible at navigating markets.

Mean Markets and Lizard Brains thus provides an answer to my question from two decades ago. Markets are irrational because of quirks in human nature. Those who understand this and harness the lizard brain can convert mean markets into money.

Acknowledgments

Jay Phelan and I have spent 10 years discussing and writing about the mismatch between Pleistocene brains and modern industrial societies. As is the case in such collaborations, most ideas are joint products. Beyond shared credit for the general concepts underlying *Mean Markets and Lizard Brains,* Jay deserves specific credit for aspects ranging from structure to style that are drawn from our coauthored book, *Mean Genes.*

Many friends donated time reading drafts and providing crucial feedback. Doug Bodenstab has read and critiqued every chapter (some of them several times). Chris Corcoran has similarly been involved at each stage, bringing his physicist's intuition to the book's underlying mathematics. Jon Goldberg applied his common sense, depth of trading experience, and apt analogies from the world of golf. Jay Phelan asked the tough questions and often supplied the answers.

In addition, others who read part of the book and made substantial contributions include: David Bear, Jeff Bodenstab, Peter Borish, Jane Burnham, Thomas and Marie Burnham, Judith Chapman, Adam Checchi, David Epstein, Brent Flewelling, Sue Flewelling, Lisa Gosselaar, Paul Greenberg, Brian Hare, Justin Holtzman, Matthew McIntyre, Michael Schwartz, Joel Smith, Martin Stapleton, Scott Stephens, and Sadek Wahba. Danielle Lake did a fantastic job of copyediting the manuscript.

Pamela Van Giessen, my editor at Wiley, deserves fundamental credit. From conception through writing and publication, Pamela has provided the support and the vision to create a book that is both deeply practical and academically rigorous. And thank you to Peter Borish for introducing me to Pamela.

Throughout every stage of the book's development, my wife, Barbara Li Smith, has been a steadfast supporter and constantly pushed me to make the work fun. Her thoughtful advice and unselfish help made the book possible. And finally, our beautiful new baby, Charlotte Valentine, has provided daily inspiration.

Thank you all.
Terry

chapter one

INTRODUCTION
Mean Markets and Lizard Brains

Where Should We Invest Our Money?

"Where should I invest my money?" So asked Adam, a former Harvard Business School student of mine. Soon after getting his MBA, Adam was working as an investment banker. His detailed knowledge of debt-laden companies had made him a bit gloomy about the economic situation. After hearing Adam's views, I asked where he had invested his money. Given his dour outlook, I expressed surprise when Adam said he had 60% of his wealth invested in stocks. In response to my shocked look, he asked for my advice.

Clearly Adam thought he was being conservative with only 60% of his wealth in stocks. Hasn't it been proven—over hundreds of years—that stocks provide the greatest long-term return? Shouldn't a patient investor, particularly a young one, put almost everything in stocks?

Maybe. Maybe not. Conventional approaches to answering Adam's question are based on the old-school assumption that people are cool-headed decision makers and that financial markets are rational. Recently, a new school has arisen that embraces hot-blooded human emotions as a core feature of our world. The reality is that financial markets have always oscillated between manias and panics, but people have not been terrifically adept at identifying them in advance. The new "science of irrationality" provides a novel way to model the future and offers investors powerful tools for growing and protecting their wealth.

Moving beyond simply describing financial irrationality, we find an underlying logic for costly behavior in what I label the "lizard brain"— an ancient, often unconscious thought process that exerts a powerful influence on us. This lizard brain has helped us reproduce, find food, and flourish, but it tends not to work so well when dealing with financial markets. The result? Mean markets that wreak havoc with our finances.

We will use the new science of irrationality and an understanding of the lizard brain to evaluate bonds, stocks, and real estate. We will find that the current situation is almost a perfect storm designed to frustrate our financial plans, and this will lead to surprising answers to Adam's question. In addition to learning *where* to invest, we will produce novel suggestions on *how* to invest. Beyond simply making more money, a goal of *Mean Markets and Lizard Brains* is to increase confidence and reduce financial stress.

The Conventional Wisdom: Bonds Are for Wimps

Adam works for a famous Wall Street investment bank. If he were to look to Wall Street for guidance on where to invest, he would find some simple advice. Buy stocks. Figure 1.1 shows the consensus of the leading Wall Street investment firms.

Wall Street says to invest the bulk of our money into stocks. In addition, economists trumpet the high return on stocks. ("Bonds are for wimps" is a quotation of Harvard Professor Greg Mankiw, head of President Bush's Council of Economic Advisors.[1]) Those of us who live on Main Street have heard the "buy stocks" message loudly and clearly.

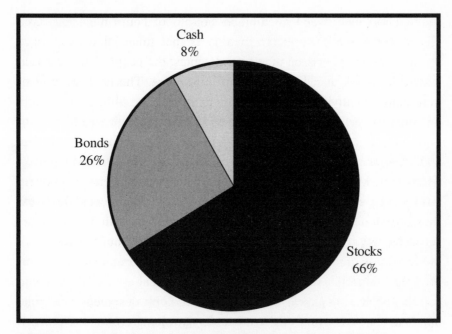

FIGURE 1.1   Bonds Are for Wimps (Wall Street's Investment Advice)
Source: Dow Jones Newswires, Wall Street financial strategists[2]

While only 5.7% of households owned mutual funds near the stock market bottom in 1980, the figure now sits near an all-time high of 50%.[3] Furthermore, the most recent Federal Reserve Survey of Consumer Finances reports that stocks represent 56% of all Americans' financial assets—a record high.[4]

So Adam's decision to invest most of his money into stocks reflects both the conventional wisdom and common practice. But should we continue to buy stocks and confidently expect high rates of return?

Wax On: The Science of Irrationality

In *The Karate Kid,* Daniel (played by Ralph Macchio) moves to California and earns the hatred of a pack of teenage bullies. In self-defense, he seeks to learn karate from Mr. Miyagi, the apartment custodian. Daniel is puzzled, however, when his training consists of performing household chores. For example, he spends many hours polishing Mr. Miyagi's cars using a particular "wax on, wax off" technique. In a frustrated confrontation with Mr. Miyagi, Daniel is surprised to find that the cleaning techniques are actually karate moves.

Similarly, we answer Adam's question by first addressing core principles and later applying them to bonds, stocks, and real estate. The conventional wisdom is based on a view that people are nearly perfect decision makers. Sane investors, the rational view suggests, would buy risky stocks only at prices low enough to promise a high return. Thus, the standard advice to buy stocks is based on the assumption that market prices are rational. If markets are crazy, however, then the "buy stocks for the long run" message might be wrong. To know where to invest, therefore, the first step is to investigate rationality.

Are people really cool-headed robots who calmly evaluate financial opportunities according to the maximizing rules of calculus? There is one place in the world where people do act this way; that place is economic theory. The standard assumption in economics is that people make such good decisions that our choices are labeled as "optimal." Conventional investment advice is based on this underlying belief that people and financial markets are rational.

In the real world, however, people are far from rational. Perhaps my own most poignant lesson came in a battle with a wedding photographer. After taking the pictures of our wedding, Juli the photographer would not give us our pictures. I appealed to Juli's morality and to her self-interest with a variety of sophisticated tactics to get our photos. I even offered to pay additional money. To all these rational tactics, she never responded. After Juli spent some time in jail, however, she relented and gave us our negatives. Was her behavior rational? No. She gained nothing from her obstinacy and suffered severe penalties. Is such irrational behavior common? Yes.

People are crazy. While we all know this, the investigation of the economic implications of irrationality began in earnest only in the late 1970s. Professor Daniel Kahneman, along with the deceased Professor

Amos Tversky, began the rigorous documentation of human decision-making errors. In 2002, Professor Kahneman shared the Nobel Prize in Economics for this new scientific approach to irrationality with my graduate school advisor, Professor Vernon Smith.

Investment advice has not kept up with cutting edge intellectual developments. While the science of irrationality has grown up, the conventional wisdom still provides investment advice based on outdated theories of sane people and rational markets.

Wax Off: Meet the Lizard Brain

Behavioral economists have proven that our financial decisions are often irrational. The obvious question is, why have we been built to be so bad at such important tasks? To find the underlying rationale for irrational behavior (which turns out not to be so crazy in some respects), we have to look beyond standard behavioral approaches to some groundbreaking work in other fields.

An important source of our troubles lies in the discord between our modern world and that of our ancestors. We are built to solve ancestral problems, and sometimes this gets us into trouble. Some of the most compelling examples of these insights come from medicine.

Consider that babies who breast-feed exclusively need to take vitamin D supplements or risk serious health consequences.[5] Nothing would seem to be more natural than to feed mother's milk to a baby. Why are we built to cause sickness in our children? The answer is that we (both as adults and as babies) manufacture vitamin D when we are hit by sunlight. People who spend a lot of time outdoors, particularly in places with strong sunlight, make plenty of vitamin D. The babies of our ancestors got enough outdoor sunlight to be healthy. Many babies (and their moms) today, however, stay indoors or out of direct sunlight to avoid skin cancer, so our natural-born system doesn't work. Thus, our babies get sick because we live differently from our ancestors.

A similar logic is found in the prevention of heart disease. Men, in particular, are told to take an aspirin a day to thin blood, reducing the risk of heart attacks.[6] Why don't we produce blood that has the correct viscosity? The answer is that "thick" blood heals wounds rapidly. Our ancestors had frequent wounds, and most died too young to worry about heart disease. Thus, our blood is too thick for us because it is built to protect us from the ravages of an ancient world where people were often wounded and died young.

So what does all this have to do with our financial decisions? Our brains, like our bodies, reflect the world of our ancestors. In particular, our lizard brains are pattern-seeking, backward-looking systems that allowed us to forage successfully for food, and repeat successful behaviors. This system helped our ancestors survive and reproduce, but financial markets punish such backward-looking decisions. Consequently, our lizard brains tend to make us buy at market tops and sell at market bottoms.

In *Pitch Black,* a sci-fi film featuring Vin Diesel, a group of intergalactic travelers crash on an ominous planet. They soon learn that the interior of the planet is filled with vicious creatures. The good news is that the creatures cannot arise in daylight, and because the planet has multiple suns, eclipses are many years apart. The bad news is that the next eclipse, with its consequent destruction, is coming in just a few hours.

Similarly, there is good news and bad news for the role of the lizard brain in our financial decisions. The good news is that the lizard brain's influence on our financial decisions is only disastrous in some particular and rare circumstances. The bad news is that we are living in one of those dangerous environments today. For the last several decades, we have enjoyed the benefits of several powerful, but unsustainable, financial trends. Our backward-looking lizard brain is most likely to impoverish us in precisely these sorts of environments. In a sense, we now face the meanest of financial markets, almost cruelly set up to frustrate and to cost us money.

Just as we can live longer by understanding the basis of our medical problems, we can make more money by understanding and taming the lizard brain.

How to Profit from the New Science of Irrationality

In *The Karate Kid,* our hero soon stops waxing cars and begins competing. Similarly, the focus of this book starts with irrationality, but then quickly applies the lessons to the most important issues facing investors—the health of the economy, budget deficits, productivity, savings, inflation, the trade deficit, bonds, mortgages, stocks, and real estate.

The first section summarizes the key findings of the science of irrationality. We review the evidence that even the smartest of people make systematic mistakes. These individual quirks create manias and panics, and markets that are far from rational.

The second section is a primer on the economy, inflation, and the value of the U.S. dollar. Will U.S. budget deficits hurt the economy? Can the productivity revolution allow us to be richer and lead better lives? How will the decline in the U.S. dollar affect investors? When will the dollar decline end? Is the Federal Reserve creating inflation? Why would anyone be worried by prices being too low?

In the third section, we apply our analysis to the most important investment decisions we face. Are interest rates going to rise substantially? Has the bull market in stocks returned, or is the early twenty-first century stock market rally a trap? Is there a housing bubble?

Our analysis culminates in the final section that provides specific investment advice. An understanding of the lizard brain provides a timeless blueprint for effective and low-stress investing. Furthermore, we reach a timely and unexpected answer to Adam's question on where to invest.

The lizard brain will be a leading character throughout our journey. Are there really $100 bills on the financial sidewalk? The answer is yes, but they are found in financial blind spots created by the lizard brain. The new science of irrationality shows us how to see into those blind spots so we can grab those $100 bills and improve our investment returns with less stress.

PART ONE

The New Science of Irrationality

The central question of *Mean Markets and Lizard Brains* is, "Where should I invest my money?" The conventional answer is that those who seek high returns must take high risk. For a patient investor with some tolerance for risk, conventional wisdom says to buy stocks.

This conventional wisdom makes sense, however, only if stock prices are not irrationally high. Those who believe in the efficient markets hypothesis claim that stock prices are always correct. The conventional wisdom is based on the assumption that markets are rational, thus stock prices cannot be too high. If markets are crazy, however, the best investments might be radically different from those suggested by the conventional wisdom.

Thus, in order to decide where to invest our money, we must first evaluate the idea that markets are rational. We do this in two parts. In Chapter 2, we ask whether people are rational, and in Chapter 3 we ask whether groups of individuals interacting in financial markets are rational. We will conclude people are not rational, and markets are often crazy.

In this section we meet the lizard brain—that part of our financial decision-making machinery that costs us money. We will find that we are built with a backward-looking, pattern-seeking brain that tends to make us want to buy when prices are irrationally high and sell when prices are irrationally low. We are built to be exactly out of sync with financial opportunity.

chapter two

CRAZY PEOPLE
Lizard Brains and the
New Science of Irrationality

Do Not Be Afraid to Meet the Lizard Brain

"'Boy, the food at this place is really terrible' . . . 'Yeah, I know, and such small portions.' Well, that's essentially how I feel about life. Full of loneliness and misery and suffering and unhappiness, and it's all over much too quickly." So says Woody Allen in the role of Alvy in the opening scene of *Annie Hall.*

Similarly, our rational skills for finance are simply terrible, filled with systematic errors and biases. As with Woody Allen's punch line about not getting enough bad food, we use our limited analytic skills far too rarely when we make financial decisions. As bad as we can be at making financial decisions with the more rational parts of our brains, we get in even more trouble when the lizard brain starts calling the shots.

In this book, I divide the human brain into two parts: the prefrontal cortex and the lizard brain. This is a dramatic simplification of an extremely complicated reality. Most, but not all, of what we think of as abstract cognition occurs in the human brain's prefrontal cortex. The term "lizard brain" includes many important human brain regions that have nothing to do with reptiles.[1]

Thus, "lizard brain" is shorthand for an important idea. It is used in the spirit advocated by Sir Peter Medewar, a scientific expert in the study of aging, in his famous article, "An Unsolved Problem of Biology":

> Being in some degree crippled by the handicap of trying to be intelligible, I am bound to make statements which, if not baldly wrong, are true only with qualifications which I shall have not time to give them. This disability is not to be avoided; one gets nowhere if every sentence is to be qualified and refined.[2]

Similarly the lizard brain is a term that I grew to use while conducting research with my Harvard Business School colleague Professor George Baker. I continue to find it productive even in discussions with experts in behavior and cognition. Because the reality is complicated, however, we must remember that "lizard brain" is verbal shorthand for the less cognitive, less abstract, mental forces that influence human behavior, most of which have nothing to do with lizards.

The lizard brain is great for finding food and shelter, but terrible at navigating financial markets. Many financial problems occur when we use the lizard brain to make monetary decisions. Instead of using the analytical part of our brain, we often default to older parts of our brain that helped our human ancestors survive for tens of thousands of years before financial markets were created. The lizard brain is not stupid, but when confronted with problems never experienced by our ancestors it can make us look crazy and cost us money.

Before we investigate how the lizard brain leads us astray in financial matters, we must first deal with another human universal: Criticism is unpleasant. Being told that we are bad at something is, for most people, about as enjoyable as a mild electric shock. As a professor, I see this with my MBA students on a daily basis. At the Harvard Business School we follow the Socratic method and an integral part of that technique is getting students to reveal their own logical errors. This approach is an effective way to teach, but one that can be painful for the student as they learn the limits of their knowledge.

As we embark on learning about the science of irrationality, the unpleasant message is that all humans are built to make certain sorts of mistakes. It's all fun and games until the irrationality comes home to roost in our own brains. Then rather than learn, our instincts direct us to close the eyes, cover the ears, and deny the truth that we, too, are irrational. In all the oral stories of Homer, the only known reference to writing comes in the form of a secret message. It is in the *Iliad,* when Queen Antea falls in love with handsome Bellerophon who spurns her love. Enraged, Queen Antea convinces her husband, King Proteus, to kill Bellerophon (Antea does not reveal her secret and adulterous love).

Proteus wants to kill Bellerophon, but shies away from doing the dirty work himself. Instead he has Bellerophon travel to another kingdom, bearing a secret message for the ruler of the neighboring land. The content of the secret note is "kill the messenger." So, one of the first mentions of writing reveals a human tendency to kill the messenger.

The reward, however, for not killing the messenger and critiquing one's own behavior can be large. After the 1997 Masters golf championship, Tiger Woods reevaluated his game. In the Masters, he had dominated the field and won by a record 12 strokes. Furthermore, in less than one year on the professional tour, Tiger won four events, earned over a million dollars, and became a worldwide celebrity.

After this initial round of fame and success, what was Tiger's view of his game? He decided that he needed to fundamentally change his swing. In an interview with *Time* magazine (August 14, 2000), looking back on the decision, he told writer Dan Goodgame:

I knew I wasn't in the greatest positions in my swing at the [1997] Masters. But my timing was great, so I got away with it. And I made almost every putt. You can have a wonderful week like that even when your swing isn't sound. But can you still contend in tournaments with that swing when your timing isn't as good? Will it hold up over a long period of time? The answer to those questions, with the swing I had, was no. And I wanted to change that.

Tiger went back to the drawing board. He revamped his swing, suffered through some disappointments, but ultimately emerged as the dominant player in the game. At one point, Woods' lead over the second-ranked player was larger than the gap between No. 2 and No. 100.[3] He went from being a great player to perhaps the greatest player of all time. The lesson is clear: Winning requires critical self-examination. If Tiger's game needed improvement and benefited from some objective review, the rest of us surely can profit from honing our investment skills.

The Science of Individual Irrationality

The debate about irrationality has two components. First, do individuals make good decisions? Second, are market prices correct? While there is still a debate about the efficiency of market prices (we'll cover this topic in the next chapter), the first question has been answered. Over the last 30 years, a significant body of research has clearly illustrated our human shortcomings.

In the late 1970s, Professors Daniel Kahneman and Amos Tversky began the rigorous documentation of human decision-making problems. One of Kahneman and Tversky's famous experiments concerns the hypothetical woman named Linda. Here's what they asked in the experiment:[4]

Linda is 31 years old, single, outspoken, and very bright. She majored in philosophy. As a student she was deeply concerned with issues of discrimination and social justice, and also participated in antinuclear demonstrations.

Which of these two alternatives is more probable?
1. Linda is a bank teller.
2. Linda is a bank teller and is active in the feminist movement.

Take a moment to answer the question (we'll get to the correct answer shortly). First, know that most people provide the wrong answer, and there is an intellectual debate over how to interpret the errors. Old-school economists have said that the errors were caused by poor experimental design. Their first response was to deny the evidence that humans make the mistakes shown by behavioral economists.

Behavioral economists refined their techniques and provided proof that people make mistakes in many important areas, going far beyond the Linda problem. Mainstream economists no longer refute this evidence, but still insist that models of robotic, cool-headed decision making are appropriate. In contrast, behavioral economists believe that conventional theories about rational behavior need to be fundamentally revised.

Back to Linda. What was your answer? The correct answer is: Linda is a bank teller. Of all the bank tellers in the world, only some of them are active in the feminist movement. This is true for any two attributes. Consider 100 college athletes. How many of them are women? How many are women and over 6 feet tall? Without knowing anything about the group of 100, the number of tall women cannot exceed the number of women. Similarly, there have to be more bank tellers than there are bank tellers who are also feminists.

People who answer number two in the Linda-the-bank-teller problem suffer from what Kahneman and Tversky label the "conjunction fallacy": The conjoined probability of two statements must be lower than for either of the individual statements. Of the people in Kahneman and Tversky's experiments, 85% gave the wrong answer. Why do we do so poorly on such simple tests?

Rocket Scientists Who Can't Figure

Part of the cause of our individual irrationality is that we aren't very good at doing calculations.

In one of my Harvard Business School classes we investigate the causes behind corporate waste. We examine situations in which executives use corporate funds to pay for individual perks. One of the most famous and well documented of these is RJR Nabisco in the early 1980s. As chronicled in *Barbarians at the Gate,* the CEO of that time, Mr. Ross Johnson, used corporate money to host lavish parties, hang out with celebrities, and build an "air force" of expensive private jets.[5]

One cause of these excesses was the fact that neither Mr. Johnson, nor his board of directors, had much stake in the company stock. In fact, Mr. Johnson owned 0.05% of the company stock, and this represented a small part of his total wealth. At a key point in my class, I ask my students to calculate Mr. Johnson's share of the $21 million purchase price of one jet in the RJR air force. So, what is 0.05% of $21 million?

In one such session I picked a student—who had not volunteered—to provide the figure. He reached over for his calculator. I said, "Excuse me, but don't you have two degrees from MIT?" He said yes. "And aren't those degrees in course six (electrical engineering and computer science), one of the toughest and most mathematical areas of MIT?" "Yes," he answered. "And you still need a calculator for this simple calculation?" The student said that yes he did need a calculator.

Most people, even those with analytical abilities sufficient to excel at MIT, are not good at even basic calculations. The calculator can readily provide the figure for Ross Johnson's $10,500 (0.05% of $21 million) contribution to RJR's jet fleet. For other problems that our brains do not solve well, however, the solution is not so simple. Consider the following two problems taken from the book *Mean Genes,* which I coauthored with my friend, Professor Jay Phelan of UCLA.[6]

Puzzle 1. Chinese families place a high value on sons, yet the Chinese government exerts extreme pressure to limit family size. Let's assume that the chance of having a girl is exactly 50%, but every couple stops having babies once they have a son. So some families have one son, some have an older daughter and a son, some two older daughters and a son, and so on. In this scenario, what percentage of Chinese babies will be female?

Puzzle 2. Imagine that you are a doctor and one of your patients asks to take an HIV test. You assure her that the test is unnecessary as only one woman out of a thousand with her age and sexual history is infected. She insists, and sadly the test result indicates viral infection. If the HIV test is 95% accurate, what is the chance that your patient is actually sick?

As with Linda the bank teller, almost everyone gets these two problems wrong, and I could pose many other brainteasers that would also trip up most people.

In fact, when doctors and staff at the Harvard Medical School were asked the question about the HIV test, the most common answer they gave was a 95% chance that the patient was sick.[7] The correct answer is under 2%. Similarly, as long as the chance of having a baby girl in each pregnancy is exactly 50%, the population will also have 50% girls. This is true regardless of any rule on when to stop having babies. If you are interested in detailed analysis of these sorts of problems, I suggest that you read the risk chapter of *Mean Genes*. The key message for this book is that most people have trouble doing mathematical calculations.

Sound investing is based on mathematical analysis that is far more complicated than the problems we just discussed. At the core of every investment is a set of costs and benefits that need to be predicted over many years and in many scenarios. Coming up with the correct price for IBM stock or for our own house involves some serious math!

All of us who get even simple problems wrong are in good company. Not only do Harvard doctors make huge mistakes on these problems, so do the most sophisticated people in the world. One of my buddies, Chris, has both undergraduate and doctoral degrees from MIT in physics. His research on lasers is so secretive that he cannot reveal the sponsor of his work. In other words, he is a twenty-first century rocket scientist (for Val Kilmer fans, watch *Real Genius* to understand this brainy culture). In spite of all his ability and training, Chris admitted that he got the HIV problem wrong.

So we aren't built to do mathematical calculations, and relatively simple problems trip up MIT rocket scientists. The news gets even worse. The second big problem we face in investing is that we are systematically overconfident. We are bad at doing the calculations required to analyze investments, and simultaneously we are unaware of our shortcomings.

Our overconfidence comes in many flavors. When people are asked to rank themselves compared to others, the average rating is always above average. For example, far more than 50% of people rank themselves in the top half of driving ability, although that is a statistical impossibility.[8] When couples were asked to estimate their contribution to household work, the combined total routinely exceeded 100%.[9]

Myriad studies have documented this bias in our self-analysis, but my favorite remains an old study that asked men to rank themselves according to athletic ability. How many men do you think put themselves in the bottom half of male athletic ability? I suspect that you know the answer—not a single man who was surveyed reported that he had below-average athletic ability.[10]

Our overconfidence extends beyond self-analysis to our views of the world. Let's take a simple test: How many people were employed by Wal-Mart in January, 2004, around the world? Without looking up any information, write down a specific estimate. That may not seem fair, as different people know more or less about Wal-Mart.

To make the question fair, in addition to your guess, write down an upper-bound and a lower-bound number. Pick these bounds so that you are 90% sure that the actual number of employees is between your extreme high and your extreme low guesses.

If you answer 10 questions of this sort, nine of the answers should fall between your upper and lower bound. Do you have your three numbers for Wal-Mart? Your best estimate of the correct number, and lower- and upper-bound numbers?

We'll get to the correct answer in a moment. Under exactly these sorts of conditions, when people are asked 10 such questions, they usually get between two and four questions wrong.[11] This poor performance comes even after they have been told to give estimates wide enough to get only one of the 10 questions wrong.

People fail in this guessing game because they place too much confidence in their own estimates. Actually I ought to say that "we" fail, as I have been tested in this manner and also came up overconfident. Before I viewed my 10 questions, I resolved to make my lower and upper guesses extremely wide. Even with that preparation, only 8 of my 10 upper and lower bounds contained the correct answer. Back to Wal-Mart: In January 2004, the firm had 1.5 million employees.

The summary is that we come to the investing game with an analytic tool kit that lacks some of the key tools required for investment analysis. To add further insult to injury, our overconfidence makes us believe we have the required skills for investing.

Split-Brain Investing

Even though our analytic investing tool kit is not complete, it is our best hope to make good choices. An amazing fact is how rarely we use analysis to make our decisions.

During the early 1990s my biggest investment was in Microsoft. One evening I was standing outside my Harvard graduate dormitory chatting with my buddy Matt. I said, "Matt, I have a puzzle that I want to discuss with you. The puzzle is that Microsoft's business is doing great, yet the stock has not gone up in months." Matt allowed me to blather on about the fantastic business of selling software to the world, and then he asked, "What is the price to earnings ratio of Microsoft?"

Silence fell as I realized that I didn't have even a rough estimate of the P/E for Microsoft. I was ignorant of a key fact in spite of spending many hours a day reading financial papers. Furthermore, the P/E for any stock is readily available. With 1993 technology it would have taken me about 5 minutes to walk to my room and find the Microsoft P/E in the *Wall Street Journal*. With twenty-first century technology, such information is available instantaneously on the Internet.

Because I am a curious person, I didn't just hide my head after my ignorance had been exposed. I started asking people about their investments. One person whom I spoke with (who was a financial professional) owned Apple computer stock, and he extolled the virtues of the easy to use operating system. I then asked him, not about the stock price (which he felt was low), but about the number of shares of stock that existed. His answer was, "Geez, I don't know. It must be millions."

The number of shares is equally as important as the stock price in figuring out the total value of the company. It is impossible to evaluate a stock if one is ignorant of the number of shares. In other words, this finance professional was as ignorant about his Apple computer investment as I had been in my Microsoft selection.

If you try this quizzing game with your friends, I suspect you will find that most of them don't know much about at least some of their investments.

These sorts of financial blind spots are, at least in theory, easily corrected. The information is available, and I am in favor of everyone making sure that they have done a solid analysis before making decisions. The investing game is more subtle, however, than these stories suggest. The reason is that human behavior, including investment choices, is influenced to a surprisingly large extent by the lizard brain.

Many rational calculations are carried out in part of the brain's prefrontal cortex, which is located above the eyes. When we think about our investments in analytic terms, the prefrontal cortex is the boss. Compared to other animals, humans have extremely large prefrontal cortexes, which explains our superior reasoning ability.[12] While we are therefore uniquely able to make rational decisions, the lizard brain is also involved, and more involved than we suspect.

Psychiatry has long examined the different parts of the brain and how they interact. Sigmund Freud is most famously associated with his split-brain view of the world, consisting of ego, superego, and id. Freud's view, of course, built on a long tradition that dates back at least to Plato. Marvin Minsky is a modern scholar who postulates a brain filled with more than Freud's three competing forces. His opinion of many mental entities is exemplified in the title of his book *Society of Mind*.[13]

When I was in one of his courses at MIT, Professor Minsky told a funny story about his own brain. He said, "I was once scheduled to have breakfast with President Gerald Ford. Although I don't normally miss appointments, I slept through this breakfast. I've never been prouder of my subconscious."

Professor Minsky was making a number of important points. First, his prefrontal cortex was not in complete control of his behavior. Second, the subconscious often has goals that are different from, and perhaps in conflict with, the goals of the prefrontal cortex. Third, and finally, the subconscious is sometimes smarter than the prefrontal cortex.

My grandfather, who was known in our family by his nickname Mandy, gave me my first lessons in the power of my own subconscious. Mandy was a moderately famous psychiatrist who trained with Sigmund Freud himself and who maintained a friendship with Sigmund's daughter Anna for many years. As a part of his training, Mandy was an accomplished hypnotist.

I was never hypnotized, but Mandy used the power of suggestion whenever I had the hiccups. He would say to me—in a particular manner that I have never been able to replicate—if you hiccup three more times, I'll give you a quarter. In all the times that he did this to me, I was never able to produce more than one additional, pathetic hiccup. I've tried the trick on other people, and it does not work for me. Apparently, something in Mandy's training allowed him to speak to my subconscious and alter my behavior.

During the Korean War, the Chinese used knowledge of the subconscious in their treatment of U.S. prisoners of war. The Chinese wanted the U.S. soldiers to collaborate with them and used a variety of extremely successful tactics ranging from brutal to cunning. In the excellent book *Influence,* Robert Cialdini describes these tactics in detail, including an incremental approach that I believe manipulated the subconscious. Almost no one was willing to collaborate fully and immediately, but over time people were pushed to more and more extreme behaviors. In the end, one in three American P.O.W.'s committed some serious form of collaboration, and some went so far as to abuse other Americans.[14]

For Americans who completely resisted, the Chinese would sometimes make a simple request. They would say, "We know that you are unwilling to make statements against the United States, but would you mind rewriting this statement by one of your colleagues? You do not have to put your name to the anti-American statement, nor tell anyone else of your actions." The Chinese found that this simple step was an important one on the road to collaboration. After a prisoner had taken this act, he was much more likely to begin making his own statements against the United States.[15] It seems that simply getting the brain to say or write something begins to change attitudes. A similar logic underlies Dale Carnegie's suggestion to "get the other person saying, 'yes, yes' immediately."

None of these examples prove that the subconscious is important. Perhaps Professor Marvin Minksy was simply lazy on the morning of his scheduled breakfast with President Ford. Similarly, we can't know for sure why my grandfather was able to stop my hiccups or why saying or writing something changes our opinion. For proof of cause and effect we need to reenter the scientific world.

Studying with people who have some sort of impairment sometimes provides insight into the brain's normal function. In our quest to understand split-brain influences, we can learn from people who literally have split brains. In most people the left and right sides of the brain talk to each other via the corpus callosum, which physically connects the two halves. Some people are born without a corpus callosum, and thus the left and right sides of their brains do not know what is going on in the other side. Studies of people with these split brains reveal that conscious parts of our brain are not always in charge. These investigations are described at length in a number of excellent books, including Professor Michael Gazziniga's *The Mind's Past*.[16]

To investigate brain function, scientists presented signs with written instructions to these patients with split brains. For example, the sign might have said, "Please wave now." The patients would comply with these requests.

The interesting aspect of these split-brain studies came when the patients were asked to explain their actions. The scientists made sure that the signs were only seen in the left visual field where it would only register in the right half of the brain. They made sure that the left hemisphere of the brain, which controls speaking, did not see the requests. Because the brains of these patients were split, one half of the brain knew that the waving was a response to a request. The other half of the brain was completely ignorant of the cause, and this half had to explain the waving.

"Why are you waving?" Now the speaking part of the brain is faced with a dilemma. It has no information about the cause of the waving. Nevertheless it can sense that the body did just wave. Rather than confess to its ignorance, the language part of the brain makes up a story. For example, it might say, "I thought I saw someone I knew." Similarly, when half the brain is instructed to laugh, the ignorant half of the brain makes up an explanation like "I'm laughing because you are funny guys."

These studies and others lead to a startling conclusion. We are built to cover up the fact that the lizard brain influences us. When we think we have decided to take an action with our rational brain, we often have simply made up a story for the cause of action. As with Professor Minsky, parts of our brain outside the prefrontal cortex often set the course and leave the explaining to other parts.

Another interesting set of studies reveals the limits of our conscious brain. This phenomenon is known as the McGurk effect; if you search the web you should be able to experience it yourself. The McGurk effect demonstrates that before sensations become consciously aware, they have been altered by the nonconscious brain systems. Here's how it works.

When we listen to others speak, we use both our eyes and our ears. This is true even for those of us who have not been trained as lip-readers. In 1976, Harry McGurk and John MacDonald demonstrated this in the following manner. Professors McGurk and MacDonald tape-recorded a person producing the sound "Ba" and then combined that sound in a precise manner with a film of the same person saying "Ga."[17]

What do you perceive when you hear the sound "Ba" while watching lips making the shape of "Ga"? The answer is a fused sound best described as "Da." The most interesting aspect of the McGurk effect is that it never goes away. If you watch the video with your eyes closed, it is clear that the sound is "Ba"; opening your eyes produces "Da." Even after watching the tape for hundreds of times, and even knowing the true sound, the effect exists. We cannot use our rational brains to override the nonconscious preprocessing of the information.

The McGurk effect demonstrates that preconscious processing affects our fundamental perception of the world. Obviously, the prefrontal cortex cannot be in complete control if it has information that is altered and shaped by the other parts of the brain.

What have we learned so far? If we divide the brain into the prefrontal cortex and the lizard brain, we have seen that our prefrontal cortexes are often far from perfect. Next, we have seen that the lizard brain has a powerful influence on our behavior. We are built to make errors and fall into a variety of traps. Finally, we are built to create a cohesive story about our behavior, which makes it hard to understand the sources of our own actions.

The Lizard-Brain Goes to Wall Street

"Democracy's the worst form of government except for all the others," said Winston Churchill. Similarly, rational investing, using our less than perfect analytic system is the worst way to make money except for the alternative of using our lizard brains. As we will see, the lizard brain pushes us toward destructive acts.

The only thing worse than having a flawed prefrontal cortex exerting weak control is not having the prefrontal cortex in charge. The most famous example of this comes from the sad tale of Mr. Phineas Gage. The incident happened on September 13, 1848, and the original newspaper article in the *Free Soil Union* tells the story.

Phineas P. Gage, a foreman on the railroad in Cavendish was engaged in tamping for a blast, the powder exploded, carrying an iron instrument through his head an inch and a fourth in circumference, and three feet and eight inches in length.

Amazingly, Gage recovered quite nicely from having this enormous metal bar pass through his brain. The bar weighed more than 13 pounds and was actually an inch and a half in diameter (larger than the circumference reported in the paper). Within less than a year of the accident, Gage felt strong enough to return to his railroad job. Furthermore, to a large extent his mental processes seemed intact.

His colleagues, however, soon found that Gage was not himself. He suffered from a number of new negative personality traits, and his coworkers concluded that he was "no longer Gage." In particular, Gage lost the ability to execute plans that he made for the future. Even if his mental functions were unimpaired, the fact that his prefrontal cortex was no longer in charge prevented him from returning to his job as foreman and he subsequently left the employ of the railroad.[18]

The list of human foibles and weaknesses is a long one. We'll now look at the most important demonstrations of individual irrationality that apply to investing. Readers who are interested in the topic more broadly are encouraged to read Richard Thaler's *The Winner's Curse,* or Nobel Laureate Daniel Kahneman's *Heuristics and Biases* (edited by Kahneman as well as Thomas Gilovich and Dale Griffin).[19]

Irrationality #1: Pride Goeth before a Financial Loss

Paul Tudor Jones II is a legendary trader who has made hundreds of millions of dollars. Some of his exploits are covered in *Market Wizards.*[20] My college roommate from the University of Michigan, Peter Borish, worked with Paul. Through Peter, I met the legendary trader and was able to spend some time with him.

You might think that great traders don't suffer from the same biases as the rest of us. That may be true, but my impression is that they are more effective at limiting the damage caused by self-destructive aspects of human nature. When I visited him, Paul Tudor Jones had two handwritten signs over his desk. I interpreted them as messages designed to help his prefrontal cortex control his lizard brain.

One sign said, "Observe that the blade of grass that resists the lawn mower gets cut down, while the blade that bends remains uncut."

In many areas of our lives, the right course requires us to swallow our pride, take a loss, and move on. If we are unwilling to bend, we, like the blade of grass, will suffer.

One of the most-studied areas in behavioral economics documents how people's stubbornness costs them money. The setting is called the "ultimatum game," and it is a very simple negotiation between two people. The game asks them to divide up a lump sum of money through a process that is decidedly unfair. One of the pair, called the Proposer, gets to suggest how the money should be divided. The second, called the Responder, is not allowed to counterpropose, but must accept or reject the ultimatum offer.

I played the ultimatum game in a workshop run by my advisor, Nobel Prize winner Professor Vernon Smith. In the version that I played, I won the right to have the proposal power by scoring well on a trivia question. I now had $100 and the right to set a take-it-or-leave-it offer to another workshop participant. Furthermore, the decision was made in an anonymous manner. Neither my counterpart nor I knew, or would ever learn, each other's identity.

So I have $100. I can make an offer to my hidden counterpart that she or he can earn $10, $20, or any multiple of $10. If my offer is accepted, I keep my part of the $100 and my counterpart goes home with whatever cash I have offered. If my offer is rejected, we both earn $0. What to do? Let's assume for a moment that one's goal is to make as much money as possible. (That was my goal in the $100 ultimatum game.)

Here's how I analyzed the game. The responder is in a tough situation. She or he can take whatever I offer or get $0. So even if I offer a small amount, the responder earns more money by taking my offer than by rejecting the offer. Based on this, I decided to offer $10 to my counterpart, while retaining $90 for myself.

Vernon Smith ran the workshop by having us first play the games for real money, then before we learned of our outcomes, we would study previous research on the topic. As I was thinking of how I would spend my $90 (I was confident that my offer would be accepted), we began learning of study after study where responders said "screw you" to low offers like mine.

Professor Werner Guth and colleagues performed the first ultimatum study, published in 1982. For stakes of 10 German D-marks (this was before the introduction of the euro), the players exhibited pride or a sense of fairness. In fact, 20% of responders rejected the offers. Furthermore, the average proposal was much nicer than mine. While I had offered a mere 10% of the financial pie, the first ultimatum game proposers offered an average of 30%.[21]

Since the original study, the basic findings have been replicated in literally hundreds of studies. In study after study, all around the world, people reveal themselves to be proud. They are willing to lose money to retain their self-esteem.[22]

Initially, many people claimed that the results couldn't be true, and suggested the rejections were artificial because the monetary stakes were so low. Vernon Smith and his colleagues tested this supposition by having U.S. participants play the game for $100. They found no difference between play for $100 and play for $10.[23]

The ultimatum game has been taken around the world, in order to test the role of culture and to increase the stakes even higher. In countries such as Indonesia, researchers have organized ultimatum games played for several months' salary. Even with such high stakes, people are willing to walk away from unfair offers.[24] And, in spite of cultural variation, Professor Guth's original findings have also been found among nonindustrialized people who still hunt animals and gather plants for a living.[25]

Are ultimatum game rejections irrational? Not necessarily, but they definitely cost the participants money. Recall that these games are generally played just one time between anonymous counterparts who will never see each other again. A decision to reject an offer under such conditions means a loss of money that will never be recouped.

In many financial situations, we are faced with taking a small loss now or digging in our heels. The best course, especially if one wants to earn money, is to admit to small defeats and move on.

I interpret Paul Tudor Jones' sign as a note to his lizard brain from his prefrontal cortex. Here is my interpretation: "Dear Mr. Lizard Brain, I know that you are built to be stubborn and proud. Although you like to behave that way, I (Mr. Prefrontal Cortex) prefer money. Therefore I'm going to force you to take the profitable and not the proud path."

New ultimatum game research in the field of neuroeconomics shows us exactly what part of the brain operates to make people lose money. Professor Alan Sanfey and colleagues had people play the ultimatum game while their brains were scanned by an fMRI machine. People confronted with small offers ($1 or $2 out of $10) had greater brain activity in the bilateral anterior insula (not part of the prefrontal cortex), and subjects with higher activation levels in this area were more likely to reject these small offers.[26]

These ultimatum game results provide us with direct, scientific evidence that parts of the human brain outside the prefrontal cortex push people down a path that costs them money. As I write this, we don't have similar evidence for the brain location of most other economic biases, but we soon will. My prediction is that most "irrational" behavior will be found to be located outside the prefrontal cortex.

Finally, in my own research, I have found that men who reject small ultimatum game offers have much higher levels of testosterone than those who accept.[27] Often associated with muscle mass, testosterone plays a crucial role in the maintenance of dominance hierarchies. For example, I measured the testosterone levels of Howard Stern and others on his team. Howard, the socially dominant male in the group, had by far the highest testosterone. My friend Vinnie Favale, a big shot at CBS and a frequent guest on the show, had the second highest testosterone level.

Both Howard and Vinnie came in above younger men (Gary, KC, John) who are lower down in the show's hierarchy.

These results suggest that the lizard brain is not so crazy after all. In natural settings where people meet over and over again, it pays high-testosterone people to use conflict as a tactic to achieve their goals. Testosterone activates the lizard brain and makes some people more willing to be confrontational. In the unnatural setting of the laboratory, however, confrontation in the ultimatum game is costly, not beneficial. Like laboratories, financial markets are unnatural environments, and this explains why our instincts often cost us cash.

What do you think happened to my offer of $10 out of $100? After learning that many people prefer no money to a small percentage, I feared all was lost. Furthermore, our group results showed that pride flowed strongly among these graduate students. Three of my fellow students had faced $10 offers, and two had rejected them. One person had even rejected $30 out of $100! By good chance, however, my puny offer of $10 had been accepted.

Irrationality #2: Fear of Losses Causes Losses

Consider your willingness to participate in the following risky gamble. A coin toss decides if you win or lose. If you lose, you pay $5. If you win, the jackpot is yours. Professor Kahneman asked people to tell him the smallest jackpot that would make this gamble worth the potential loss of $5.

What is your answer? If your answer is more than $5, you hate losses. In fact, the average answer to this question is more than $10. Professor Kahneman interprets this to mean that people hate losses much more than we enjoy equal gains. We are not willing to lose $5 for the possibility of gaining just $5; we need a bigger jackpot to justify the risk.[28]

Professor Kahneman calls our answers to this question, and the results from related research, "loss aversion." Among all the findings that led to his Nobel Prize, loss aversion is one that Professor Kahneman rates as among the most significant. While hating to lose money might seem like a good thing, it can cause us to lose money.

The infamous trader Nick Leeson exemplifies the troubles that loss aversion can cause. Leeson was the "Rogue Trader" who brought about the collapse of Barings Bank. Interestingly, Leeson himself wrote a book detailing his mistakes that was made into a movie starring Ewan McGregor.[29] (I suppose I'd be tempted to commit some misdeeds if I could be sure to be portrayed by a dashing actor.)

Barings Bank was one of Britain's most prestigious financial institutions. It was destroyed when Leeson lost nearly 1 billion British pounds in a failed speculation. Although there are many reasons for the behavior, it is consistent with that caused by loss aversion.

At first glance, loss aversion sounds rational. Who likes losing money? No one. But consider what happens when you have lost a little bit of money. Now, the strong hatred of losses creates perverse incentives. That is to take big, stupid risks with the possibility of avoiding the label of loser.

Nick Leeson didn't lose his billion pounds in one go. In fact, he made a financial bet that lost a relatively small amount of money. Rather than accept his small loss, Leeson dramatically increased his bet. He continued to add to his losing position, hoping that he could get back to even. In the end, it was precisely his hatred of losses that led him to massive and destructive losses.

More than loss aversion caused the Nick Leeson blowup, but the general lesson is valid. Our hatred of losing money can push us toward taking bad risks, which in turn causes us to lose money.

Irrationality #3: Finding Patterns in Random Walks

One of B.F. Skinner's most famous experiments created what he labeled "superstitious" pigeons.[30] The experiment provided food to the pigeons at regular intervals. In many of Skinner's experiments, he rewarded pigeons for particular acts. By reinforcing certain behaviors, Skinner was able to produce pigeons that could play ping-pong, or even pilot bombs. In his superstition experiment, however, Professor Skinner gave the pigeons food without attempting to reinforce any particular behavior. In fact, he gave the pigeons food "at regular intervals *with no reference whatsoever to the bird's behavior.*"

The outcome of this experiment was superstitious pigeons. Even though the food was given out on a fixed schedule, the pigeons attempted to make sense of the outcomes. (Of course, they didn't really try to make sense of the outcomes; they have tiny brains and even tinier cortexes.) They did, however, change their behavior in ways that may seem quite rational. The pigeons tended to duplicate their own processes that preceded food. Skinner writes,

> One bird was conditioned to turn counter-clockwise about the cage, making two or three turns between reinforcements. Another repeatedly thrust its head into one of the upper corners of the cage. A third developed a "tossing" response, as if placing its head beneath an invisible bar and lifting it repeatedly. Two birds developed a pendulum motion of the head and body, in which the head was extended forward and swung from right to left with a sharp movement followed by a somewhat slower return.

These pigeons were classic "stimulus response" machines. They replicated actions that led to good outcomes and avoided actions that led to bad outcomes. The actual result was quite amazing. Each pigeon developed its own superstitious behavior. These superstitious pigeons are crazy, because their outcome was not affected by their actions. Nevertheless, the small-brained creatures sought a pattern in their experimentally mad world. Professor Skinner concludes,

> The experiment might be said to demonstrate a sort of superstition. The bird behaves as if there were a causal relation between its

behavior and the presentation of food, although such a relation is lacking.

Surely, we humans are much smarter than these pigeons? Yes, with our large prefrontal cortexes we are indeed much smarter. Outside the prefrontal cortex of our brains less rational notions thrive in the lizard brain. We humans retain brain structures that are little different from the homologous parts of brains in other animals, even some that we might label as quite primitive. The lizard brain is an active, albeit often silent, actor in human decision making.

Consider the following two sequences of heads (H) and tails (T):

Sequence A: H-T-H-T-H-T-T-T-H-H-T-T-T-T-T-T-H-T-H-H
Sequence B: T-H-H-T-T-H-T-H-H-T-H-H-T-H-H-T-T-H-T-T

I just created A and B by using two very different processes. I constructed one of the two sequences analytically. I produced the second sequence by flipping a quarter 20 times just now in my office. So one of the sequences was randomly generated by coin flips, while the other was constructed.

So which sequence, A or B, is a random sequence of coin flips? Take a guess before I provide some hints.

Let me tell you more details about the nonrandom process, and you'll be able to figure it out. In the constructed sequence, I never allowed more than two consecutive heads or tails. Similarly, in this constructed version, I did not allow a strictly alternating sequence of heads, tails, heads to persist for more than three times.

So sequence A, which contains a long string of consecutive tails is part of the random sequence. Sequence B is the nonrandom sequence. In experiments of this nature, people tend to pick the wrong sequence.[31]

The point is that our lizard brains seek a logical pattern to illogical behavior. Stock prices have a large random component, yet we are all built to search for patterns in that noise. Many investment strategies are no better (and perhaps no less entertaining) than the dance moves of our superstitious pigeons.

Irrational Nobel Prizes

The academic battle over irrationality at the individual level is largely complete. There is overwhelming evidence that we do crazy things that defy the laws of logic. The 2002 Nobel Prize in economics, awarded jointly to Professor Daniel Kahneman and Professor Vernon Smith, is symbolic of the victory of those who believe that irrationality is a fundamental part of human nature. In the next chapter, we will see how these quirks and biases play out in financial areas.

Before moving on, however, we must address what may be the mother of all irrationalities, that of self-control. In almost all models of rational behavior, people coolly trade off the future against the present. Should I, for example, pay more money up front on my mortgage and thereby buy myself a lower set of future payments? The single, correct answer is to weigh the cost against the benefit, using the appropriate formula.

While this rational view of decision making is appropriate, and I actually use it from time to time, many other choices are made by far more whimsical processes.

Consider the discussion that I have with my wife, Barbara, about four times a week. As we drive home in the evening, I suggest that we pull into the empty gas station and top off our tank. Unless the gas gauge is banging on empty, she argues against stopping. "Please, don't stop. I'm really tired, and I need to get home right now."

The result of not topping up is that when we are about to leave on a trip, we need to go to the gas station. These trips often occur during busy afternoons and take much more time and stress than the late-night top off. On each night, however, Barbara looks forward to a blissful future with no time constraints and no fatigue.

Our little game where I threaten to stop in the evening has taken a humorous turn analogous to the "cheese shop" game of Monty Python. That game is played as follows. One person, the customer, asks for a variety of cheese. The second person, the store owner, gives an excuse for why the cheese isn't available (for example, "the cat just drank it" was one answer in the original skit for a particularly runny cheese). Each player has to come up with a unique cheese or excuse, and the game ends when one side runs out of new ideas.

In our gasoline station variant, I propose new reasons why we have to stop and Barbara gives reasons why the present is a uniquely bad and inconvenient moment.

The gasoline game is simply a trivial demonstration of a self-control problem. Most of our bad decisions involve an inappropriate trade-off between today and tomorrow. We know that we should work hard now and play later, but we are just so busy now.

Behavioral economists have documented our self-control problems. In a variety of interesting settings we place too much weight on the present and too little on the future.[32] We use our lizard brain when we ought employ our prefrontal cortex.

Woody Allen says that the brain is his second favorite organ. As we have seen, our brains are not monolithic bastions of rationality. While we have a powerful prefrontal cortex with special analytic power, it has only limited ability to control the wild and powerful lizard brain.

chapter three

CRAZY WORLD
Mean Markets and the New Science of Irrationality

How Can a Market Be Mean?

There's a Wall Street adage that "markets move to frustrate the most people." There is some suggestion that this is true. Contrarian lore tells us that when people are optimistic markets are likely to fall and pessimist sentiment is said to predict rallies. The more extreme the investors' emotions, the more powerfully the market will move—but in the opposite direction of sentiment.

A "mean market" is one in which people are systematically out of sync with opportunity. In a mean market, our lizard brain screams at us to buy just before a collapse and makes us want to sell in terror just before a rally. If markets did create such emotional cruelty, especially because it costs us cash, they would indeed be mean. Are markets really mean, moving to frustrate us systematically?

There is one kind of market that can never be mean, and that is a rational market. To prove this point, try to be really wrong in predicting coin flips. For example, flip a coin 100 times and predict each flip. It is almost impossible to get significantly more than half wrong. This is true regardless of what system is used to predict the outcome of each flip— astrology, tips from friends, or always predicting heads. Because a fair coin is unpredictable, it is equally cruel (and kind) to all efforts at prediction.

In a rational market, prices move like coin flips. In such a market, the chance of an up move in a short period of time should be almost exactly 50%. Furthermore, as with coin flips, nothing is supposed to be able to predict price moves. In such a market, all strategies to predict future price changes will be no better than chance. The bad news is that only those who are very lucky can do really well in a rational market. The good news is that it is also almost impossible to do really poorly in a rational market.

Therefore, for markets to be mean they must be irrational. We tackle the issue of market rationality first, and then return to mean (and nice) markets.

Are Markets Crazy?

We know that people are crazy. In addition to the scientific evidence that has piled up over the last several decades and that we reviewed in Chapter 2, surely our daily experiences confirm, at least anecdotally, that we are just not as rational as we think we are (or at least not as rational as old-school economists assume).

While the case against individual rationality is closed, this is not sufficient to prove that markets are irrational. Consider what happens when you put a bunch of crazy people together. Is the result more chaos, or can order emerge even from a group of irrational people? It turns out that both chaos and order are possible.

In February 2004, hundreds of people were killed in a stampede outside of Mecca, Saudi Arabia. As part of the hajj, huge numbers of Muslim pilgrims were participating in a rite where each one throws a pebble at a historical pillar symbolizing the devil. The crowd crushed the victims as people in the back pressed forward to reach the pillar within the appropriate time frame for the ceremony. With its large crowds, the hajj has a history of deadly stampedes.

Rock music fans can be almost religious in their fervor, and many concerts have turned deadly. In 1979, 11 fans were killed at the Who concert in Cincinnati. The causes of stampedes are often very minor; things turn deadly only when many individuals compound the original problem.

A survivor of a stampede at a Pearl Jam concert that killed eight said, "Things were really great, and we wanted to move up." As people moved closer to the stage, everything was fine until, "The pressure from behind was too great" and the desire to have a better view led to death. Similarly a post-concert stampede in Belarus that killed 53 was caused by a hailstorm that made people rush to enter a metro station. In the dash for cover, a few young women in high heels fell and thus began a deadly chain reaction.

In the case of stampedes, groups of individuals, each one of whom may even be acting rationally, end up with very bad outcomes. The overall system works to magnify problems.

In contrast, there are other situations in which the right guidance can turn a mob of unruly individuals into an efficient team. I think of one such example whenever I board an airplane. My standard experience is that the boarding process is extremely inefficient. As soon as allowed, everyone surges forward, rushing to stuff their bags into overhead compartments. Invariably, as I work my way to my seat, I have to wait for the aisle to clear.

In contrast to this inefficient, clogged mess, I had one boarding experience that was almost magical. I was flying from Frankfurt, Germany, back to the United States on a flight that was extremely crowded. Rather than let us mob the plane, one of the gate agents organized an efficient boarding.

With just a few moments of effort, this agent organized us so perfectly that passengers in row 56 were at the front of the boarding line, followed by those in row 55, and so forth. With this setup, there were no clogs in the aisles and hundreds of people boarded the plane effortlessly in just a few minutes. It was a miracle, and one that I wish for on every flight.

On the way to his Nobel Prize, Professor Vernon Smith demonstrated that this phenomenon extends beyond boarding planes. There are situations in which the outcome is efficient beyond any reasonable expectation. Professor Smith's work concerned the magical ability of supply and demand to meet.

The question that Professor Smith addresses relates to the following joke: How many economists does it take to screw in a lightbulb? None; the invisible hand will do it.

Similarly, how is it that I can walk into the small convenience store in my condominium building five minutes before it closes and know that I will find Ben & Jerry's chocolate fudge brownie ice cream? The answer is that, as Adam Smith wrote, the self-interest of the store owner, working within a framework of law, almost magically provides the goods that I desire (or in this case, the ice cream that my wife Barbara desires).

Professor Smith found that supply and demand work even better than expected. Economists have proven that supply and demand work well when people are rational and have excellent information about the world. Professor Smith's work showed that even when people know nothing about their world (and are irrational), supply and demand do work their invisible magic. Collective efficiency sometimes arises from individual ignorance and irrationality.[1]

Even with the evidence that individuals are crazy, it is possible that collections of individuals, operating in markets, will make rational financial decisions. The question remains: Are financial markets more similar to stampedes where small problems multiply, or to miraculous plane loadings where crazy people are guided to efficient outcomes?

The Efficient Markets Hypothesis

The standard view in finance is that markets remove individual irrationality. This "efficient markets hypothesis" says that just as self-interest allows me to find my wife's ice cream in the local store, prices are pushed to the "right" level by an efficient and invisible hand.

I recently employed a variant of the efficient markets hypothesis in a mundane setting. The trustees of my condominium complex renovated a little exercise room and during the process removed the chin-up bar: the one piece of equipment that I used regularly. To lobby for a new chin-up bar, I attended a trustees' meeting. During the meeting, I was surprised to find that the trustees were considering spending almost half a million dollars (some of it mine) to buy an apartment for our superintendent.

Among the justifications for this purchase was an analysis that said buying the apartment was a "can't lose" proposition. Since our building is near both Harvard and MIT, demand for housing was sure to be strong and the apartment's price would definitely increase, or so the argument went.

Even though I wanted to discuss biceps, I found the lure of the "can't lose" investment compelling. Accordingly I asked, "If the price of the apartment is so low that it will definitely rise, why is the owner willing to sell?"

The trustees found great wisdom in this question and invited me to attend future meetings. There is indeed wisdom in my question, but the credit goes to a Frenchman named Louis Bachelier, not to me.[2] While he was a graduate student about 100 years ago, Bachelier asked a variant of this question about financial markets.

When two people trade with each other, Bachelier suggested that a good deal for one means a bad deal for the second. Thus, when two people each seek profit, all trade between them should take place at the right prices.

Price changes must occur, Bachelier reasoned, because of new information. In other words, only unexpected news should change the prices of stocks, houses, bonds, and other assets. Since price changes only come from unexpected new information, Bachelier deduced the heretical claim that it is impossible to predict price changes. Similarly, efficiency in the housing market would suggest that "can't lose" propositions are not available.

Interestingly, Bachelier's idea, which is now the conventional wisdom, was extremely unorthodox in his time. Even his advisors criticized his work, and his results were ignored to a large extent. Bachelier lived out the rest of his life in relative obscurity, and he died without fame in 1946. Not too long after his death, however, the concepts that Bachelier invented were reformulated as the efficient markets hypothesis that swept through universities and onto Wall Street in the 1970s.[3]

In the words of Burton Malkiel, author of *A Random Walk down Wall Street,* the modern version of Bachelier's insight is "Even a dart-throwing chimpanzee can select a portfolio that performs as well as one carefully selected by the experts." Malkiel's book was published in 1973, and it was part of an enormous intellectual wave that restructured the investment world.[4]

If the efficient markets hypothesis is true, then an investor need never fear buying overpriced stocks. According to the hypothesis, stocks are never overpriced and markets can never be mean.

During the great bull market of the 1980s and 1990s, belief in market efficiency and stock ownership soared. On the 1998 edition of Professor Jeremy Siegel's *Stocks for the Long Run,* the dust jacket proclaims, "stocks are actually *safer than bank deposits!*" (Emphasis and exclamation point in the original.)[5]

The idea that stocks are safer than bank deposits sounds a bit silly today (and has been removed from the dust jacket of later editions of Professor Siegel's book). Nevertheless, if markets are rational, then Professor Siegel's advice that "stocks should constitute the overwhelming proportion of all long-term financial portfolios" might be reasonable.

If markets are not rational, however, then investors ought to worry about buying stocks at irrationally high prices. They should also worry about selling stocks at irrationally low prices. They should also be concerned about the prices of houses, bonds, gold, and all assets.

The essence of the efficient markets hypothesis is realizing that a good deal for one person implies a bad deal for the other. Thus, no one should be willing to sell at irrationally low prices and no one should be willing to buy at irrationally high prices.

The efficient markets hypothesis is a beautiful theory. Is it true?

If She's Got Pictures, Deny It! . . .

It wasn't me.

The pop star Shaggy gives this advice to men caught cheating. "Honey came in and she caught me red-handed, creeping with the girl next door." The correct response to being caught cheating, according to Shaggy? Deny by saying "it wasn't me." Even if caught on camera, Shaggy sticks to his defense of "it wasn't me."

The great comic Lenny Bruce expressed a similar philosophy in one of his routines: "There's this kind of guy who says: 'When I chippie on my wife, I have to tell her, I can't live a lie, have to be honest with myself.' "

To which Bruce replies, "Man, if you love your old lady, really love her, you'll never tell her that! Women don't want to hear that! If she's got pictures—deny it! . . . Gee, honey, I don't know how this broad got in here—she had a sign around her neck, 'I am a diabetic—lie on top of me or I'll die.' No, I don't know how I got my underwear on upside down or backwards."

Those who defend the efficient markets hypothesis use a similar tactic of denial. In response to evidence of market irrationality, the response is denial. (It wasn't me.)

There are examples of market irrationality that appear as convincing as photographic documentation of infidelity, and they are everywhere around us. For example, financial bubbles have occurred in every society throughout history that has had markets. The most famous case is the seventeenth-century Dutch "tulipmania." In 1635, at the height of speculative frenzy, the price for a single tulip bulb exceeded that of a nice house in Amsterdam.[6]

How could it be rational to buy a tulip bulb for the price of a house? This seems particularly strange given that one tulip bulb can produce an infinite number of baby tulip bulbs. While tulips may not breed like rabbits, they do multiply rapidly and thus high prices are impossible to sustain. In fact, the Dutch tulip crash came swiftly, with some varieties losing 90% of their value in a matter of weeks. (By comparison, after its peak in 2000, it took Sun Microsystems two years to lose 90% of its value.)

The high price of tulip bulbs before the crash and their rapid decline appear to be evidence of market irrationality. As we will come to see, true believers of the efficient markets hypothesis deny that bubbles and crashes imply that markets are irrational. (It wasn't me.)

While markets continue to behave as they have for centuries, the debate on irrationality has changed dramatically in recent years. The field of behavioral finance has produced new, scientific evidence of market irrationality. In many cases, the new studies provide statistical confirmation of folk wisdom.

Let's take a look at some compelling evidence of market irrationality—both historical and new—and the response of those who deny it. (If you are already convinced that markets are irrational, you can jump down to the section entitled "Why Professors Fly Coach and Speculators Own Jets.") I argue that it is impossible to prove that markets are irrational, but the evidence is compelling. To which, of course, true believers in the efficient markets hypothesis will reply: It wasn't me.

Claim #1: Stock Market Crashes

On Monday, October 19, 1987, the Dow Jones Industrial Average lost 23%. By noon of the following day stocks faced a crisis where some people feared a total collapse of the stock market. The U.S. Federal Reserve, led by a recently appointed Alan Greenspan, rode to the rescue by guaranteeing certain trades. The market recovered in the afternoon of October 20.

Many people have investigated the 1987 stock market crash. Of note, independent studies were performed by Professor Robert Shiller, the author of *Irrational Exuberance,* and by his friend Professor Jeremy Siegel, the author of *Stocks for the Long Run.*[7]

These two leading academics are often on opposite sides of the stock debate. Professor Shiller argued (correctly so) that stocks were overvalued in the late 1990s. On the other hand, Professor Siegel has maintained a uniformly positive view of stocks, before, during, and after the bursting of the bubble in 2000. Because of their opposing views on the prospects for stocks, they are often contrasted as leaders of the bear and bull camps.

When it comes to the crash of 1987, however, Professors Shiller and Siegel agree. The crash was not caused by any rational factor such as a news event. Professor Shiller summarizes his findings as, "No news story or rumor appearing on the 19th or over the preceding weekend was responsible for investor behavior."[8] Similarly, Professor Siegel writes, "No economic event on or about October 19, 1987 can explain the record collapse of equity prices."[9]

As most of us know all too well, starting in 2000 the NASDAQ suffered a decline that was less dramatic than the 1987 crash, but more severe and longer lasting. Table 3.1 shows the performance of leading stocks sometimes called the "four new horsemen of the NASDAQ."

These figures suggest that either precrash prices were irrationally high or postcrash prices irrationally low. When Cisco was priced at $80, the evidence suggests that the stock price was irrationally high. Similarly, when Cisco was trading at $8, after the bubble burst, the evidence suggests that the stock price was irrationally low.

The Denial: The believers in the efficient markets hypothesis deny that sudden price changes indicate irrationality. Furthermore, they claim that

TABLE 3.1   The Decline and Partial Recovery of the Four New Horsemen of the NASDAQ

	Bubble peak (2000)	*Post-bubble low*	*Current (7/2004)*
Cisco	Over $80	$8	$23
EMC	Over $100	$4	$11
Oracle	Over $45	$8	$12
Sun Microsystems	Over $60	Under $3	$4

Source: The Wall Street Journal

Cisco's stock price (and all other prices) were correct at the time. Thus, they argue that the decline in Cisco's price from $80 to $8 was caused by unexpected information that was unknowable at the peak.

This claim is based on the fact that stocks discount the future. For example, the value of Cisco in 2000 depends on China's attitude toward imports in 2010, so even small changes in investors' expectations about China's future import policy can cause big changes in Cisco's value. Even huge price changes can be rational when nothing concrete changes in the world.

Thus, even though Professors Shiller and Siegel cannot identify the cause of the 1987 crash, it can be explained as a rational response to expectations about the future. Since we can't know what those expectations are, we can't conclude that the sudden changes in stock prices are irrational.

Photographic Evidence: Asset Bubbles in the Laboratory

In the real world, we can never prove that bubbles and crashes are caused by irrationality. It is possible that real world crashes are caused by changes in unknowable variables. To investigate bubbles, economists have built artificial stock markets where everything is known. In these laboratory markets, bubbles and crashes, if they exist, must come from inside people.

In fact, Professor Vernon Smith and others have found that even artificial stock markets exhibit bubbles and crashes. In these experiments, people trade a stock for real money. In contrast to the actual stock market, the traders in these artificial markets know the true value of the stock. Nevertheless, traders in these artificial markets push stock prices up to irrationally high prices and then the prices crash.[10]

In the artificial markets, there is no explanation for the bubbles and crashes other than the fact that they arise naturally as part of human nature. True rational market believers argue that the markets are artificial and, in the real world, people who trade at irrational prices would be weeded out.

It wasn't me.

Claim #2: Markets Are More Than Simply Irrational—They Can Be Mean

Investors seem to have an uncanny ability to be wrong about investments. We tend to be optimistic about stocks just before market collapses and pessimistic just before bull markets. Consider the experience of U.S. investors in the period from 1965 to 1981 as shown in Figure 3.1.

The Dow Jones Industrial Average ended 1965 at 969, and 16 years later the index stood at 875. Almost an entire generation passed with the stock market going absolutely nowhere. Near the end of this period, people essentially forgot about stocks, and in 1980 only 5.7% of households owned any mutual funds.[11]

In 1979, *BusinessWeek* printed its now infamous "Death of Equities"

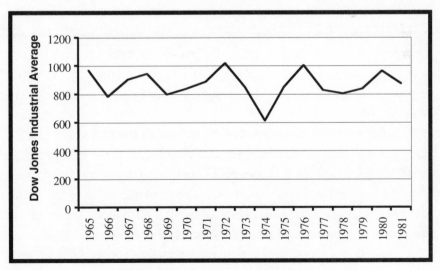

FIGURE 3.1   A Generation without Stock Market Gains
Source: Dow Jones

issue suggesting that investors avoid stocks. The cover image was a crashing paper airplane, created from a stock certificate. Stocks were destined to be bad investments, opined the magazine, for the foreseeable future, and "the old attitude of buying solid stocks as a cornerstone for one's life savings and retirement has simply disappeared."[12] The pervasive pessimism about stocks in the late 1970s coincided with the best buying opportunity of the century as shown in Figure 3.2.

As we see in Figure 3.2, from the end of 1981 until today, the Dow has yielded more than 1,000%, and this calculation does not factor in dividends. As the stock market rose throughout the 1980s and 1990s, the attitudes toward stocks shifted from gloom to glee. Investors gradually increased stock purchases. By the time the stock market peaked in 2000, almost half of U.S. households were invested in mutual funds.[13] At the same time, Wall Street firms were advocating 70% investment in stocks, among the highest figures on record.[14] The peak enthusiasm for stocks reached in 2000 corresponded with the beginning of one of the worst bear markets since the Great Depression.

Sentiment is a predictor of future returns. Optimistic periods tend to be followed by bad performance, whereas pessimism tends to dominate

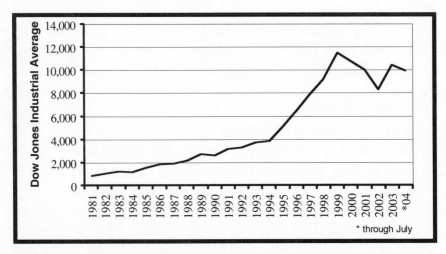

FIGURE 3.2   The Mother of All Bull Markets Started When Stocks Were Hated
Source: Dow Jones

before good things happen. Wall Street is driven by greed and fear. The funny thing is that our lizard brains tend to make us greedy when we ought be fearful, and fearful when we ought be greedy.

Our ability to be excited at the wrong time extends to individual stocks. Professor Terrance Odean examined the actual trading records of 10,000 ordinary investors.[15] He focused part of his study on investors who sold one stock and then bought another stock within a few days. He compared the performance of the stock that was sold with that of the stock that was purchased.

How did the investors in this study perform? Remember that if markets were rational, then the stocks that these investors sold would have had the same return (on average) as the stocks that the investors bought. What happened? Professor Odean writes, "over a one-year horizon, the average return to a purchased security is 3.3 percent lower than the return to a security sold." So these investors became excited enough to buy and pessimistic enough to sell stocks at the wrong time. Their sentiment was an inverse predictor of success.

The efficient markets hypothesis is usually employed to suggest that bargains are impossible. "Don't waste your time looking for cheap stocks; if they existed someone else would already have bought them." The converse is also true, but rarely mentioned; if markets were rational, then it would be equally impossible to make systematically bad decisions. "Don't waste your time worrying that you might get excited at the wrong time and buy expensive stocks; if they existed someone else would already have sold them."

Professor Odean found that markets were mean to these people. The investors studied were completely out of sync with the market. They sold stocks that went up and bought stocks that went down. None of this is supposed to occur if the world ran according to the rules of the efficient markets hypothesis. All stock prices are supposed to be correct, so it should be impossible to make systematically bad choices.

In an episode of the futuristic cartoon, *The Jetsons,* there is a mobile, robotic slot machine that rolls around enticing would-be gamblers by saying, "I'm due." The implication is that no one has hit the jackpot in a while so now is a good moment to invest a few bucks to try to win. The punch line of the scene comes when some lucky gambler actually does win the jackpot. The robot pays out the money and then scoots off proclaiming, "I'm due."

In reality, slot machines are never "due." They are designed to completely forget the past; in the language of probability, slot machines are "memoryless." The chance of winning immediately after a jackpot is the same as on a slot machine that has gone years without a winner.

The efficient markets hypothesis states that stock markets should be memoryless like an idealized slot machine. Nothing should predict the next day's stock price changes. So if it were true that optimism preceded stock (and stock market) declines, then that would be evidence of market irrationality and market meanness.

The Denial: The believers in the efficient markets hypothesis deny that sentiment provides any information about future price changes. They claim that the evidence of disdain for stocks in the late 1970s (e.g., the "Death of Equities" cover story) is anecdotal and thus not scientific. Professor Odean's study demonstrating irrationality must be flawed.

Photographic Evidence: Scientific Evidence of Sentiment Predicting Stock Price Changes

Professor Richard Thaler, doyen of the behavioral school, and Professor Werner DeBondt performed a systematic analysis of sentiment.[16] They hypothesized that people would feel good about rising stocks and feel bad about falling stocks. Therefore, they predicted that the future performance of stocks that made investors feel bad (the losers) would be better than that of stocks that made investors feel good (the winners).

Professors Thaler and DeBondt thus predicted that a way to make money is precisely to buy the hated stocks that had been losers. They performed a systematic study of hundreds of stocks over many years. In each period they constructed a portfolio of previous winners and previous losers. They then compared the performance of their winner and loser portfolios.

The rational and irrational views of markets make competing predictions in this situation. If the efficient markets hypothesis were true, then nothing would predict the future changes in price. If the market were rational, then the winners' portfolio would have the same performance as the losers' portfolio.

But, Professors Thaler and DeBondt found that individual stocks exhibit the same pattern as the market as a whole: Pessimism precedes rises, and optimism precedes falls. In their words, "Loser portfolios of 35 stocks outperform the market by, on average, 19.6%, thirty six months after portfolio formation. Winner portfolios, on the other hand, earn about 5.0% less than the market." This study was published in the prestigious *Journal of Finance.*

The winner and loser study contradicts the efficient markets hypothesis, which predicts that memoryless markets don't care about previous performance. Many other behavioral finance studies have produced evidence that contradicts the efficient markets hypothesis. (Professor Thaler collected and published 21 such studies in *Advances in Behavioral Finance.*[17]) To which the true believers argue that the studies are contrived and people who trade at irrational prices would be weeded out.

It wasn't me.

Claim #3: Some People Get Rich by Selling High and Buying Low

Over the last 40 years, Warren Buffett has increased the value of Berkshire Hathaway at a compounded rate of 22.2% per year. Over the same period, the S&P 500 stocks have increased by 10.4% a year; $1,000 invested with Warren Buffett at the start of this period would have been worth $2,594,850 at the end of 2003 versus $47,430 for an equivalent investment in the S&P 500.[18]

So Warren Buffett seems to have a pretty good record of buying and selling at favorable prices—prices that the efficient markets hypothesis suggests should never exist. Furthermore, Warren Buffett seems to have done a lot better than a dart-throwing monkey.

Warren Buffett actively seeks undervalued investments. In his 2003 letter to shareholders he writes:

> When valuations are similar, we strongly prefer owning businesses to owning stocks. During most of our years of operations, however, stocks were much the cheaper choice. We therefore sharply tilted our asset allocation in those years towards equities . . . In recent years, however, we've found it hard to find significantly undervalued stocks.

So Warren Buffett believes that undervalued stocks sometimes exist. He also says that there are not many good values in the stock market these days. If the efficient markets hypothesis were true, there would not be any better or worse time to buy stocks; all prices would be fair at all times. So Warren Buffett has made his fortune by acting precisely in a fashion that would be silly if markets were rational.

The Denial: The believers in the efficient markets hypothesis deny that Warren Buffett's success is due to skill. Their argument is as follows: Put 1,024 people in a room. Have each of them flip a coin 10 times. On average, one of them will have produced 10 heads in a row. Now call that person Warren Buffett.

In other words, there are lots of money managers and by sheer dumb luck someone will have a great track record. That great track record, in this view, predicts nothing about the future.

Photographic Evidence: Predicting Coin Flips

If Warren Buffett's success in the past was luck, then the efficient markets hypothesis suggests that for next year he is not expected to outperform the market or a dart-throwing monkey. In this thought experiment the "winner" who produces 10 heads in a row has exactly a 50% chance of producing an eleventh head on the next coin flip, the same odds as a loser who produced 10 tails in a row.

Professor Thaler has created a money management firm (run with Russell Fuller) that seeks to systematically exploit irrational market opportunities. The firm makes investment decisions guided by the findings of behavioral finance. Although the firm is young, the results are interesting; as of the end of 2003, the firm's six funds are outperforming their benchmarks by an average of 8.1% a year.[19] To which the true believers argue that the performance of these funds, like the performance of Warren Buffett, is luck and not skill.

No one can really know if a particular performance is due to skill or luck. However, the interesting point is that the efficient markets hypothesis cannot be proven false by any investor's performance. Regardless of how many more good years Warren Buffett or Fuller-Thaler have, defenders of the efficient markets hypothesis can argue that superior performance is sheer luck.

It wasn't me.

A Hypothesis Masquerading as a Theory

During the war of 1812, the Native American Chief Tecumseh captured the fort of Detroit through an interesting ruse. In the conflict, federal and state troops, under the command of Major-General Hull, vastly outnumbered about 1,000 Native American warriors. Tecumseh had his fighters run out of the woods and then secretly circle back to emerge again. General Hull saw—and counted—the same warriors over and over and was fooled into thinking he faced a vastly larger force. He surrendered without a shot.

In any endeavor it is important to have an accurate estimate of the opposition. General Hull gave up before the fight started because he treated a small force like an army. Similarly, the idea that markets are efficient is at best a hypothesis, which is a weak statement. Investors who surrender to dreams of market efficiency give up before the investing battle has begun.

Proven scientific views of the world are called theories. For example, all of us know that gravity is true, yet it is categorized as a theory. In contrast to proven theories, new ideas that may or may not be true are labeled "hypotheses." Importantly, even those who defend market rationality label their idea as only a hypothesis, acknowledging that it has not been proven.

In fact, the belief in market efficiency might not even qualify for hypothesis status. The great philosopher of science, Sir Karl Popper, writes, "In so far as a scientific statement speaks about reality, it must be falsifiable; and in so far as it is not falsifiable, it does not speak about reality."[20]

In order to reach the standard of hypothesis, an idea must be provable, which means that there must potentially be evidence that could disprove it. As we have seen, there is essentially no way to disprove the idea of efficient markets. Popper excludes unfalsifiable ideas as being outside of science, mere dogma.

"Double, double toil and trouble; Fire burn, and cauldron bubble," say the witches in *Macbeth,* associating bubbles with troubles. However, these same witches also note that in some situations "foul is fair and fair is foul." When someone sells a house to buy a ridiculously expensive tulip bulb, for example, another person gets to buy a house for the rock-bottom price of one tulip bulb.

Investors who accept the dogma of market efficiency give up the opportunities that exist precisely because markets are irrational. Such surrender might be merited if the idea of market efficiency was a proven theory, but it is at best a hypothesis, and at worst a nonscientific assertion.

Why Professors Fly Coach and Speculators Own Jets

"I have made my living from market inefficiency," so the financier Alfred Checchi told me during a visit to my Harvard Business School classroom.

In contrast, most of the professors at the Harvard Business School are believers in market efficiency, and one told me (with apparent sincerity) that technology stocks were not overpriced in 2000.

Although Mr. Checchi is frequently invited to visit the Harvard Business School, he is so offended by the assumption of market efficiency that he refuses to attend finance classes. (Similarly, the Nobel Prize–winning economist Professor Ronald Coase told me that his only objection to the idea of "bounded rationality" is that the word "rational" should not be used in any sentence describing human behavior.)

So who has been more successful in finding market opportunity, efficiency-preaching professors or irrationality-exploiting financiers? Alfred Checchi was able to spend $30 million of his own money on a run for governor in California. Furthermore, while professors usually fly on commercial airlines, Alfred Checchi's success not only provided him with enough money to buy a private jet, it even allowed him to buy a substantial stake in Northwest Airlines.

The lesson is that those who seek profit should stop looking for absolute proof that markets are not efficient. Such proof is not possible. In contrast, those who seek superior performance should, like Mr. Checchi, accept market irrationality as the first step toward profit.

Furthermore, Mr. Checchi shows that crazy markets don't have to be mean. They can, in fact, be very nice. The key is to be on the right side of irrationality—to sell at high prices and buy at low prices.

Sell the Fads, Buy the Outcasts

Opportunities occur periodically in many different markets. In all cases, winning requires a willingness to challenge the conventional wisdom. During the inflationary 1970s, Andrew Tobias, the personal finance guru, literally had to deal with a mob in order to profit from an irrationally high silver price.[21]

Throughout the inflationary 1970s the price of silver rose by more than 1,000% until it exceeded $40 an ounce. At the height of the frenzy, Tobias decided to sell some of his physical silver. He went to a retail location that bought and sold precious metals including silver and gold. As he approached the store he saw a huge crowd and thought it was too late. Everyone, he supposed, had realized that the price of silver was too high and had gathered to sell.

When Tobias reached the store he discovered to his delight that the crowd was gathering to buy! Soon afterwards, silver prices plummeted and more than 20 years later silver still sells for under $10 an ounce. Similarly, in 1970s gold prices soared toward $900 ounce before crashing, and today it sells for less than half that price.

In the late 1970s precious metals were the investment craze, and they were terrible investments. In order to profit, Tobias had to lean into the prevailing opinion by selling while all of those around him were buying.

Usually the mob is not physically present, but rather represented in the prevailing views of "the knowledgeable." In 2000, I began dating Barbara. As a joke, I told Barbara that we would have enough money to get married and have a baby if the stock price of EMC fell from $100 to below $50 (I was betting against EMC's stock price by shorting the shares).

Barbara is an archeologist and before this baby challenge she had never paid any attention to financial media. Now she began to listen, and the more she learned about EMC, the more she worried. Every single mention of the stock, in every venue, detailed the virtues of the EMC and predicted that the shares would continue to rise. Wall Street analysts and mutual fund managers appeared on TV and described how EMC's markets were growing and the stock was a "no-brainer," and a "must own."

Under the deluge of praise, Barbara asked me what I knew that these pundits did not. Did I think EMC had bad products? No. Did I have some inside information that EMC sales were bad? No. Did I know of competitors that would steal EMC's customers? No. Well, she demanded, what did I know? I told Barbara that I knew all the analysts and mutual fund managers loved EMC and that was enough. Barbara responded with "that is so Zen." With universal praise and love, the stock had nowhere to go but down, and down it went from over $100 a share to below $4.

The story of precious metals in the 1970s, and EMC more recently, form a universal pattern. Both Wall Street and Main Street have an amazing ability to be wrong about investments. At about the same time that Andrew Tobias was selling silver at ridiculously high prices, unloved stocks were being sold for rock-bottom prices.

Job Listing: Street Sweeper to Pick Up Surplus $100 Bills Left Lying in the Street

This is one of the job descriptions that you will never see posted. For obvious reasons, $100 bills cannot remain visible for long. Because $100 bills tend to get picked up, believers in efficient markets assume that they can't exist. An alternative, however, is that there are opportunities to make profits, but they persist only in what can be thought of as the lizard brain's financial blind spots.

Market opportunities will be difficult to find. There are no easy roads to making money. In *The Godfather: Part II,* a young Vito Corleone does the favor of hiding some guns for his neighbor Clemenza (Vito goes on to become the Don and Clemenza one of his trusted lieutenants). After the guns are returned, Clemenza says, "A friend of mine has a nice rug. Maybe your wife would like it. . . . It would be a present. I know how to return a favor."

As the two men go to pick up the rug from the "friend's" house, it becomes clear that they are actually stealing. In the process, a policeman comes to the door and Clemenza prepares to shoot the officer. Fortunately, the scene resolves itself without any violence, but the quest for possessions, whether by legal or illegal means, isn't an easy one.

While the $100 bills we seek are not easy to find, interestingly sometimes the hardest things to spot are those hiding in plain sight. For example, with modern electronic-search capabilities, the FBI can track most people down very easily. Special agents enter some information about the suspect into the computer, click a few keys, and voila, the suspect is found. Among the hardest to find, however, are people with common names like John Smith. So one of the few ways left to hide from the FBI is to hide in plain view, by being part of a crowd. This problem has complicated U.S. efforts to prevent bombers from boarding planes. There are a large number of people, for example, with the name Mohammad. Thus, many international flights have been cancelled because of mistaken identity.

In the case of markets, the opportunities exist, but the lizard brain is built not to be able to see them. During the dot-com bubble, the unprofitable Internet retailer Etoys was worth more than the profitable, and much larger, Toys R Us. Recognizing that Etoys was irrationally priced (and in fact soon went out of business) didn't require any fancy math.

While profitable investing doesn't require mathematical prowess, it does require a willingness to learn about the irrationality in oneself, in others, and in markets. Becoming a successful investor requires a keen understanding of human frailty, including one's own limitations.

We've encountered many of those limitations in Chapter 2. Two additional aspects of the lizard brain are harmful to investing success. The first is our desire to conform, and the second is the fact that our emotions really do seem to be out of sync with financial markets—both of which tend to lose us money.

The Loneliest Man in San Diego

One of our human limitations is the desire to conform to the majority. This seems to be something built into us and it works against us since popular investments tend to be unprofitable.

I learned something about this a few years ago at a football game between my Detroit Lions and the San Diego Chargers. My Lions lost the game, which was not surprising, as they've had a long tradition of mediocrity. What was surprising was the level of pain that I felt. The game was played in San Diego, and I was almost the only Detroit fan in a sea of Charger fans. The pain of losing in this setting was far greater than any I had experienced in home losses.

The human desire to conform to those around us extends beyond sports stadiums. A line of psychological research performed by Professor Solomon Asch and others demonstrates the pressure to conform.[22] In one setting for this research, six people enter a room and are asked to answer a question for which there is a clear answer. For example, here is a reference line:

X   ————————————————————

Which of the following lines matches the length of the reference line?

A   ————————————————
B   ——
C   ——————————

Of the six people answering the questions, five are "confederates" of the experimenter, which means they give false answers designed to manipulate the behavior of others. In this case, the experimenter first asks the confederates to rate the lines, and they all give the same wrong answer. In this case they might say, "Line C matches line X."

After the five confederates have made these obviously false statements, the sixth person (who is not in on the experiment) is asked the same question. Now this person faces a bit of a quandary. Should he or she pick the obviously correct answer (A) or pick the same answer as everyone else (C)? In the original experiments, 75% of subjects sometimes conformed to what is labeled the "false consensus" by picking the obviously false answer (C).

More recently some of these original results have been challenged, but the basic finding seems intact. We seem built to want to be part of the crowd, even when doing so contradicts our direct observation.

In the case of the lines, the correct answer is obvious. In the case of investments, the correct view is rarely so evident. Consider again the situation of Etoys versus Toys R Us. While it appears obvious in retrospect that Etoys would go bankrupt, imagine the pressure to conform. Day after bubble day, people (many of them professionals) bought the stock at high valuations. In such cases, our brains seem built to start believing what others are saying.

To do well, an investor has to purchase exactly that which is unloved. This requires an ability to take the emotional pain of being different. I recall my broker's mocking laugh when I placed an order to buy Treasury bonds in early 2000. Bonds had been going down consistently and all the "smart money," he said, was selling not buying.

Unlike my Detroit Lions story, the bond story has a happy ending. As usual, the common consensus was wrong, and the bonds that I bought soon increased in value. The successful path was the path that was scorned.

An Instinct for Losing Money

A cartoon I saw posted over a trader's desk on Wall Street read, "Definition of a quandary: Should I sit back and watch the market soar or buy now and cause it to plummet?"

In some areas our natural tendencies take us to good outcomes. My wife's recent pregnancy comes to mind as one such area. During the early part of pregnancy, the growing fetus is especially sensitive to certain naturally occurring toxins.

According to Margie Profet, who won a MacArthur Foundation "genius" award for her work on this subject, pregnant women are built to avoid foods that include fetus-damaging toxins (teratogens).[23] She provides evidence that pregnant women are nauseated by such foods, particularly cabbage-family vegetables like broccoli and cauliflower that have high levels of damaging compounds. If Profet is correct, then in the area of food choice, pregnant women ought to follow their instincts and eat whatever tastes good.

When it comes to investing, the message is exactly reversed. The trades that feel good tend to lead to losses. For example, my older sister Sue recently sent me an e-mail saying, "I have gone crazy buying stocks! . . . No informed rationale for purchases, just a feeling. Reminds me of the slots at Vegas!" Sue's lizard brain was screaming at her to buy.

After almost a year of watching the market rally with only a small ownership in stocks, sister Sue was fed up. It was time for her to get in on the gravy train. Unfortunately, this impulsive purchase was timed for losses. In fact, within a few weeks of the e-mail, the stock market had its biggest decline in a year.

My buddy Doug had a similar experience recently. Doug appears in a few chapters of this book and has had excellent results overall (in the stocks chapter, you can read about the day he earned $500,000 in an afternoon of surfing). In early 2002, Doug did some careful analysis of a few firms that he knew well. He decided to buy some Nortel stock at around $1 a share. This turned out to be a great purchase as the stock went up steadily.

In the months after Doug's purchase of Nortel, I heard not a single peep from him about his successful investment. Then one day, the following note arrived with the subject line of "a little bragging." It read, "I was pushing Nortel big back at around $1. Well Nortel is over $8 today; up $1. Call me Warren :-)"

After months of watching Nortel stock climb, Doug's lizard brain made him send this e-mail at this particular moment. A Wall Street cliché is that "nobody rings a bell when it's time to sell," but this bragging e-mail was a perfect time to sell. Within a short period after the e-mail, Nortel's stock returned to $3, going down even faster than it had risen.

The message is that unfettered emotions are not the investor's friend. Doug's decision to buy was driven by analysis in his prefrontal cortex, his decision to gloat, by his lizard brain.

A recent study documented the physiological reaction that people have to market information. Professor Andrew Lo and Dmitry Repin wired up a group of professional traders.[24] With a setup not too different from a heart stress test, these MIT researchers were able to measure minute changes in body temperature, skin conductance, and a host of other variables. The traders they wired were trading real money for an investment firm.

What happened to our wired traders when news broke? Lo and Repin report two interesting findings. First, all the traders—even the most experienced—had measurable emotional responses to news. Second, the more experienced traders had weaker emotional responses than their less-experienced colleagues.

These physiological responses may help us understand mean markets. When people see stock price changes or read about world events, we have physiological responses. If we act on those emotions, we tend to make precisely the wrong moves. In other words, we need to shackle the lizard brain in order to make money.

To be successful we have to damp down our emotional response (toward the lower response of the experienced professional traders in the MIT study) or we need to prevent our emotional reactions from impoverishing us. The "timeless tips" of Chapter 10 focus on ways to shackle the impulsive and unprofitable lizard brain trader who lurks inside us.

A Guide for Bubble Hunting

As the title would suggest, the *Incredible Shrinking Man* portrays the life of a person as he goes from normal size to tiny. As the protagonist continues to shrink he faces danger from a house cat and—when even smaller—from a spider. Eventually our hero realizes he cannot cower indefinitely. He confronts the spider, and even though the beast is much larger than the shrunken man, he kills it with a pin. After this victory, the movie ends as our hero prepares to leave his former house with a cocky walk and a blood-covered weapon slung over his shoulder.

Similarly, we reach the end of the first section of this book and push off into a dangerous and unknown future. The science of irrationality has proven that people make a variety of errors. Furthermore, markets do not always iron out those errors and people sometimes stampede into and out of markets at precisely the wrong time. Markets can indeed be mean, but because markets can be crazy, opportunities exist for profitable investments.

While markets are irrational, the profits are hard to obtain precisely because $100 bills persist in the lizard brain's financial blind spots. Just as we must use a mirror and other tricks to see into the blind spots on our cars, we need help to spot market opportunity. We have one tool so far and that is sentiment. We know that in order to make money, we must make the unpopular moves and attempt to constrain the lizard brain.

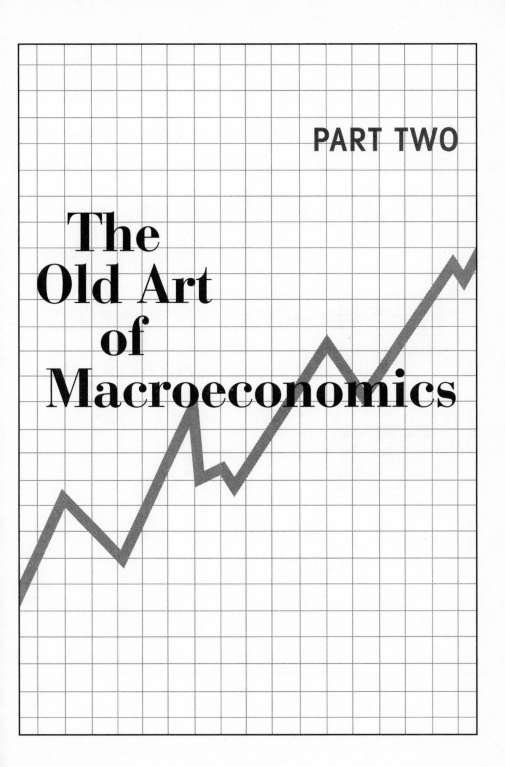

PART TWO

The Old Art of Macroeconomics

We ended Part One with the conclusion that both individuals and markets are far from rational. Thus, the answer to the Mean Markets and Lizard Brains question of, "Where should I invest my money?" varies depending on the circumstances. Sometimes the conventional wisdom of stocks will be correct, but sometimes other investments will be better bets.

Part Two sets the macroeconomic stage for choosing investments. Because markets can be far from rational, we cannot assume that prices are fair. Rather, we need to evaluate the prospects for bonds, stocks, and real estate. This section analyzes the fundamental forces that drive investment returns.

Chapter 4 presents an economic snapshot of the United States. Will government deficits hurt the economy? Can the productivity revolution allow us to be richer and lead better lives? Chapter 5 examines the prospects for inflation and deflation. Is the Federal Reserve creating inflation? Why would anyone worry about prices being too low? Chapter 6 looks at the U.S. trade deficit and its implications for the value of the U.S. dollar. How will the decline in the U.S. dollar affect investors? When will the dollar decline end?

chapter four

U.S. ECONOMIC SNAPSHOT
America the Talented Debtor

Financial Hangover versus the American Spirit

"It was the best of times, it was the worst of times." So wrote Dickens in his famous opening to *A Tale of Two Cities*. Dickens continues with, "it was the age of wisdom, it was the age of foolishness, . . . it was the season of Light, it was the season of Darkness, it was the spring of hope, it was the winter of despair."

Dickens intended that this description be applicable to all times. And, not surprisingly, his sentiments provide a good summary of modern times, both generally and economically. In this chapter we examine competing arguments regarding the U.S. economy. In one camp are the worst-of-timers—the doom and gloomers who predict a financial hangover that will last for years or decades. On the other side are the best-of-timers—the bright-eyed new-agers who predict a magical world filled with material abundance and leisure.

Revolution lurks just offstage throughout *A Tale of Two Cities*. The story begins in 1775, and Dickens' readers knew that by the end of the century the streets of Paris would run red from the reign of terror. Revolution also lies at the heart of the debate about the modern economy. While the current revolution is less bloody than that experienced in eighteenth-century France, it is no less fundamental.

The Industrial Revolution loosened the connection between physical labor and economic wealth. With machines we no longer needed to work like animals. Even with machines, however, we still needed to work. Now the information technology revolution promises material luxury without work.

Even though he had never seen a computer, the famous economist John Maynard Keynes summarized the optimistic view in his 1930 essay, "The Economic Possibilities for Our Grandchildren."[1] In it Keynes looks forward to a materially rich world filled with leisure. He imagines that his grandchildren will have so much abundance they will work very few hours and spend the rest of their time on artistic and intellectual pursuits. In fact, Keynes worries about the lack of work to fill the day:

> we shall endeavor to spread the bread thin on the butter—to make what work there is still to be done to be as widely shared as possible. Three-hour shifts or a fifteen-hour week may put off the problem [of too little work] for a great while. For three hours a day is quite enough.

If such a world is to exist for our grandchildren, information technology seems destined to play a major role.

Published in 1859, *A Tale of Two Cities* contained a cautionary tale. It warned that those who do not prepare for change well might end up at the wrong end of a guillotine. Specifically, Britain had to be careful to avoid the bloody aspects of change that befell (and beheaded) French society.

Similarly, the specter of the Japanese economy hangs over the United States. In the late 1980s, the Japanese economy was surging and analysts confidently predicted future greatness. Over the last 15 years, the Japanese economy has stagnated, unemployment has risen dramatically, and confidence has waned. Japan still leads in many economic categories, but also has a suicide rate that is among the highest for industrialized countries.

So what path will the United States follow? Will it be Keynes' vision of examined leisure created by information technology, or will we stumble down a painful path similar to that taken by post-bubble Japan?

We will develop the answer to this question throughout this chapter. To understand the problem we will have to wade knee-deep in economic statistics of debts, deficits, and productivity. When I ponder the U.S. economy, however, I do not think only of economic data. In addition, I think often of a high school classmate of mine—Steve—and his behavior in the fall of 1975.

In 1975 I was a junior in high school on a mediocre cross-country running team. Actually both the team and I were mediocre—so bad that our archrivals and state champions, Grosse Pointe North, used our competitions as practice days. Rather than drive to our competitions, "North" would run eight miles just to get to the starting line. They'd then run the three-mile race, defeat us handily, and run the eight miles back home. They didn't want to waste a training day by running just a few miles against such a pathetic team as ours.

Into this gloom came the "new guy," Steve, a young man with a great natural talent for running. Although he had not been on the team in previous years, he showed early promise and soon became the best runner on our team.

The funny thing about Steve, however, was that he didn't sacrifice much to be a great runner. While my friend Jim and I made sure to eat right and go to bed early, Steve was not averse to having a few drinks the night before a competition. He would even sometimes arrive at a Saturday morning race hungover, his natural talent usually allowing him to outrun the rest of us. Though on the mornings after particularly hard evenings, we were not sure whether Steve's talent or Steve's hangover would prevail. Had the excesses of the previous night been extreme enough as to overwhelm Steve's ability?

The U.S. economy faces a similar battle between hangover and talent. The United States has demonstrated an unmatched ability to innovate and produce. Our economic system seems to have a natural talent for making products both cheaply and well. Impeding that talent, at least over the next several years, is the financial hangover caused by the excesses of the 1990s.

What condition will win out? The hangover or the talent? To find out we'll delve into some macroeconomic issues. When I was an MBA student at MIT, the economist Lester Thurow said, "If you like reading [dry] data tables, then you should consider becoming an economist." The shoe that Lester described fit me perfectly; after a few years I returned to get a Ph.D. and became an economist.

When I tell people at social functions that I am an economics professor, a very common response is "that was my worst course in college." I have met literally dozens of people who took one economics course, found it distasteful, and stopped. Part of this dislike of economics comes from the standard teaching style (boring!), but part is due to the very nature of the subject (including dry data tables). As hard as it is for me to understand, I have learned that some people do not enjoy reading economic statistics.

Furthermore, some people can succeed financially without studying economic numbers. Take my friend David who works as an oil trader in the New York Mercantile exchange. He does his trading in a crowd on the floor of exchange—just like the people shown screaming at each other on TV and in movies, David makes his living by buying and selling oil. In fact, David once joked that his epitaph ought to read, "He yelled for cash."

David's yelling has resulted in quite a bit of cash. His lifetime earnings are north of $10 million, and he has earned more than $1 million in some years.

How does David make his money?

In the early days of trying to figure out David's secret, I used to grill him. "Do you think that the United States will start constructing new nuclear power plants and thereby reduce demand for oil? How did the

1991 oil fires set by Saddam Hussein's troops affect the future capacity of Kuwaiti production?" To all of these questions, David would calmly answer, "I do not know." He even joked that to make money he wouldn't even need to know the number of gallons in a barrel of oil (42).

What is David's secret? He summarizes it by saying, "I know when the buying is real and the selling is real." David stands in the crowd, listens, observes, and acts. He capitalizes on emotional signals from his counterparts, and he uses little or no formal economic analysis.

So is it possible to make money just by exploiting knowledge of sentiment, with no economic analysis? The answer is yes, but I believe it is possible to make even more money by combining economic analysis with the science of irrationality. That is the course that we will follow in the rest of this book, and it requires that we delve into the economic details.

We begin with the economic evidence in favor of the worst of times, and then move to the arguments in favor of the best of times.

Bear #1: Animal House Fraternity Goes National

"Fat, drunk, and stupid is no way to go through life, son," says Dean Vernon Wormer on his way to expelling the members of the Animal House fraternity. When learning of his expulsion, John Belushi's character Bluto remarks, "Seven years of college down the drain!"

The first argument against the U.S. economy suggests that an economic path that is the equivalent of fat, drunk, and stupid cannot have a good ending. The three "pillars" of the U.S. economy are: (1) government deficit spending, (2) the Federal Reserve's easy money policy, and (3) profligate spending by U.S. consumers.

Pillar #1: Deficit Spending

When the federal government runs a budget deficit, it sells U.S. Treasury bonds to make up the slack. From the beginning of the 1960s up until the late 1990s, the U.S government generally spent more than it collected in taxes so the supply of bonds grew. By the late 1990s, however, the government was actually running a budget surplus and using the extra cash to buy back lots of its bonds. During the technology bubble, the government was raking in lots of taxes (often paid on stock market gains).

Surprisingly, some economists thought that the U.S. debt was becoming too small! They feared that persistent U.S. government budget surpluses would lead to paying off the entire national debt and make U.S. Treasury bonds extinct. This could cause problems because some investors buy U.S. Treasury bonds as key parts of their financial strategy (e.g., insurance companies). As we see in Figure 4.1, the fear of government surpluses leading to a debt *shortage* was unfounded.

In an amazingly short time, the fear of government surpluses evaporated and we have returned to the good old days of deficit spending. In just four years, the budget swung from a surplus of more than $200 billion to a projected deficit in excess of $500 billion.

Pillar #2: Loose Money

After the stock market bubble popped, the Federal Reserve cut interest rates dramatically to soften the economic pain. The popular press believes that monetary policy can come to our rescue. Alan Greenspan is often

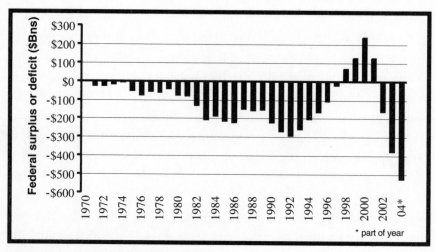

FIGURE 4.1   Uncle Sam the Borrower
Source: Office of Management and Budget

called the second most powerful person in the United States. Every statement by the Federal Reserve is scrutinized for the slightest nuance of monetary policy.

Pillar #3: Consumer Spending

Every month the government reports on American consumer spending. Wall Street cheers every report showing that we are continuing to spend like 1920s bootleggers and boos any hint of frugality. The assumption is that the more the U.S. consumer spends, the better for the U.S. economy.

Can a country really become rich by spending more than it earns and by printing money?

No. Government deficits promote waste. Loose money creates inflation, not wealth. Finally, it is possible for consumers to spend too little (e.g., Japan), but the U.S. personal savings rate is close to zero. If profligacy and printing presses were the way to grow an economy, then many countries that are now bankrupt would be economic superpowers. Similarly, seven years of fat, drunk, and stupid would be a good start to college.

Bear #2: Financial Hangover

When I was a graduate student, I played on the Harvard Ultimate Frisbee team. One of our rivals, Williams College, had an excellent team for some years until most of their star players graduated in the same class. The next year, the Harvard team destroyed Williams. In their dazed and defeated state, the Williams players gathered to regroup. One of the optimistic players said, "We can learn and improve," to which another responded, "But who is left to teach us?" The pessimistic answer: no one.

The financial hangover argument looks at the purchasers of U.S. products and asks who will buy? The pessimistic answer: no one.

To make the effects of financial hangover clear, Figure 4.2 classifies the purchasers of U.S. production. The diagram looks at actual purchases.

For example, the money that the government collects for social security is almost immediately sent back from the government to individuals. Thus, social security taxes collected by the government are counted in the U.S. consumer category. Similarly, U.S. consumers' purchases of foreign goods are not included.

There are four major groups of purchasers of U.S.-made products and services. We'll look at the financial health of these four groups of buyers and see that most buyers are not in a position to increase purchases: (1) U.S. consumers; (2) U.S. businesses; (3) foreigners; and (4) governments.

U.S. Consumers

Consumer spending is driven by both wealth and income. That is, how rich we are and how much we earn.

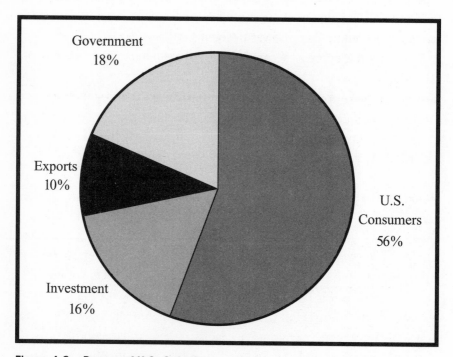

Figure 4.2   Buyers of U.S. Output
Source: U.S. Department of Commerce Estimates, 2004

Because of financial market declines, the total wealth of U.S. families in 2004 was almost identical to that in 2000.[2] Even as wealth has not increased, U.S. consumers have continued to spend. Unfortunately, income growth has also slowed considerably. The average annual growth rate of disposable personal income dropped from 4.0% in the five years ending in 2000 to 2.7% so far in the twenty-first century.[3]

So if U.S. consumers are not getting richer, and have less income to spend, is there hope of continued spending? Yes, but it will have to come by decreasing the savings rate. Figure 4.3 shows the savings behavior of U.S. consumers.

From a historical level of around 10%, the U.S. personal savings rate has declined toward zero. While it is possible for the savings rate to decline even further, I read the chart to indicate a possible rebound in savings. A return to a higher U.S. savings rate is a positive development for the long run, but it means that the U.S. consumer is unlikely to be the engine of economic growth over the next few years.

This idea that increased savings hurts the economy is known as the

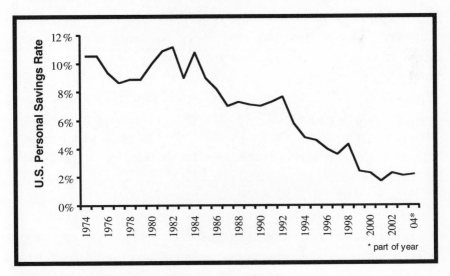

FIGURE 4.3 Americans Do Not Save Very Much
Source: U.S. Commerce Department

"paradox of thrift." Saving money is prudent and good for the individual, but the more people save, the less they buy.

To summarize the state of the U.S. consumer, both wealth and income growth have slowed. For U.S. consumers to continue to support the economy, the savings rate would have to decline even further. If consumers return to their more traditional, higher rates of savings, their rediscovered frugality will place a serious drag on the economy.

Conclusion: The U.S. consumer is unlikely to be a major source of economic growth.

U.S. Businesses

What about investment by U.S. businesses? One of the important factors driving business investment is the amount of idle production capacity. Simply put, companies with idle facilities are not likely to be aggressive purchasers of new equipment. Figure 4.4 shows the percentage of idle capacity for U.S. businesses.

U.S. businesses have about one-quarter of their capacity sitting idle, and this level has increased rapidly since the bursting of the bubble. Companies have enough spare capacity to accommodate years of economic growth without any additional investment.

The two recessions of the early 1980s and 1990s also had high levels of idle capacity. The personal savings rate diagram (Figure 4.3), shows that those recessions ended when U.S. consumers sharply decreased their savings rate throughout the 1980s and 1990s. In previous recessions, high levels of idle business capacity were put to use when consumers increased spending.

Thus, a key to U.S. business spending lies with the U.S. consumer. If consumers increase their spending, business investment will follow. If the U.S. consumer cannot be an engine of growth, then businesses are unlikely to increase their investment spending.

Conclusion: U.S. businesses may follow, but they are unlikely to lead economy recovery.

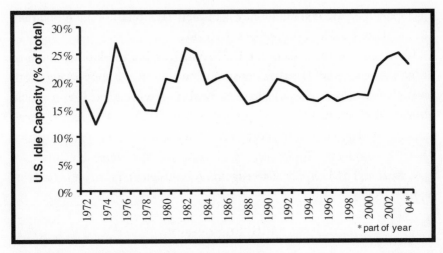

FIGURE 4.4   Lots of Excess Capacity in America
Source: Federal Reserve

Foreigners

In the midst of the 1990s' stock market bubble, one of the common justifications for ridiculous stock prices was the entry of China into the world economic system. Cisco's high stock price, it was widely said, made sense because Cisco would sell a lot of product to China. More broadly, the hope was that U.S. companies could export products to many foreign markets and thus not depend on the U.S. consumer.

While this export-based argument was wrong with regard to stock prices (Cisco shares have lost 75% of their value), a significant and growing proportion of U.S. output is indeed sold to foreign consumers. With U.S. consumers possibly looking to save, and U.S. factories sitting idle, perhaps the foreign consumer will provide growth.

Unfortunately, important foreign economies are not in great shape. Japan and Germany—the world's second and third largest economies—continue to struggle to recover from economic slumps. The German economy is barely growing at all, and the German unemployment rate is near 10%.[4]

The Japanese economy is not in much better shape. Since the late 1980s, the Japanese stock market average has declined from 40,000 to just over 11,000 (July 2004). This decline far exceeds both the length and depth of the U.S. stock market troubles. The Japanese stock market decline provides a measure of Japanese economic weakness. It also reduces the wealth of Japanese people and puts further downward pressure on the global economy.

Even the effect of Chinese economic liberalization has been negative for U.S. producers. Chinese workers make products more cheaply than U.S. workers. The export of those Chinese products has negative effects on the U.S. economy.

Conclusion: Exports are a potential source for economic growth, but given their relatively small role in the U.S. economy, the effect may not be significant.

Governments

The final significant piece of economic consumption is local, state, and federal governments. With overburdened U.S. consumers, idle factories, and less than robust foreign economies, can government spending fuel the economy?

Most of the discussion about government spending revolves around U.S. federal spending. It is important to note that state and local government spending is almost as important as that of the federal government.

In his campaign for California governor, Arnold Schwarzenegger famously remarked, "The public doesn't care about figures."[5] That may be an accurate assessment of voter sentiment, but governors themselves must care about numbers. Most state and local governments are legally required to run balanced budgets so when times are tough, their spending must be reduced.

All around the country, state and local governments are cutting services and raising taxes. In order to close its budget gap, New York City raised property taxes. California Governor Gray Davis earned the hatred of many by tripling the tax on car registration. A similar story is unfolding across the country. The conclusion is that state and local governments will be a drag on economic recovery, not a stimulant.

What about the federal government? As we discussed earlier in the chapter, the federal government has been the major supporter of economic growth by heavy deficit spending. Can the federal government increase the deficit even more and provide more economic growth? Yes. A $500 billion deficit is large by any measure. When compared to the size of the economy, however, the current deficit is much smaller than historical extremes.[6] Thus, if needed, the federal government can increase purchases.

There are, however, risks to increased federal deficits. The most obvious is the possibility of rising interest rates. If large, additional government borrowing forces up interest rates, the increase in mortgage rates will depress the housing sector. The U.S. market for homes has remained strong because it has been fueled by low mortgage rates. The housing market will be hurt if mortgage rates rise in response to additional federal spending.

Conclusion: The U.S. government has the potential to increase deficit spending and provide a boost to the economy. However, additional deficit spending may cause an increase in mortgage rates and damage the housing market.

The United States is struggling with a financial hangover. The effects of the 1990s' excesses will reduce economic growth.

Bull #1: Economic Eyeglasses for the Short-Sighted

The first optimistic defense of the economy simply looks at the longer trend instead of the recent past. If we cast our eyes back to the immediate post-bubble past, the picture painted above is quite grim. We are told that things are often darkest before the dawn. It is easy to repeat such phrases, but harder to feel optimistic during tough times. This lesson was demonstrated by one of General George Custer's men at the Battle of the Little Big Horn.

There is a story that has been passed around about the battle. As is well known, General Custer's men were wiped out and none of his troops survived. According to this story—which would have come from Sioux warriors—one of the cavalrymen had an opportunity to escape. He was riding away and had enough of a lead over his pursuers that his odds were good. At precisely the moment when he looked likely to escape, however, he pulled out his pistol and committed suicide.

The U.S. economy has taken some severe blows in recent years. Yet we may be on the cusp of recovery and ought not despair at what might be our darkest hour. If we take even a slightly longer-term perspective, most economic statistics look quite good. The U.S. stock market as measured by the S&P 500 index is down about one-third from its all-time high (as of July 2004). It has, however, gained almost 1,000% since the stock market bottom in the early 1980s.

A similar pattern emerges across almost all the seemingly dire economic landscape. Interest rates have risen from their lows (including one amazing 50% rise in little over a month), yet rates remain near 50-year lows. Inflation has become so low that the Federal Reserve has spent considerable effort wondering how to stop prices from falling.

Rising unemployment is perhaps the worst aspect of current economic troubles. The unemployment rate has risen by almost 50% and literally millions of people have lost their jobs. Even in this area, the longer-term news is good. As recently as 10 years ago, the current unemployment rate of about 6% would have been considered good news.[7]

What about the enormous federal government deficit? Surely the rapid swing from large government surplus to gaping deficit cannot be overlooked. Surprisingly, even in this area, the longer-term perspective is very positive. If we measure the amount of U.S. government debt as a percentage of the total economy, the debt is significantly smaller than it was in 1993. Measured this way, the current federal debt is only about one-half as big now as it was at the end of WWII.[8]

Conclusion: While the last few years have been painful, there is no proof that the longer-term economic miracle has ended.

Bull #2: Vince Lombardi Meets the Computer

"Winning isn't everything, it is the only thing."

This quote is misattributed to legendary Green Bay Packers' Coach Vince Lombardi who actually said, "Winning is not everything—but making effort to win is." It is an odd quirk of history that Lombardi is most remembered for something he didn't say. What he did say on a variety of topics is great, and much of it is relevant to investing. Among my favorites is, "Winning is a habit. Unfortunately, so is losing."

When it comes to economic growth, productivity isn't everything, it is the only thing. Even though Coach Lombardi probably never said this either, it is a mathematical fact.

There are two roads to wealth: One is to work harder, and the second is to work smarter. Obviously working smarter is the preferred route; productivity measures the economy's ability to work smart. Thus productivity becomes the key to long-term economic growth.

Optimists can make a good argument based on U.S. productivity as shown in Figure 4.5.

This young decade has had higher U.S. productivity growth than any other in the post-WWII era.

Is productivity really higher now than in the past and can the good news continue? It seems possible. Some economic historians make an analogy between the Industrial Revolution and the information technology revolution. It took many decades to learn how to harness machines effectively. Thus the benefits from the Industrial Revolution were not immediately visible.

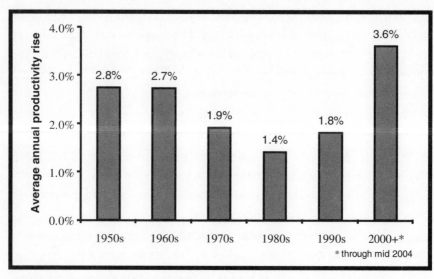

FIGURE 4.5 U.S. Productivity Growth Is Very Rapid
Source: U.S. Bureau of Labor Statistics (non-farm business output per hour)

We may just be getting to the time when information technology is being understood well enough to make us richer. If so, it is possible that the recent high productivity will not only continue, but could even accelerate.

Is the recent rise in productivity really a big deal? Yes, because of the magic of compound interest. My favorite example of compound interest comes from Charles Darwin. In Chapter 3 of the *Origin of Species,* he writes:[9]

> The elephant is reckoned to be the slowest breeder of all known animals, and I have taken some pains to estimate its probable minimum rate of natural increase: it will be under the mark to assume that it breeds when thirty years old, and goes on breeding till ninety years old, bringing forth three pairs of young in this interval; if this be so, at the end of the fifth century there would be alive fifteen million elephants, descended from the first pair.

Darwin was calculating compound interest. If something grows at just over 2.3% a year, it doubles in 30 years. The magic of compound interest means that even with slow rates of growth, given enough time, the overall growth is stunning. The inability of the world to support so many elephants was an important step on Darwin's intellectual road.

To appreciate what different productivity rates mean, let's take Keynes at his word. What are the economic possibilities of our grandchildren? In particular, let's contrast the wealth of our grandchildren under two possible scenarios. In the high-growth scenario, productivity grows at the 3.62% average of this decade. In the lower-growth scenario, productivity grows at the 1.72% average of the period 1970 to 1999.

Does it matter much for your grandchildren which of these two productivity rates exists for the next 40 years? Let's test your intuition. How many hours per week will your grandchild work to have the same lifestyle as could be earned by working 40 hours now? Here are four possible answers.

(1) 29.3 hours per week.
(2) 20.2 hours per week.
(3) 15.9 hours per week.
(4) 9.6 hours per week.

Pick an answer for each of the two productivity scenarios—high growth and lower growth. If the world turns out as in (2), your grandchildren will be roughly twice as rich as you for each hour that they work. That means twice as many cars, TVs, fridges, and vacations per hour of effort.

Before we get to the correct answers, let's take a step back and understand that even a productivity growth rate of 1% is remarkable and rare.

What is the productivity growth rate for our closest living ancestor, the chimpanzee? This may seem like a strange question, but the answer is easy to calculate. Take a modern-day chimpanzee, and calculate the number of hours of work to obtain a fixed amount of food.

To calculate change in productivity, compare the modern chimpanzee's workload with the comparable figure for a chimpanzee from a thousand or a million years ago. Of course, we do not have any historical data on chimpanzees, but the answer is clear. The productivity growth rate for chimpanzees (and all other animals) is zero. Animals, even those with culture, show no progress across generations.

The economic opportunities of the grandchildren of modern chimpanzees will be no higher than today's chimpanzees (and probably far worse because of environmental destruction). Perhaps it is obvious that animals have zero productivity growth. Less obvious is the fact that the human rate of productivity growth throughout much of history has also been almost exactly zero! Through most eras, humans have done no better than chimpanzees or even bacteria for that matter. Keynes makes this point in his grandchildren essay noting, "the absence of modern technical inventions between the prehistoric age and comparatively modern times is truly remarkable."

The archeological record reveals that Keynes's observation applies to most periods. For most of human existence, the rate of technological change was essentially zero. Our modern ability to create more material goods per unit of effort is nothing short of amazing.

Let's return to our grandchildren. The answers are 20.2 hours per week for the lower-growth case and just 9.6 hours per week for the high-growth case. If the next 40 years look like the period 1970 to 1999, our grandchildren will have to work half as hard as we for the same material outcome. Alternatively, if productivity grows at the rate of the last few years, our grandchildren will only have to work one-quarter as hard as we do. If the high productivity path happens, our grandchildren could work Keynes's 15 hour weeks and be considerably richer than we. Note that productivity growth doesn't just mean more TVs, it also allows for better medical care and education.

In terms of economic wealth, small improvements in productivity translate into big improvements to our lives and those of our children and grandchildren. When it comes to economic wealth, productivity is the only thing. Thus, our economic wealth depends almost entirely on the rate of productivity growth.

There are, of course, a number of important caveats to this productivity argument that go beyond the scope of this book. First, average economic wealth may mean very little if it comes in a world that is environmentally damaged. Second, the distribution of wealth may be more important than its total. Third, and most fundamentally, there is scant evidence that increases in wealth make people any happier. In fact, studies from around the world suggest that while most of us believe money will make us happier, wealth does not cause happiness.[10] All of these are important topics, but not for this book, which is dedicated to the mission of helping investors make money.

Conclusion: If the last few years of extremely high productivity are a sign of good times to come, we will be much richer, and our large debts will not be a problem.

America: The Talented Beggar

We started this chapter by asking what path the United States will take. Will it be Keynes's vision of examined leisure created by information technology, or will we stumble down a painful path similar to that taken by post-bubble Japan?

Those who believe that these are the worst of times are right to recognize the U.S. financial hangover from the bubble years. The aftereffects of the 1990s are clearly visible in shaky consumer finances, idle factories, and large government deficits. However, those who believe these are the best of times are right to recognize the central importance of extremely high productivity growth.

Thus, productivity is the key. If there is to be a happy financial ending for the United States, it must come through information technology and productivity growth. For investors, this converts to simple advice. Watch the productivity figures. If productivity can stay above 3% for the coming years, then like my talented running teammate, the United States should be able to work through its hangover. If productivity drops substantially, however, the pain of recovering from the excesses of the 1990s will be much greater.

chapter five

INFLATION
Rising Prices and Shrinking Dollars

Return of the Inflationary Monster?

During the German hyperinflation of the early 1920s, banknotes had so little value that people had to carry money around in giant sacks. So worthless had the money become that one man who left a wheelbarrow full of money unattended for a moment returned to find that thieves had left his money but had stolen his wheelbarrow. While this story is funny, the hyperinflation itself was not; it wiped out the lifetime savings of millions of families.

My first experiences as an investor came in the inflationary 1970s. In those days, inflation was a mysterious monster ravaging the U.S. and global economies. When I was in college in the 1970s, my friends and I used to retire to the student lounge after dinner each night to watch Mel Brooks' classic comedy show, *Get Smart*. Because the lounge had just one shared TV, a form of adolescent democracy selected the channel. Other students who wanted to learn and not laugh sometimes outvoted my friends and me, and on some evenings we were forced to watch the nightly news.

When it came to inflation in the 1970s, the TV news was bleak. Every month the government would announce the growing rate of inflation. We sat and feared that we would not have enough money to enjoy life. Even presidents seemed impotent to defeat the inflationary monster. In 1974, President Gerald Ford manufactured millions of "WIN" buttons to exhort the American public to "Whip Inflation Now" (although he never told us quite how we were supposed to accomplish this task). In sour economic times, President Ford lost to Jimmy Carter in the 1976 election. President Carter in turn lost his 1980 election to Ronald Reagan—a casualty, some say, in the Federal Reserve's campaign to defeat inflation.

As shown in Figure 5.1, the 1970s' U.S. inflationary monster was tamed, and for the last two decades, the United States has enjoyed a low inflation rate. Stories of inflationary problems might therefore seem to apply only to those living in Latin American countries or those with a long memory. Recently, however, gold prices have risen dramatically,

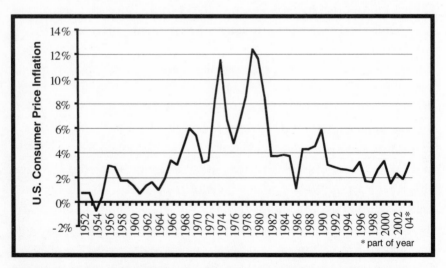

FIGURE 5.1   The United States Has Enjoyed Low Inflation for Many Years
Source: Bureau of Labor Statistics

and the value of the U.S. dollar has declined substantially. These are classic signs that inflation might be building. What are the prospects for inflation, and what sorts of financial investments are likely to prosper?

As in most areas to do with money, the best insights on inflation come from Professor Milton Friedman. Winner of the 1976 Nobel Prize in Economics, Professor Friedman is the leader of the monetarist school that seeks to understand the financial world through the creation and removal of money from the economy.

The seminal work, *A Monetary History of the United States, 1867–1960,* written by Professors Friedman and Anna Schwarz, states, "Money is a fascinating subject of study because it is so full of mystery and paradox. The piece of green paper with printing on it is little different, as paper, from a piece of the same size torn from a newspaper or magazine, yet the one will enable its bearer to command some measure of food, drink, clothing, and the remaining goods of life: The other is fit only to light the fire. Whence the difference?"[1]

As Professor Friedman suggests, to understand inflation we must remove some of the monetary mystery. Accordingly, our investigation into inflation starts with an analysis of the reason we use money in its current form. In this journey, we begin by examining a modern market that does not use money at all.

The Creation of Money: This Kidney Is Not for Sale!

Kidney transplantation is a potentially life-saving surgery that transfers a kidney from one person to another. Sometimes the kidney comes from a donor who has recently died, while many others come from living donors. Most people are born with two kidneys but can live quite well with just one.

My Harvard Business School colleague, Professor Al Roth, has become involved in improving the kidney transplantation system. At first glance, the situation seems quite simple and not applicable to the tools of economics. People in need seek a relative or friend willing to donate a kidney. Those needy patients who do not find a willing donor wait in line for kidneys from cadavers. Why is Professor Roth, an economist, involved in a medical process?

There are special circumstances that make the kidney market particularly problematic and appeal to an economist's special skills. Kidney donors and recipients need to match on a number of physiological measures. So while a needy patient might find a willing donor in, for example, his or her spouse, tissue incompatibility may preclude a transplant. In these cases, a willing donor cannot help his or her loved one because of biological mismatch.

A potential solution for couples suffering from this mismatch is to find a complementary couple in a similar situation. In the simplest case, two such couples might find that they can swap organs. So, for example, Mrs. Smith wants to donate a kidney to Mr. Smith, but they are biologically incompatible. Similarly, Mr. Jones wants to donate a kidney to Mrs. Jones, but cannot. If, by chance, they are mutually compatible, the solution is to have Mrs. Smith donate to Mrs. Jones, and Mr. Jones to Mr. Smith. Thus, both patients get the kidneys they need.

This sort of "matching" problem is well understood by economists and is a particular area of expertise of my colleague Al Roth. In some of his previous work, Professor Roth helped reform the system of matching medical residents to positions at teaching hospitals.[2] Thus, the kidney transplantation system, which appears at first to be purely medical, has an underlying "matching" problem that has been studied by economists.

Such organ-swapping is legal, and it is beginning to happen. Here is a summary of a news story about one such arrangement (*The Reporter*, Vanderbilt University Medical Center, November 21, 2003):

The lives of two West Tennessee families have been changed forever by the generous act of organ donation, but not in the way they had originally planned. Kay Morris, 53, was to receive a kidney from her daughter, Melissa Floyd, and Tom Duncan, from his friend and neighbor, Patricia Dempsey. But, there was a positive cross match within each couple so the transplants couldn't take place. Debbie Crowe, Ph.D., an astute Nashville immunologist, discovered that by swapping kidneys between the two pairs, the transplants would work.

In this case, Melissa donated her kidney to Tom, a man she had not previously met, while Tom's friend Patricia donated her kidney to Melissa's mother. These organ-swapping arrangements allowed transplants that could not take place otherwise. In this case, two recipients received new kidneys that they could not have had without involving the other pair. Fantastic.

There are, however, some difficulties with kidney swaps. First, sometimes it takes more than two pairs to find compatible matches. For example, Johns Hopkins recently performed a three-way swap. Involving more couples makes the matching process more difficult, particularly since donor and recipient need to be in the same hospital for the surgery. Second, surgeons who do swaps have a rule that all the surgeries must take place simultaneously. In the West Tennessee case, that meant four simultaneous operations (two donors, two recipients) and the Johns Hopkins triple swap involved six operating teams working on the three donors and the three recipients at the same time.

Why do the surgeons require simultaneous exchange? They fear that if the exchanges are not simultaneous, then some of the donors might change their minds. Perhaps, for example, Mr. Jones might become unwilling to donate his kidney after Mrs. Jones has received her new kidney. Obviously, it is impossible to compel someone to donate a kidney against his or her will.

To avoid this problem of failed exchange, surgeons require that all of the operations take place at the same time. The requirement for simultaneous exchange makes the actual operations much more complicated. Recall that each operation involves many medical staff. So the requirement to have four or more full medical teams working simultaneously is very challenging.

Furthermore, simultaneous exchange prevents some swaps entirely. For example, a patient's compatible donor might not be available until next year. If there were some way to store value over time, such swaps could take place. For example, a donor could give one kidney to a stranger now, and get credit for future exchange when the matching donor is discovered. Such swaps that involve delays are impossible if all exchanges must be simultaneous.

Using his expertise on matching, Professor Roth is working to improve the quantity and quality of these exchanges between couples. His work has the potential to greatly improve the system, but is limited and complicated by the requirement for simultaneous exchange.

Now imagine what the world would be like if all economic transactions required simultaneous exchange. A simple task like filling a car's gas tank would require a negotiation involving delivery of some good or service to the gas station owner. Perhaps the most profound effect would be the difficulty retirement would bring about. During later years, most people spend years or decades living off previously accumulated wealth. The ability to store up favors of the magnitude required to retire would be impossible if all exchanges needed to be simultaneous.

The world of simultaneous exchange is not mythical; it is called a barter economy. Before the invention of money, all human societies used barter. Even recently, some nonindustrialized societies existed without money. As the kidney example illustrates, the need for simultaneous exchange in barter societies places a serious damper on economic activity. Consequently, barter economies are less productive than societies that use money. Importantly for financial planning, barter economies make it very difficult to store up wealth to use in the future for retirement or other activities.

The Form of Money: Rice, Cheese, Stones, Gold, and Paper

Money is truly an amazing invention that lubricates economic exchange. As Milton Friedman writes, money in its current paper form is almost magical. With money, one is able to obtain real goods—food, drink, transportation, and housing—in return for flimsy pieces of paper. Furthermore, the ability to store wealth means that retirees can live for decades off their savings.

I am reminded of the power of money when I travel to exotic locations. Emerging from a busy and frequently dusty airport, I am immediately able to get help from strangers simply by offering a piece of paper. These strangers are willing to help me because other people will, in turn, grant them valuable goods and services in exchange for the paper that I provide. Both transactions are made possible by the fantastic tool of money.

For all of its wonderful positive effects, money immediately creates the potential for trouble that is not possible with barter. Recall that because of simultaneous medical operations, our kidney-swapping couples are sure that the other couples will do their part. In contrast, in any transaction using money, one side gives up something of immediate value in return for the promise of future value. Those who trade a hamburger today for a dollar they will spend next Tuesday (or 10 years from next Tuesday) risk the prospect that the dollar will lose some of its value before it is spent.

Part of the risk of money lies in its somewhat ephemeral nature. Modern paper money has value only because others perceive it to have value. As Professor Friedman writes, "Why should they [dollars] also be accepted by private persons in private transactions for goods and services? The short answer—yet the right answer—is that each accepts them because he is confident others will. The pieces of paper have value because everybody thinks they have value."[3]

Unlike dollar bills, some earlier forms of money had intrinsic value.

Rice and other grains were used in a variety of cultures.[4] The recipient of "rice" money knows that even if everyone else stops accepting payment in rice, he or she can eat the money. For similar reasons, some northern European cultures used cheese as currency.[5]

While rice and cheese solve the problem of future repayment, they have their own problems. They can be bulky, hard to store, and subject to decay. Imagine the difficulty of keeping your retirement account entirely in the form of rice, or hauling a giant sack of cheese to the car dealer. Other forms of money can improve upon these "commodity" currencies.

Throughout the ages people have been willing to die and kill for gold. On the surface, this might seem ridiculous, as gold has very few actual uses (and cannot be eaten!). Gold has value not for what it can do, but because it solves many of the problems with commodity-based currencies like rice and cheese.

If we were to imagine ideal money, what characteristics would we seek? Ideal money would be easy to verify, impossible to counterfeit, portable, and not subject to decay. Gold has been an important currency throughout human monetary history because it has many of these characteristics. It is scarce enough that small amounts have value, thus making it portable. It is relatively easy to detect fake gold, and gold does not rot when stored. This seemingly simple set of features explains why gold can launch (and sink) armadas, ruin friendships, and dominate dreams.

For all of its advantages, gold and other naturally occurring forms of money still have problems. Residents on the Pacific Island of Yap discovered this through an interesting experience.[6] This is an old story that has become famous because it is included in Professor Gregory Mankiw's best-selling textbook (called simply *Macroeconomics*).[7] (Professor Mankiw taught in the Harvard economics department and is currently the head of President Bush's Council of Economic Advisors.)

The residents of Yap use money called "fei" that consists of large stone wheels shaped liked coins that can reach up to 12 feet in diameter. These fei have many of the optimal characteristics of money. They are difficult to counterfeit and they do not decay. While the fei are not portable, they are stored in the equivalent of banks and do not get moved very frequently. The fei can change ownership without being physically moved. Because the society is sufficiently small, everyone knows who owns which fei, and consequently there is no risk of theft.

Many years ago one of the fei was washed away during a storm. The people of Yap faced a choice. Should the person who owned the money be liable? If so, that person would suffer, but so would the whole society. As Professor Friedman has shown, the amount of money affects economic activity. Thus a decrease in the amount of money would likely harm the overall economy. The residents of Yap decided that the lost fei should still be credited to its owner. So while the actual fei remained lost, all the residents simply acted as if it were still on the island. They kept track of who owned the fei and—many years later—this virtual fei still existed in everyone's mind and was used in transactions.

The story of stone money on the island of Yap illustrates the problem with any tangible currency. If such currency is used, then the ability to create money is taken out of the government's hands. So in the case of Yap, the entire society would have had less money if the washed-away fei had been declared lost. In the case of gold, the quantity of metal is determined not by government, but rather by the foibles of discovery and mining technology.

As we'll see, government control of money is frequently the source of monetary misery. Nevertheless, few leaders want their economy to be subject to the ebb and flow of gold production. The United States was effectively on a gold standard from the Bretton Woods agreement in 1944 up until 1971. Because President Nixon wanted to stimulate the economy, something that was difficult to do under the rules of Bretton Woods, he removed the fixed link between U.S. dollars and gold. Today, every major country has made a similar move, and money has been decoupled from anything tangible. We live in an era of so-called "fiat" money where the supply of currency is dictated by government command (or fiat).

With the proper controls on counterfeiting, fiat money has a seemingly perfect set of characteristics. Fiat money is of known value, lightweight, and easy to store. Unlike gold, the supply of fiat money is controlled by the government and so can be modulated to fit economic needs.

Shrinking Money: The Trouble with Inflation

Economics is often characterized and summarized as "supply and demand." When it comes to money, there are clear consequences to changes in supply. The residents on the highlands of Papua New Guinea learned this in the early part of the twentieth century.

Papua New Guinea is a large island north of Australia. The coasts are populated with people who have been in contact with their neighbors in other countries for centuries. Soon after leaving the coastal region, the land rises steeply to a mountainous and elevated plateau that was thought to be too rough for human habitation.

In the early part of the twentieth century, a group of Australians decided to investigate the highlands in search of gold. There are several fascinating aspects to this story. First, the highlands were far from empty, but rather contained close to a million people who had been almost completely isolated from other cultures for centuries. Second, the Australians brought a movie camera with them. This may be the only film recording of a first contact with a nonindustrialized people. Some of the original footage can be viewed in an academic movie appropriately titled *First Contact*. Third, and particularly relevant to our story, the people of the highlands placed a high value on seashells.[8]

Why would anyone use seashells as a form of money? For most cultures this would be silly, as no one would exchange anything of great value for seashells. In the highlands of Papua New Guinea, however, seashells make as much sense as gold did for ancient Greeks. Almost completely isolated from the sea, shells in the highlands were scarce enough that small amounts had high value. It is easy to detect fake shells, and shells do not rot when stored. These are exactly the characteristics that make gold valuable all over the world.

As long as the highlands were separated from the seashores, a seashell money standard made sense. However, it did not take the Australian gold miners long to understand the opportunity. There was some gold in the highlands, but it required hard work to extract. The Australians flew in planeloads of seashells they used to pay wages of the highlanders who mined the gold. The highlanders worked for seashells until shells became so common as to lose value.

There is no question that the Australians exploited the Papua New Guinea highlanders, but the highlanders did not want to be paid in paper currency. With shells the highlanders could buy anything they wanted within their community; banknotes were worthless. This changed when the Australians opened up trade stores where banknotes could be exchanged for pots, pans, axes, and shovels. One of the original Australian miners, Dan Leahy, opened up a trade store and stocked it with a variety of goods. What do you suppose was his most popular item? It was the big "*kina*" shells used as part of courtship.

The Papua New Guinea highlanders exchanged their hard work in return for money. These workers were hurt because their money came in the form of seashells, and the rapid increase in the supply of shells pushed their prices down. Thus, the decision to trade work for shells was made with an expectation of a particular value to the shells. The increased supply of seashells made this a rotten deal for the workers.

The highlanders continued to value shells for years. This may seem silly, but imagine our response if extraterrestrials with unlimited quantities of gold came to earth. It would probably take us some time to prefer their paper money to gold.

Inflation is defined as a loss of purchasing power for a particular amount of money. Before the Australians arrived, one beautiful shell had considerable value and could even constitute the bulk of the money paid to find a marriage partner. After shells became common, their value plummeted. Thus, the Papua New Guinea highlanders experienced a severe period of inflation. Those who had accumulated wealth in the form of stored shells saw the value of their savings devastated by the inflation.

Residents of Weimar, Germany, in the 1920s ran into a similar problem.[9] People who accepted paper money in return for work or goods soon found that the paper money had no value. The magnitude of the German inflation is almost impossible to comprehend. In 1920, the cost to send a letter was under one mark. By 1923, the cost had risen to 50 billion marks! In this period, prices could double in a day.

Based on stories like these, John Maynard Keynes quipped that in inflationary times, people ought to take taxis, whereas in noninflationary times, buses are preferred. His logic? You pay at the end of a taxi ride and at the beginning with buses. In times of hyperinflation, the later you can pay a fee, the lower its true economic cost. Similarly, in the inflationary 1970s, my friend Jay's father taught him to always defer payment by using credit cards.

My grandmother, who lived through the German hyperinflation, described some of its effects. As soon as the family earned a paycheck, she would immediately rush to a store to buy as much as possible before prices rose. My grandmother's modest earnings for teaching converted into so many stacks of bulky bills that she used a baby pram to transport the cash.

Stores could not change prices on goods fast enough to keep up with inflation, so some implemented a multiplication factor system.[10] A grocery store, for example, might mark a can of soup at 10,000. The actual cost of the soup at the time of purchase would be the price (10,000) times a factor posted at the front of the store. So if the factor were 3, the soup would cost 30,000. This system allowed the store to mark up all prices immediately by changing the factor. A change from 3 to 4, for example, immediately increases prices by 33%. My grandmother told of the stress of waiting in line and fearing that the prices might be increased before she could pay.

The effect on German savers was dramatic. Imagine someone who worked his or her whole life to amass a pile of savings. To be concrete, imagine someone who had stashed away 20 million marks. In 1920, this would have been a fortune, allowing a life of opulent leisure. Just three years later this fortune would not even come close to buying a single postage stamp. German savers who kept their money in marks were completely wiped out.

No cloud, it is said, is without a silver lining. While some were wiped out by the German hyperinflation, others were made much richer. In fact, hyperinflation works to wipe out all debts. The Bible writes of "jubilee" years when all debts are forgiven: "Then you shall cause the trumpet of the Jubilee to sound . . . And you shall consecrate the fiftieth year, and proclaim liberty throughout all the land to all its inhabitants." In a Jubilee year, all debts are forgiven.

Hyperinflation is an effective jubilee. For example, during German hyperinflation the total value of all German mortgages as measured in U.S. currency declined from $10 billion to under one U.S. penny.[11] Debtors were able to pay off their debts with the wheelbarrows full of nearly worthless marks. Thus, one important effect of inflation is to hurt savers and help debtors (more on how to profit from this later). This could be considered good or bad, depending on whether one favors the savers or the spenders.

While the erasing of debts helps some and hurts others, a second effect of high inflation is simply bad. Because of the uncertain value of currency, many people simply stop accepting money. Thus, the economy returns to barter with all the consequent inefficiencies of simultaneous exchange.

So an economy like that of 1920s Germany can go in a full circle. Before the creation of money, all exchanges are done by barter. Then commodity money replaces barter with gold, and then with paper money. If the paper money loses value because of high inflation, the economy returns to barter with its inherent inefficiencies.

Goldilocks and Inflation That Is "Just Right"

Goldilocks entered the house of three bears. In the kitchen, there were three bowls of porridge. Goldilocks was hungry. She tasted the porridge from the first bowl. "This porridge is too hot!" she exclaimed. So, she tasted the porridge from the second bowl. "This porridge is too cold," she said. So, she tasted the last bowl of porridge. "Ahhh, this porridge is just right," she said happily and she ate it all up.

Just as Goldilocks liked porridge that was neither too hot nor too cold, economists think that the optimal level of inflation is neither too high nor too low. While high inflation has obvious costs, falling prices also have their "costs." During a recent visit to Japan, my wife Barbara and I were discussing Tokyo rents with a friend. Our host told us that every year she meets with her landlord to discuss the magnitude of the rent *decrease* for the following year. Over recent years, prices of land have fallen dramatically, and consequently landlords have found it necessary to cut rents.

Rent reductions may sound delicious, but the broader consequences can be quite negative. It turns out that falling prices can cause trouble. In fact, the Japanese economy has suffered from deflation since the bursting of its financial bubble in the late 1980s.

An obvious problem with deflation is that it rewards frugality—to an extent that can harm the economy. My friend Jane, for example, never wants to buy a computer because she knows that she can buy it for a lot less next year. In a deflation, all sorts of prices are falling and this can create a destructive cycle. Falling prices encourage people to wait to buy, and this in turn reduces demand, which causes prices to fall even further. This is precisely the opposite of the effects of hyperinflation that encourage people to spend money minutes after they are paid.

A second problem with deflation is that people really hate taking pay cuts. While this seems obvious, the amount of hatred can be surprising, and the consequences severe. One striking example involves the labor negotiations between the workers and the management of Hormel Foods in the early 1980s. Hormel's products include the meat product Spam, which inspired the name for junk e-mail. We teach this example in our negotiations class at the Harvard Business School, and the saga is recorded in the excellent documentary *American Dream.*

In the early 1980s, the areas surrounding Hormel's plant in the midwestern United States were hit by a severe recession. Accordingly,

Hormel plant workers agreed to temporary wage cuts. In the next contract negotiation, the workers and management met to reach a more permanent labor agreement. After some intense and protracted negotiation, management offered $10/hour, an offer that was less than a dollar below that contained in the pre-recession contract. The workers insisted that the new wage be at least as high as the wage in the previous contract.

With pennies per hour separating the two sides, the union went on strike. The results were devastating. The strikers were fired. Many of the fired strikers were forced to move out of the area. The company found plenty of replacement workers (the prevailing wage for similar jobs in the area was around half of management's offer).

The Hormel strikers were unwilling to take a small wage cut even though the economic conditions were severe. The unwillingness to accept management's offer led to severe disruptions in the workers' lives.

What does this have to do with money and inflation? The relationship between inflation and the Hormel strike is as follows: Imagine that the workers were given back their old wages but that inflation has eroded the value of their wages to the level offered by management. Would the workers have gone on strike, lost their jobs, and moved out of state to prevent inflation from reducing their pay by less than a dollar per hour? No one can know the answer, but evidence suggests that the Hormel workers would have not gone on strike to prevent a few cents' worth of inflation.

If inflation changes a decision, it is labeled "money illusion." In most economic theory, workers are expected to react identically to a pay cut by management, and the same effective pay cut due to inflation. If, however, workers treat the two situations differently, mainstream economists say that they are acting irrationally. (Behavioral economists suggest they are acting like normal people.)

In real world situations, one can never be sure of the causes. So perhaps there was more to the Hormel story than worker stubbornness. In laboratory experiments, however, economists can create artificial inflations and deflations. The result from recent experiments by the team of professors Ernst Fehr and Jean-Robert Tyran indicate that people do exhibit money illusion.[12]

A more mundane version of money illusion is the tendency for people to set watches and clocks a few minutes fast. The clock on my computer has been six minutes fast for years. If I were completely rational, I would immediately know the real time. Even after years, however, my lizard brain is still fooled by my fast clock. While I can rapidly calculate the correct time, my first glance takes the clock at face value. Consequently, I get out the door a little sooner than I would with a clock with the right time.

Money illusion is one reason economists believe that some inflation is good. Inflation allows the adjustment of prices without triggering anyone's emotional stand against getting a worse deal. For example, increased competition from China might cause the "appropriate" wage for U.S. textile workers to go down. This real-wage drop can occur either through an actual pay cut (which is likely to be resisted) or through a wage increase that is less than the rate of inflation. The true economic impact is the same in both cases, but one is more palatable.

Wage rigidity appears to hold outside the laboratory as well, and some believe it was an important source of the extremely high unemployment rate during the Great Depression.[13] Because of money illusion and deflation, some scholars argue that Depression wages did not fall to levels low enough to induce employers to hire more workers.

This Goldilocks view of inflation has been studied extensively by a large number of economists.[14] In 1996, Larry Summers gave a talk on his views on the optimal inflation rate. Larry Summers is currently the president of Harvard University, and although still quite young, was a tenured economics professor at Harvard before holding a variety of nonacademic positions, including Secretary of the Treasury. In his discussion, he summarizes this sticky wage situation as follows: "You can't get real-wage reductions without nominal wage cuts, making it harder to get the needed labor market adjustments." For this and other reasons, Professor Summers concludes that an inflation rate of 1 to 3% "looks about right."[15]

Yogi Berra and Milton Friedman Share a Pizza

Where do we stand in our monetary journey? First, we have learned that money is a financial tool invented to lubricate the economy. Without money we would be forced to use inefficient and complex simultaneous exchange as in the kidney transplantation market. Second, we determined the attributes of ideal forms of money, which helps us understand the progression of types of money. Third, we have learned the Goldilocks rule that some inflation, at a low rate, is "just right."

A mystery remains, however, and it is the one that worried me in the 1970s. All of our knowledge about money and inflation is great, but what is the use if inflation is an uncontrollable monster capable of toppling presidents and destroying societies? Knowing the enemy may have some benefits, but it would be much better if that enemy could be shackled.

The real mystery of inflation is that there is any mystery at all. There is no magic behind the cause and control of inflation. In *The Wizard of Oz,* the magic of the land is revealed when Dorothy pays attention to the man behind the curtain. Similarly, there are people who determine the inflation rate. Far from being an uncontrollable beast, inflation is a tame dog both created and completely controlled by monetary authorities.

Milton Friedman appropriately gets credit for the academic understanding of inflation. As in many other areas, however, Yogi Berra captured its essence without a Ph.D. in economics. When asked how many pieces he wanted a pizza cut into, Berra replied by saying, "Just four, I'm on a diet." (Whether he actually made this joke is subject to dispute. Berra claims to be misquoted frequently. He coauthored a book titled *I Really Didn't Say Everything I Said.*)

Regardless of its origin, the joke recognizes an obvious truth. A pizza contains the same number of calories regardless of how it is divided. Thus, the choice of the number of slices merely determines the size of each slice, not the size of the overall pizza.

Professor Friedman made the same discovery when it comes to the value of money. The decision on how much money to create doesn't have much effect on the overall size of the economy, but it does have an enormous effect on the value of money. He wrote, "Inflation is always and everywhere a monetary phenomenon."[16]

When the amount of money is increased, the result is inflation. Inflation destroyed the value of seashells in Papua New Guinea. When their "money supply" increased because of the importation of planeloads of seashells, the value of each seashell decreased. Similarly, the German hyperinflation was caused by a massive increase in the supply of German marks.

Inflation is simple. When more money is created, the value of each piece of money declines. That is inflation.

What about the U.S. inflation of the 1970s? I was particularly scared by news reports that suggested inflation was some mysterious force. As Figure 5.2 shows, this inflation was not mysterious at all. It was, to quote Milton Friedman, "a monetary phenomenon."

The inflation of the 1970s was caused by a rapid growth in the money supply. Just as there is no mystery (to those in the know) for the cause of inflation, there is no mystery for its cure.

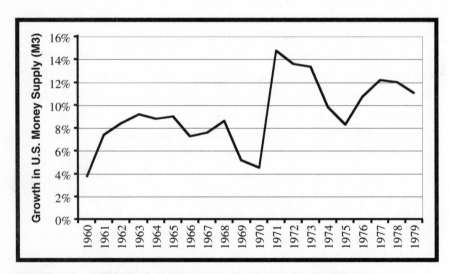

FIGURE 5.2   1970s' U.S. Inflation Was Created by "Loose" Money
Source: U.S. Federal Reserve

In 1979, Paul Volcker became the chair of the U.S. Federal Reserve. With inflation running at about 13% a year, Chairman Volcker decided to stop the insanity. He slowed the growth of the money supply, and by 1983 inflation was down to 4%. *Time* magazine's cover from October 22, 1979, pictured Volcker under the heading "The Squeeze of 1979." This squeeze cranked up interest rates so that some rates exceeded 20%. Imagine getting a car loan or a mortgage in such an environment, and it is easy to see how tight money slowed the economy and reduced inflation.

It's Good to Be the King

In *The History of the World, Part I,* Mel Brooks remarks, "It's good to be the king!" The king has unique powers to achieve his goals (either nefarious as in the movie, or noble). Similarly, the Federal Reserve has unique rights that allow it to control the money supply, and through the money supply, to control inflation.

The injection of money into an economy can have a powerful effect. A simple personal example came when I was living in western Uganda in the summer of 1997. I was spending some time at a chimpanzee research station run by Harvard professor Richard Wrangham. Things were going fine, but I decided that I couldn't rely upon the station's truck for transport, and that I needed to buy my own vehicle.

Accordingly, I had my parents wire funds to a local bank so that I could purchase a motorcycle. With the help (and protection) of several of the research station's employees, I negotiated the purchase of a used motorcycle at the exorbitant price of $2,400.

As I rode the motorcycle along the local roads, people would greet me and then laugh to each other. They found the situation funny for many reasons. First, I was ridiculously large for the small motorcycle. Second, I had paid at least $1,000 more than a local would have paid (in Swahili, they said that I paid the "Mzungu," or European, price). Third, there were stickers on either side of the bike that showed a hunter with a spear. I was unaware that the spear was metaphorical, and that these stickers were public service messages to exhort the people to use condoms. So I became a mobile source of humor.

The actual purchase took place as follows. After reaching a deal on price, I went to the bank, took out the $2,400 in local currency. I was acutely aware that this represented close to a decade's wages for the locals. I had guards on either side as I took my backpack full of bills and picked up my condom-advertisement machine. The previous owner asked me to hurry so that he could return the funds to the bank before closing time. In fact, he then returned the bills to the exact same bank manager who had given them to me earlier in the afternoon.

As I lay under my mosquito netting that night, I marveled at the power of electronic entries in the banking system. My parents sent an electronic message to a bank in western Uganda. Less than 24 hours later, I had a motorcycle and the electronic bookkeeping showed that the motorcycle's previous owner had credit for $2,400. So by just moving a few electrons, I now controlled a motorcycle.

My motorcycle purchase created a whole cascade of effects. The previous owner was now rich with the proceeds of his sale. He used the money to buy a variety of products. The sellers of those products in turn purchased more goods. By injecting some money into the economy of western Uganda, I created a mini wave of prosperity. In my case, Uganda's prosperity came at the expense of some in the United States. While I was $2,400 richer, my parents were $2,400 poorer. This was a zero-sum game where gains were offset by losses.

Being the king of the monetary world, however, the Federal Reserve plays by its own rules. For me to get money, my parents had to lose money. When the U.S. Federal Reserve buys something, no one's account is reduced. The Fed controls the electronic system of bank credits. Thus, the Fed can increase an account by $2,400 or $240 billion with no offsetting reductions. While the Federal Reserve uses its power to buy U.S. Treasury bonds, and not motorcycles, the effect is the same as my mini wave of prosperity.

Except, the Federal Reserve can create money from nothing. It simply pays for its purchases by crediting the seller's account. While private transfers are zero-sum activities, the purchases of the Federal Reserve are not.

Through these monetary operations, the Federal Reserve determines the growth rate of the money supply, though the decisions of other people impact the effect of monetary operations. For example, the speed at which people spend their new riches has implications for the economy. Even after taking account of the "velocity" of money, the Federal Reserve controls the money supply and thus determines the rate of inflation.

Reading the Body Language of the Federal Reserve

In *Rounders* Matt Damon plays a reformed poker shark forced back into gambling by circumstances. Damon's poker prowess lies in his ability to read other players and thus know what cards they have. Most professionals agree that the ability to size up opponents is a crucial skill needed to win at competitive poker. In these games, knowledge of human nature, not of the mathematical odds, provides the key advantage.

Predicting inflation also requires understanding the human actors controlling the situation. The rate of inflation is determined by the growth of the money supply. In the United States, the Federal Reserve controls the money supply. To make predictions about U.S. inflation, therefore, one must have a good idea of the future actions of the Federal Reserve.

Many people are willing to make bold predictions of future inflation rates. On one hand, you find books about how to protect yourself in the coming deflation. On the other hand, some foresee an inflationary world where investors must buy gold to protect themselves.

I remain unconvinced by those who make clear predictions about a future inflation or deflation. U.S inflation rates will be determined by the future decisions made by the Federal Reserve. A prediction of inflation must be based on future decisions of the monetary authorities. Furthermore, the current chairman, Alan Greenspan, was born in 1926, so he might not even make it to the end of his current term in June 2008. Thus, all longer-term investments will be affected by the inflation rate determined with a new chair of the Federal Reserve.

Consider the historical period between World War I and World War II. Between the wars, Germany experienced a hyperinflationary depression, while the United States had a deflationary depression. The German monetary authorities created huge amounts of money and destroyed the value of the German mark. The U.S. monetary authorities did not create inflation—quite the contrary, U.S. prices declined throughout the Great Depression.

These extremely different outcomes suggest that the people in power determine the inflation rate. Although this may appear obvious, it is possible that the German authorities had no alternative. Similarly, some believe the current Japanese monetary authorities are powerless to prevent the current deflation. To the contrary, Milton Friedman believes that the Japanese can end deflation by simply increasing the money supply. I side with those who believe that the individuals in charge of monetary policy determine the inflation rate, constrained, but not controlled, by circumstances.

Thus, a good prediction of inflation requires detailed understanding of the forces that will pull and push the people who determine inflation. Furthermore, as in high-level poker, inflationary predictions depend on the ability to predict human behavior. While it may be possible to predict the behavior of the next Federal Reserve chair, even before she or he is appointed, I have not seen a convincing prediction.

Missouri on My Inflationary Mind

Missouri is the "show-me" state, where residents are reported to wait for proof and not act on promises. When it comes to inflationary predictions, I suggest a show-me attitude. Rather than speculate on the future actions

of monetary officials who have not yet been selected, a preferable financial strategy is: (i) based in the facts, and (ii) likely to perform well in
either an inflationary or deflationary world.

First, let's look at the monetary facts. Figure 5.3 depicts U.S. money
supply growth over the last decade. Monetary growth has accelerated, so
the facts provide some support for those who predict rising inflation.
Monetary changes create inflation only after some time, and the Federal
Reserve may have planted some seeds of inflation that will sprout in the
years to come. Both gold prices and the value of the dollar confirm that
inflation may be stirring. Gold has risen from $250 an ounce to over $400
an ounce. Over a similar period, the dollar has fallen significantly against
many currencies and to an all-time low against the euro.[17] These moves
suggest that the Federal Reserve's loose money policy is decreasing the
value of the U.S. dollar.

The inflationary case is not, however, complete. First, money supply
growth over the last decade is still slower than the rates of increase in the
1970s. Second, money supply growth has slowed. So perhaps the Federal

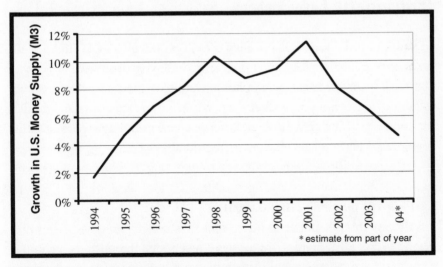

FIGURE 5.3   Is the Federal Reserve Creating Inflation Again?
Source: U.S. Federal Reserve

Reserve's policy is perfect. This optimistic view is that the Federal Reserve created lots of money to soften the effect of the bursting stock market bubble. Now that the economy may be emerging from that dour period, the Federal Reserve is easing up on money growth. If this optimistic scenario is correct, then inflation need not reappear.

To repeat the mantra of this chapter as expressed by Milton Friedman, inflation is always and everywhere a monetary phenomenon. Thus, as long as we keep a clear eye on money growth, we should have early warning of any major change in inflation. If money growth increases, then inflation will follow and investments should be in tangible assets including gold and land, and in currencies other than the U.S. dollar. If deflation becomes likely because of slow monetary growth, then financial assets, particularly certain bonds, should do well. For example, the simple U.S. Treasury bond, even with a yield of just 5% per year, could be extremely profitable in a deflationary environment.

Buy Your Inflation Insurance at Irrationally Low Prices

In addition to looking out for changes in the money supply, there are a number of financial steps that make sense in any environment.

Recall from our discussion of human nature that our lizard brains tend to put too much weight on recent experience. Since Paul Volcker stopped inflation in 1979, the United States has experienced nearly perfect inflation rates. This suggests that most investors will be too little concerned with the possibility of either inflation or deflation. Having spent 20 years in a Goldilocks zone of low and stable inflation rates, we are likely to overlook the possibility of problems.

A funny thing happens to the stock of insurance companies after disasters. When a hurricane, fire, or earthquake hits, the insurance companies pay claims that can add up to billions of dollars. What do you think happens to the stock price of these companies immediately after disaster strikes? You might expect the stock prices to decline to reflect the billions of dollars in claims. Quite often, however, the result is exactly the opposite and the stocks rally.

Why do insurance company stocks rise on bad news? The answer is that people tend to buy insurance after big disasters. So the insurance firms are indeed hurt by the claims that they pay, but they also gain from the marketing of their product. Often the gains exceed the losses, and this can cause the stock price of insurance companies to go up after a disaster.

This response to disaster points out that in insurance, just as in other areas, most people tend to be exactly out of sync with the money-making strategy. The time to buy insurance is obviously before the event, when no one is buying and the insurance rates are low, not after the event when everyone is buying and rates are high.

Twenty years of Goldilocks has lulled most of us into exactly the wrong position. We have come to expect price stability. That means our lizard brains are likely to be underprepared for price instability, in the form of either inflation or deflation. To the extent that many of us are in the same position, now is the time to insure ourselves against price instability on favorable terms.

Here are three strategies to protect your wealth against both inflation and deflation. They are all ways to buy insurance in case we leave the Goldilocks world of low and stable inflation.

Buy at Today's Prices

The first technique is simply to buy at today's prices. If you buy the home that you plan to live in for some time, then you are protected against price swings. While you may suffer as compared to your alternatives, you will be safe within your home. Similarly, some states allow you to pay college tuition ahead of schedule.

If you buy the stocks of companies that own natural resources, then you are protected from commodity price changes. For example, if you own the stock of oil companies, then you will benefit from any subsequent rise in oil prices. If you buy the correct amount of such stocks, you can completely protect yourself from the effects of commodity price changes.

If You Borrow, Lock in Current Rates

Recall that high inflation is a jubilee where debts are effectively erased. The higher the inflation rate, the lower the true cost of repaying debt. In the 1920s, German debtors were able to pay off their mortgages with marks that were essentially worthless. Thus, high inflation provides a financial windfall to debtors.

This inflationary benefit to debtors is only true, however, for those with fixed-rate debt. A growing percentage of Americans are financing their debt with adjustable-rate loans. If inflation rises, these people will find that their payments have increased commensurately with the new inflation.

If you want to insure yourself against price changes, choose fixed rates for all of your debt. With fixed rates, your debts decrease in real value in inflationary environments. What about in deflationary times? In deflationary times, you can refinance your debts at lower rates.

So fixed-rate loans are better than variable-rate loans in inflationary times, and fixed-rate loans are no worse than variable-rate loans in deflationary times. Are fixed rates, therefore, a free lunch? The answer is they are not, because the fixed-rate loans are offered at higher rates than variable loans. The extra monthly payment for a fixed loan can be viewed as purchasing insurance against price changes. If the previous analysis is correct, then the world may be pricing such insurance at unusually low and attractive prices. Thus borrowing at a fixed rate may not be a free lunch, but it might represent a value meal.

Buy Inflation-Protected Securities

The U.S. government sells bonds that provide complete protection against inflation. The amount that these bonds pay is adjusted each year for the prevailing inflation rate. If inflation is high, the bonds pay more to reflect the lower value of each dollar.

Let's compare the payoff to an investment in a 10-year inflation-protected bond to an investment in a traditional bond without inflation protection. To be concrete, we will compare a $1,000 investment into U.S. government bonds with and without inflation protection. Both bonds pay interest over the years and then make a lump-sum payment at the end. Whereas a traditional, noninflation-protected bond simply returns $1,000, the inflation-protected bond adjusts the $1,000 based on the amount of inflation.

Thus, the inflation-protected bond returns at least $1,000, and perhaps more. How much more? That depends on the inflation rate. To see the specifics, Table 5.1 compares the final payment for the inflation-protected and the noninflation-protected bonds under four different inflation scenarios.

Scenario 1 is no inflation. Scenario 2 is a continuation of the Goldilocks environment of 3% inflation per year. Scenario 3 is a return to the late 1970s in the United States with 13% inflation per year. Just for fun, scenario 4 considers prices rising at 500% a year (although this inflation rate is high, it is far lower than the rate in Germany during the hyperinflation). So what do our bonds pay in these four scenarios?

TABLE 5.1   TIPS Provide Inflation Protection (Payment at Maturity per $1,000 Investment)

	Standard U.S. Government Bond— no inflation protection (10-year maturity)	*Treasury Inflation Protected Securities (TIPS) (10-year maturity)*
0% inflation	$1,000	$1,000
3% inflation	$1,000	$1,344
13% inflation	$1,000	$3,395
500% inflation	$1,000	$60 billion

Table 5.1 shows that when the original $1,000 is returned, the inflation-protected bond is always at least as good as the standard bond and usually much better. Even in extreme conditions, the inflation-protected bond ensures that the investor is protected.

This inflation protection, however, comes at a price. That price is the lower interest rate paid on the inflation-protected bond. Currently that difference is about 3% a year. Therefore the most that inflation insurance could cost you is about $30 a year for each $1,000 investment. This maximum price will be paid only if there is no inflation at all. If there is even modest inflation, however, the price of insurance is even less than $30 a year for each $1,000 investment.

Because inflation protection has been unnecessary over the last 20 years, the behavioral economic research suggests that our lizard brains, and consequently the market, may be undervaluing the inflation-protected bond. Furthermore, U.S. government bonds are fantastic investments in deflationary times. Therefore the inflation-protected bonds are almost unique in being great investments under both inflation and deflation. Thus, I believe that the inflation-protected bonds represent good value.

There are two types of U.S. government, inflation-protected bonds. They are the I-series of U.S. savings bonds, and the Treasury Inflation Protected Securities or "TIPS." There are some legal differences between the two types of bonds. For example, the savings bonds are restricted both in the amount of purchase and the type of investor (mainly U.S. citizens). Both bond types, however, are essentially identical when it comes to inflation protection.

What about stocks as a protection against inflation or deflation? At first glance, this seems like a crazy suggestion. Consider three of the most famous periods of inflation and deflation. They are the current Japanese deflation, the U.S. deflation during the Great Depression, and the U.S. inflation of the 1970s. In all three periods, stocks were terrible investments. So stocks would appear to be a very bad way to protect wealth against an end-of-the-Goldilocks era of price stability.

While stocks were bad investments in past periods of price instability, they may be good investments now. Company profits have a built-in inflation protection, just like the U.S. government bonds. Inflation, without other economic change, simply inflates a company's revenue and costs. Thus company profit—the difference between revenue and cost— ought to rise in lockstep with inflation.

If corporate profits are inflation protected, why have stocks done poorly in previous periods of price instability? The answer may be that in those previous periods the inflation and deflation were symptoms of deeper problems. For example, the poor stock performance in the United States during the 1970s may not have been caused by inflation. Perhaps the oil shocks of the time caused both inflation and poor stock performance. Thus, in future periods of price instability, stocks may provide protection.

Magic Paper

As Professor Friedman suggests, money is a fascinating topic. The magical little pieces of paper and electronic entries in bank computers allow us to leave behind the inefficiencies of barter and to amass wealth that we will use over many years.

The form of money has changed over time from commodities to precious metals to the current standard of fiat currencies. These modern forms of money are perfect with the exception of one enormous risk. That risk is that monetary authorities will misuse their power to determine the rate of inflation. In the past, such monetary mischief has bankrupted many families.

The United States has lived through 20 Goldilocks years during which inflation has hovered near optimal levels. The science of irrationality suggests that these halcyon years will have left most of us unprepared for any future price instability. Therefore, when most people's lizard brains feel that the risks of price instability are negligible, we may have an opportunity to buy low-cost protection for our wealth. Fortunately, there are both traditional and innovative investments that allow us to protect our wealth.

chapter six

DEFICITS AND DOLLARS
Uncle Sam the International Beggar

Neither a Borrower Nor a Lender Be

A few years ago I went to dinner in Los Angeles with a group of close friends and a couple whom we had recently met. Because some people had very expensive meals with cocktails while others consumed very little, we decided not to divide the bill equally, but rather to each pay for our own consumption. When the bill came we all pitched in what we felt was our fair share (or so we thought).

We came up about $40 short of the tab. Since I had eaten a very modest dinner consisting of a turkey burger and a diet coke, I was pretty sure that I had not made a major mistake in calculating my share; nevertheless I pitched in an extra $5. So did most everyone else, and we paid the bill.

A few days later we revisited the embarrassing shortfall, and we began to piece together the puzzle. Because we were all good friends, we soon figured out that the new couple had consumed the most extravagant meals and had drunk the fancy cocktails yet had contributed almost nothing to the bill. We thus labeled the man "Cheapskate" (he had "paid" for the couple's dinner).

We resolved that in future interactions, we would not allow Cheapskate to take advantage of us. We even practiced confronting Cheapskate over the bill. "I had the turkey burger, what did you have?" Even though such displays are deeply embarrassing, we found them preferable to having Cheapskate take us for more money.

Our role-playing was never put to use with Cheapskate because he met a fate similar to Elvis. He died on the toilet from a heart attack just weeks after shorting us on the bill. After his death, his girlfriend discovered that she had a big mess to clean up—Cheapskate owed money to almost every single person he knew.

A small-scale con artist with a drug dependency, Cheapskate had put "the touch" on everyone by borrowing money and never repaying it. Interestingly, although he owed many people money, his total debt was only a few thousand dollars. People were quick to cut him off. Just as he was never going to get more than $5 from me, others were not willing to make repeated loans.

A lesson from Cheapskate's life is that it is hard to be a perennial borrower. People are built with instincts that prevent and limit exploitation. When we loan money, we expect repayment and stop lending to deadbeats.

The same is true of countries. Those that consume more than they produce must return the favor or get cut off. The "current account" describes whether a country is consuming more or less than it is producing. Countries with current account surpluses, like Japan, are producing more than they consume. The excess Japanese production is being sent to other countries in return for IOUs in the form of money. The current account is the broadest measure of a country's consumption and includes everything from cars to movies, legal services, and investment income. Thus the current account includes the trade deficit and all other international transfers.

As shown in Figure 6.1, unlike Japan, the United States has a *large*

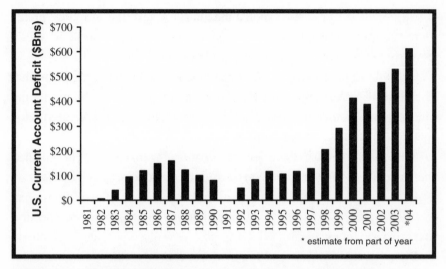

FIGURE 6.1   The United States Consumes Far More Than It Produces
Source: U.S. Commerce Department

current account deficit. We've had a deficit for so long that we show the negative current account deficit as positive numbers. Because we can't imagine a world where the United States consumes less than it produces, we measure the amount of profligacy, not its existence. Residents in the United States consume far more than they produce. In return for Saudi oil, Japanese cars, and Canadian lumber, the United States sends the producers IOUs to the tune of about $500 billion a year.

How big is $500 billion a year? The short answer is: the biggest current account deficit in history. The longer answer is: The current account deficit is about 5% of the size of the U.S. economy, which still makes it one of the biggest current account deficits in history. How did we get here?

Current account imbalances are influenced by currency values. When Canadian lumber is made cheap by a strong dollar, for example, we import more logs from Saskatchewan. To understand the U.S. current account deficit we begin by looking at exchange rates.

When I was first learning about money, the British pound was always worth about $2.50. What I didn't realize then was that currency prices were fixed by agreement between governments. Thus the $2.50 was a government-mandated price, not a market price.

In 1944, governments decided that exchange rates were too important to be left to market irrationality. Economists put part of the blame for the Great Depression of the 1930s on wild fluctuations in the value of currencies. Toward the end of World War II, the major economic powers met in Bretton Woods and fixed the value of their currencies. The governments wanted to make sure that the excesses that led to global economic collapse would not reappear.[1]

In 1971, Richard Nixon devalued the dollar and destroyed the Bretton Woods pact. Freed from its fixed price, the dollar was free to fluctuate between irrationally low and high values, and to create current account imbalances. As seen in Figure 6.1, from the 1980s until now the dollar's value has led to large and growing U.S. current account deficits.

Current account deficits are a form of borrowing. There's nothing inherently evil about borrowing in general nor in running a current account deficit. College students borrow to further their education, companies borrow to expand factories, and countries borrow to undertake projects that may take years to repay.

For example, the Hoover Dam outside Las Vegas was built in the 1930s and now generates very low cost hydroelectric power. Only a curmudgeon would argue against borrowing for the Hoover Dam on financial grounds (there are, of course, legitimate environmental arguments against dams). Borrowing to develop something is often better than the alternative of no borrowing and no development.

While IOUs are nice, and loans can be good, eventually the piper must be paid. Notice that Wimpy in the Popeye cartoon says, "I'd gladly pay you Tuesday for a hamburger today." He doesn't say I'd gladly eat a hamburger on Tuesday for a hamburger today.

"Neither a borrower nor a lender be" says Polonius to his son Laertes in Hamlet. While this advice appears sound, many scholars think Shakespeare wrote it as an example of a father droning on with obvious and unsolicited comments. In the case of borrowing, the advice is essentially empty. Debts must be repaid, so borrowing and lending are just different phases, not permanent states. It is impossible to go through life as a borrower (although I suppose Cheapskate did).

The implications are clear. Countries with current account deficits must at some point swing to surplus. Thus the United States, currently the world's biggest net consumer from other countries, will become a net producer. In the coming years we will be discussing the size of the U.S. current account *surplus*. Because the U.S. current account deficit is huge, the inevitable adjustment to surplus will have profound effects on the world's economy and on individuals' investments. Let's look at how this is likely to play out and the implications.

A Euro for Your Thoughts

In November 2002 my wife and I visited Milan. Walking along the famous shopping street of Via Montenapolean, Barbara spotted a Bottega Veneta purse for the price of 700 euros. At the time, one dollar bought just over one euro so this purse was being offered at the price of about $680.

Both Barbara and I found this $680 purse price to be ridiculous but for different reasons. "Don't you realize that I saw this same purse on sale in New York for over $800!" she said. Biting my lip and suppressing my horror, I said, "I think you should snap it up." On our way back from Europe we flew out of the airport in Cologne. A young German woman about 23 years old was working the customs desk. She said, "You have declared an item worth 700 euros; may I see it?" I showed her the purse, and she gasped, "That's it?" "Yes, isn't it a ridiculous value?" I replied. We returned to the United States with Barbara's beautiful bargain, thereby contributing $680 to the U.S. current account deficit.

Were we to go to Europe in 2004 we would find that purses costing 700 euros translate to a dollar-cost of $850. Costs to U.S. consumers have increased dramatically because the dollar has lost value relative to the euro. Currency devaluations change people's purchasing decisions. Add up enough 700 euro purses not purchased, throw in a few Mercedes that Americans don't buy, and pretty soon a falling dollar leads to a smaller current account deficit.

A current account deficit means that a country is consuming more than it is producing. A simple way to cut back is to raise the price of consumption. This can be accomplished almost magically by changing the value of the currency. Against the euro, the U.S. dollar has lost almost a third of its value over the last few years. As compared to the Japanese yen, the U.S. dollar has been in decline for decades. Thus without any change in dollar wealth, U.S. consumers are now much poorer than we were a few years ago. This weakening of the dollar works to make us consume less from abroad. It also makes the American products cheaper, thus boosting purchases by foreigners.

A cheaper dollar decreases imports and increases exports, reducing the current account deficit.

Real and Nominal Exchange Rates

While exchange rates are a bit abstract for many people, for others they are of visceral importance. I learned this during a 1992 visit to Victoria Falls. I was staying in Zimbabwe across the Zambezi River from Zambia (Zimbabwe used to be called Rhodesia, and Zambia was Northern Rhodesia). One day I rented a bicycle and crossed a bridge into Zambia, intending to peddle a few miles to the museum in the town of Livingstone.

Two interesting things happened on the road to Livingstone. First, my bicycle got a flat tire. There was no place to fix the tire, so I decided to ride on the metal rim and pay the owner for any consequent damages. This meant that my already slow pace in the hot sun was further reduced.

Second, a group of Zambians descended on me. The Zambians were hungry to get their hands on some Zimbabwean currency. I found this interesting because I was able to get so much Zimbabwean currency for my U.S. dollars that I felt like a rich man in Victoria Falls. While the Zimbabwean currency was weak compared to the U.S. dollar, it was rock solid compared to the currency of Zambia. So motivated were these Zambians to get some "hard" currency that they chased after me for more than a mile—running beside my damaged bicycle in their street clothes and hard-soled shoes.

If one were to visit Victoria Falls today, the situation would be reversed. The Zimbabwean currency is now extremely weak compared to that of Zambia. What happened? The current inflation rate in Zimbabwe is over 640%. By comparison, the Zambian rate of 18.5% looks positively tame.[2] Because of the different inflation rates, the Zimbabwean currency is dropping on a daily basis. People who want to store their money in a stable currency are willing to work hard to avoid Zimbabwean currency.

Of the two currencies, the Zambian is now rock solid because of the difference in inflation rates. The lesson from this is that whenever we discuss exchange rates, we need to be sure to consider relative inflation rates. We care about the purchasing power of our money (the *real exchange rate*), not the number of bills we can get (the *nominal exchange rate*). The real exchange rate takes into account inflation rates.

With high inflation rates, the difference between nominal and real exchange rates can be enormous. In January 1913, one U.S. dollar converted into 4.2 German marks. In October 1923, the same dollar was worth over 25 billion German marks! Because German prices had risen even faster than the exchange rate, however, the purchasing power of these 25 billion marks was less than the 4.2 marks in 1913.[3] The *nominal* value of a U.S. dollar in marks had gone up astronomically while the *real* value actually fell.

Wouldn't it be nice if we could just ignore the difference between real and nominal exchange rates? Yes, and we will. Most of our discussion focuses on the three big currencies: the U.S. dollar, the euro, and the Japanese yen. All three regions have similarly low inflation rates these days.

When countries have similar levels of inflation, it is okay to use nominal exchange rates.

Two Roads to Times Square

In *The Out of Towners,* the protagonists George and Gwen Kellerman (played by Jack Lemmon and Sandy Dennis in the 1970 original; Steve Martin and Goldie Hawn in the 1999 remake) make a hellish trip to New York City.

When their flight intended for New York is diverted to Boston, the Kellermans improvise and push on to Manhattan by train. After a very long night including a mugging, a police chase, and sleeping outdoors, the Kellermans run into one of their fellow passengers from the original flight. Unlike the frazzled Kellermans, their calm compatriot rested overnight in Boston and took a morning flight. Both parties ended up in Manhattan for breakfast, but by very different routes.

Similarly, there are various paths the world can take as we adjust from the United States having the biggest current account deficit in history to a future with U.S. current account surpluses. Two relevant and recent examples exist in North America. In these sagas, Mexico took a painful Kellermanesque path of adjustment, while Canada eased through its transition with many fewer aches and pains.

In the 1960s and 1970s my family used to vacation in Canada's Point Pelee National Park. As an industrious child, I scavenged for discarded bottles with my sister Miranda to make money on the deposits. On good days, we would gather more than 100 bottles, which, depending on the brand, each carried a 2 cent or a 3 cent deposit. We were able to get our hot little hands on 2 or 3 dollars for a few hours of work. But there was one small catch; we earned Canadian dollars (now also known as "loonies"), not U.S. dollars.

When we began our bottle collecting, the loonie was worth slightly less than its U.S. counterpart.[4] So we had a bit of disdain for the Canadian currency. Furthermore, because some of the coins were of similar size (particularly the quarters), people who lived in Detroit and the neighboring Canadian town of Windsor would often exchange the coins at an even rate. I was always happy if I could unload my Canadian quarters at full value, whereas I felt cheated when someone slipped me a Canadian quarter.

In the early 1970s something magical happened. The Canadian dollars that we earned from our bottle work became worth more than a U.S. dollar.[5] Although the adjustment was quite small, the movement to more than a buck was accompanied by tremendous pride. Instead of shyly sliding my Canadian dollar across the counter at Harry's hobby shop and hoping I wouldn't get yelled at, the crisp Canadian bills became something that I could proudly display.

Were I to earn some Canadian dollars today they would be worth far less than a U.S. dollar. In late 2001, the loonie dropped to 63 U.S. cents. What happened to my beloved loonie?

For many years, particularly in the 1980s, Canada ran a large current account deficit.[6] In the post-1973 world, without governments controlling exchange rates under Bretton Woods, Canada's current account deficits were among the largest for an industrialized country. In other words, Canada in the 1980s was consuming more than it produced to a degree almost as extreme as the United States in 2004.

In the 1980s, Canada was enjoying its Wimpy burgers with the promise of repayments on Tuesdays to come. The decline of the Canadian dollar indicated that it was Tuesday and time for repayment. The subsequent fall in the value of the Canadian dollar made Canadians less able to import products from abroad. The cheap currency also made Canadian products into excellent values. In short, Canada went through a textbook process. Years of consuming more than it produced were followed by repayment; this repayment, in the form of a current account surplus, was accompanied by a cheap currency.

Canada consistently runs a current account surplus, and the adjustment process was gradual.[7] Over a quarter of a century, the Canadian dollar fell from just over 1 U.S. dollar in 1976 to a low of 63 cents and has remained below 75 U.S. cents for almost 10 years.

Canada's adjustment process was not painless, but it was relatively gradual and did not involve any panics. In contrast, Mexico took the Kellermans' route.

In the mid-1980s, my buddies and I used to make surf trips from San Diego down to Mexico's Baja peninsula. Along the way we saw advertisements for Mexican investments "guaranteed" to return 40% per year. This seemed like an amazing deal, and some of my friends took up the offers.

For a time, my surf friends earned high interest rates on their Mexican investments. The process was very simple: Convert some U.S. dollars into Mexican pesos and invest the pesos for a year. Earn 40% on your pesos in a year, get them back, and convert your pesos into dollars. A $1,000 investment returned $1,400 just 12 months later. Not too shabby! Furthermore, the deposits were guaranteed to return 40% more pesos than invested.

There are few things more expensive than free lunches, especially in the investing world. The catch is that the Mexican deposits were guaranteed to return 40% more *in pesos*. The dollar value of those pesos was not guaranteed. Not to worry, though, how much can a peso devalue in a year?

As you might expect, this story involves the Mexican current account. In the early 1990s, Mexico was running a current account deficit that was 7% the size of its economy. As we have learned, such deficits are unsustainable and the road to repayment usually includes devaluing the currency.

In late 1994, a Mexican peso was worth about 30 U.S. cents. One year later it was worth about 12 cents.[8] Now consider the 40% guaranteed return on your peso investment. Your $1,000 still earns 40% in pesos, but when the proceeds are converted back into dollars the investment returns about a total of $500. Rather than earning a 40% positive return, this "guaranteed" investment lost half its value in one year.

While the Mexican peso devaluation was bad for foreign investors, it was a crisis for Mexicans and many others. In simplest terms, the adjustment from current account deficit to surplus requires a change in wealth.

Both Canadians and Mexicans became poorer because of their currency devaluations. The speed of the Mexican decline caused panic and severe readjustment costs.

The U.S. current account deficits will end. The adjustment path can be rocky or smooth. The U.S. situation is different, and in many ways better, than either the Canadian or the Mexican current account deficits. These differences lead many pundits to confidently predict a smooth path. Because the U.S. current account deficit is the largest in history, however, there is no precedent. Therefore predictions of the adjustment path are simply speculations, some well grounded, but speculations nonetheless.

The Country with the Golden Brain

Since the United States is in a dominant economic position, perhaps the best predictor of the coming current account adjustment lies neither north nor south of the border, but in our own history. In the early 1980s, the U.S. current account deficit reached then record highs (although Figure 6.1 shows that these deficits pale in comparison to more recent deficits).

What happened after record U.S. current account deficits in the early 1980s? Well, the most common effects of large current account deficits are clear in this case. First, the current account deficits shrank. Second, the move away from deficit was accompanied by a substantial weakening of the dollar.[9]

This 1980s' bout of U.S. current account adjustment was very smooth; much more like the Canadian experience than the Mexican peso crisis. Should we then infer that the coming adjustment will also be relatively smooth? Perhaps, but the current situation differs for two reasons. First, the current U.S. deficits are much larger than those in the 1980s. Second, in the last few decades the United States has moved from being the world's biggest creditor to the biggest debtor.

The protagonist in Alphonse Daudet's "Man with the Golden Brain" is born with a skull full of precious metal—his brain is literally made of gold. Throughout his life, he spends his birthright to help his parents and then his beautiful wife. He is particularly lavish with his spouse and spoils her with gifts paid for by depleting his finite supply of metal. For each purchase, he must remove part of his brain and sell the precious supply for cash.

When the man with the golden brain's wife dies, he spares no expense on the funeral. On his way home from the cemetery, he stops to buy a pair of blue satin boots. The store clerk hears a scream and rushes to find the man clutching the boots in one hand, while the other hand is covered with blood and contains gold scrapings at the ends of the nails. His golden birthright was gone; his entire brain sold off bit by bit over the years.

In a far less dramatic manner, but to a far greater degree, over the last several decades the United States has spent its golden treasure. Figure 6.2 depicts how the United States has changed from an international creditor to a debtor. The figures are calculated by adding up all the U.S. investments abroad and then subtracting foreign investments in the United States.

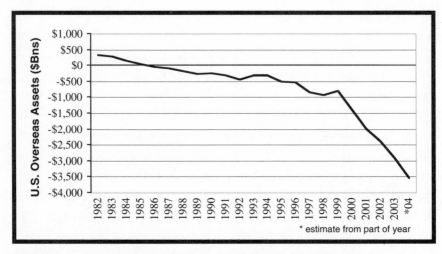

FIGURE 6.2   The United States Is the Biggest Debtor in the World
Source: U.S. Commerce Department

In the early 1980s, and throughout most of its history, the United States was a creditor. The value of U.S. investments abroad exceeded the value of foreigners' investments in the United States. The positive figure in 1982 of $328 billion represented accumulated U.S. savings.

When a country runs a current account deficit, it is borrowing. In the case of the United States, it began borrowing from a position of strength. The early years of borrowing just reduced the savings that had built up over decades. In the late 1990s and beyond, the growth in accumulated debt became extreme. The U.S. debt to the world at the end of 2004 stood at $3.5 trillion.

As with the current account deficit, the debt that the United States owes to the world is the largest amount in history. As with other figures, there are nuances where the figures are adjusted for the size of the economy and the current value of the assets (the data in Figure 6.2 use the historical cost of the investment, not the current market value). When these nuances are taken into account, the trend is identical. The United States has had a dramatic change from global creditor (and saver) to debtor (and consumer).

Loan Sharks and Latin American Defaults

The accumulated U.S. debt to the rest of the world stands at $3.5 trillion. While this is a lot of money to you and me, the real puzzle is why such a *small* amount of debt is any trouble at all. After all, $3.5 trillion is only about 3 months' worth of U.S. economic output.

Compared to how much individuals frequently borrow, the U.S. international debt seems small. For example, my brother in-law Henry racked up about $150,000 in debts during graduate school. At the time, the loans represented many years of income. However, his education allowed him to become a physician so the borrowing was justified. When people borrow for houses, we borrow many years' worth of income.

Therefore, the puzzle is why such a puny amount as $3.5 trillion is considered a problem for the United States. The answer, as my Harvard

Business School colleague Professor George Baker points out, is that the amount of credit available is a function both of the income of the borrower as well as the ability of the creditor to force repayment.

"Charlie, the bedbug took my thumb," says Paulie (played by Julia Roberts' brother Eric) in *The Pope of Greenwich Village.* The "bedbug" is the local Mafioso chief and by a series of poorly executed steps, Paulie owes more than he can pay. The bedbug actually goes easy on Paulie because of family connections. Nevertheless, debts that aren't repaid in this world invite severe punishments.

Why would anyone borrow money from a loan shark? As one might expect, people who borrow from loan sharks usually have no alternative. Some desperate circumstance leads them to need money, and with all other doors shut, the loan shark fills the void. The puzzle then is not why people borrow from loan sharks, but why loan sharks are willing to loan money when all others aren't.

The ability of the bedbug to take Paulie's thumb explains why loan sharks will loan money to people who cannot borrow from anyone else. Because loan sharks are willing to collect in extreme ways, most people try really, really hard to repay them.

The financial situation of the borrower as well as the tools available to collect debts are the keys to understanding credit limits. With this perspective, it is easy to see why the biggest loans in most people's lives are associated with their houses. Banks lend a lot of money, relative to salary, for housing because it is relatively easy for banks to get their money back by repossessing the property. When creditors cannot take thumbs or houses to ensure repayment, they are not willing to lend very much.

International lenders always have to consider the possibility of default. In December 2001, Argentina defaulted on its loans and stopped repaying agencies such as the International Monetary Fund. At the time, Argentina owed more than $100 billion. Could Argentina repay these debts? Absolutely—they represented about one year's worth of production.[10] So just as a homeowner can pay down a similarly sized debt over the years, Argentina could have repaid the money it owes.

But countries will default on loans when it is in their interest to stop making payments, not when debts become too large. Argentina's President Néstor Kirchner said that he would rather bear the consequences of default rather than cut spending; he stated that repayment would be "paying with the sweat and toil of the people."[11]

John Maynard Keynes said, "If you owe your bank a hundred pounds, you have a problem. But if you owe your bank a million pounds, it has." The United States owes the world $3.5 trillion and Keynes suggests that this is a bigger problem for the creditors than for the United States.

Because the creditors appreciate their trouble, they are reluctant to loan even more. This is one reason why the U.S. debt is problematic even though it is a relatively small sum for such a large economy. A second reason is that no bank or country has the ability to come to the United States and force repayment, so lending money to the United States relies upon its good graces for repayment. By this second measure alone, the United States is the worst sort of borrower. No one can force the United States to repay debts.

While the United States looks like a bad debtor for these two reasons, it has another feature that makes it a low risk for default. When it gobbles down the world's oil, cars, and other products, the United States issues IOUs denominated in U.S. dollars. Now, guess who controls the ability to create as many U.S. dollars as are needed to ensure repayment? The answer is the United States. Because the United States can create an infinite supply of dollars, it is impossible for it to default.

Many other countries, including Argentina, promise to repay in a currency they don't control (usually U.S. dollars). When Argentina needs to come up with U.S. dollars to repay a loan, Argentina has to trade something valuable in order to get those dollars. In contrast, the United States has the ability to make U.S. dollars for nothing (both by actually printing banknotes and by electronic entries in the Federal Reserve system).

In some respects, therefore, the United States is the best possible debtor. No lender need fear a default. U.S. creditors can be absolutely certain to get back every penny of the $3.5 trillion in loans. Because dollars can be created by the United States at no cost, the same would be true if the U.S. debt totaled $35 trillion or $350 trillion. So we still haven't figured out why anyone would be worried about the United States' debt to the world.

In an early scene in *Waterworld,* Kevin Costner enters a community in search of trade. Costner offers to sell some dirt, a precious resource to a floating world that needs to grow plants. In return for his dirt, Costner is offered money and after some haggling, a deal is reached. When he goes to buy something with his money, however, Costner is angered to find that the amount that he has just earned is too little to buy anything useful.

Hey, I'll give you 16 quadtrillion "credits" for your car. Is that a good price? Obviously it depends on what real goods you can buy with a credit. Costner's behavior makes no sense. Haggling over price only makes sense if the money has known value. Similarly, the people who have lent the United States money do not need to fear default. They will get whatever amount of dollars they are owed.

The real value of those dollars, however, is very much in doubt. As we discussed regarding inflation, the U.S. Federal Reserve determines the value of the U.S. dollar. The larger the total debt, the more incentive there is for the Federal Reserve to create money to erase those debts. Even though $3.5 trillion is a small debt for the United States, creditors have reason to fear getting repaid the full value of their debts.

Where Do We Stand in the Cycle of Irrationality?

What is fair value for the U.S. dollar? In the long run, countries can be neither borrowers nor lenders. Because the United States has accumulated a massive debt that will be repaid, the United States will need to run many years of current account surpluses. This change from current account deficit to surplus will be accompanied by a fall in the value of the dollar. Let's look at some major currencies in detail. Figure 6.3 shows that the dollar has already lost a lot of value against the euro.

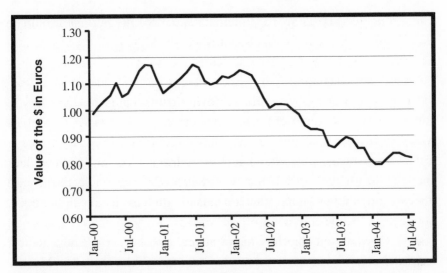

FIGURE 6.3   The Dollar Has Lost One-Third of Its Value against the Euro
Source: Federal Reserve

The dollar looks to have hit an overvalued high in late 2000 and 2001. The dollar rose in value almost every day for years, and the airwaves were filled with negative comments on the euro. On October 17, 2000, Tony Norfield, currency analyst with ABN Amro said, "It is simply ridiculous for people to keep suggesting the euro is fundamentally undervalued. It isn't." At the same time, Jane Foley of Barclays Capital went on record with: "It is still the case that Europe needs to implement structural reforms more quickly. Until that happens and productivity improves, investors will still want to be in dollars."[12]

As is so often the case in mean markets, you'll note from Figure 6.3 that these experts were exactly wrong. In contrast with Mr. Norfield's opinion, the euro was fundamentally undervalued, and even though Europe hasn't implemented structural reforms, Ms. Foley was wrong in predicting that investors would still want to be in dollars.

Obviously the dollar was overvalued against the euro in 2000. Since then, the dollar has lost one-third of its value in euros. Is that enough? If markets were rational we might expect the decline to end when the price of products in the United States equaled those in the euro area.

The Economist magazine, for example, calculates the average cost of a Big Mac hamburger in the United States to be $2.90, and the cost in the euro area to be $3.28.[13]

Since everyone prefers to buy Big Macs for $2.90 instead of $3.28, the theory of purchasing power parity (PPP) suggests that prices in different countries are pushed closer together. In the case of Big Macs, the dollar would have to rise in value against the euro to equalize the two prices. Thus, this burger application of PPP is saying that the dollar has fallen enough against the euro. If the Big Mac prices were indicative of all prices, particularly of goods that are actively traded, then the dollar does not need to decline any more.

So the dollar might be close to fair value against the euro (there are, of course, far more comprehensive analyses of PPP beyond Big Macs). What other currencies are particularly relevant to reducing the U.S. current account deficit? Figure 6.4 shows that the dollar has lost about one-quarter of its value against a basket of major currencies.

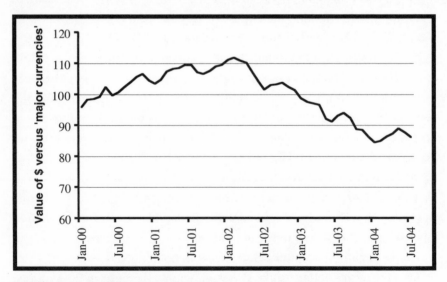

FIGURE 6.4   The Dollar Has Lost One-Quarter of Its Value against Major Currencies
Source: Federal Reserve

The Japanese and Chinese economies are so large that their currencies deserve special attention. The Chinese currency is fixed to the U.S. dollar by Chinese government mandate. China runs a significant current account surplus. There is speculation (both whispered and in the futures' prices) the dollar will eventually weaken against the Chinese currency (known as yuan, it is officially called renminbi or RMB).

The large current account surplus of China suggests that the dollar will fall in comparison to the yuan. What about the Japanese yen? In 1980, I saw a talk by Douglas Fraser, then president of United Auto Workers. Fraser said that the reason Japanese cars sold well in the United States was because the dollar was too strong against the yen. At the time, you could buy more than 250 yen for one U.S. dollar. If only the dollar would weaken to about 200 yen, Mr. Fraser suggested, American-made cars would be a better value than those made in Japan.

The U.S. dollar soon weakened to far beyond Mr. Fraser's target and currently fetches about 110 yen. In spite of this weakening of the dollar, Japanese cars and other products remain so cheap that Japan runs a large current account surplus with the United States. Thus, the expectation is that the U.S. dollar will continue to weaken against the yen.

Furthermore, both the Japanese and Chinese currencies are kept at artificially low levels by their governments. Because such government interventions always fail in the long run, these currencies are likely to rise to their correct levels over time. The Bank of England attempted to keep the British pound at artificial levels in 1992. Speculator George Soros earned a reported $1.1 billion by betting that the Bank of England could not maintain artificial levels—he was right. So the dollar is likely to fall against the Japanese yen and the Chinese yuan.

Putting these facts together, I conclude that the decline in the dollar that began in 2001 is not over.

The U.S. current account deficit remains near its historical high. Furthermore, sentiment toward the dollar is not negative enough for a market bottom. Recall that at market extremes, our lizard brains tend to be exactly out of sync. Even if rational financial calculations suggest that the dollar's decline is over against some important currencies, mean markets don't stop at fair value. Just as the dollar became wildly overvalued before it stopped rising, the science of irrationality suggests that it will have to become undervalued (and scorned by experts) before its decline can end.

How to Invest in a World with Fluctuating Exchange Rates

Cartoon characters have neat tricks that help them avoid disaster. When one of our heroes is trapped in a falling house, the solution is simple. Just as the house is about to crash into the ground, Bugs, Daffy, the Road Runner, and others simply step out of the house. They walk away from the wreck with nary a scratch.

While we cannot exit falling houses without injury, we can leave behind declining currencies. For the last few years, my wife and I have owned a good-sized position in bonds issued by the German Central Bank. The bonds pay low interest rates of no more than 4.5% annually. In spite of the low interest rates we have been earning more than 10% a year on our German bonds.

The payoff from owning euro bonds is the interest rate plus the change in the currency. For example, we bought some of these German bonds in 2001. At the time each U.S. dollar bought 1.1 euros. For each $1,000 that we invested we received more than 1,100 euros' worth of bonds. When those bonds matured a year later, the 1,100 euros had grown to 1,133 euros (3% interest rate). Furthermore the dollar had declined in value so the dollar value was almost $1,150. So in one year these euro bonds earned 3% interest plus more than 10% in currency change for a 15% return.

To avoid being hurt by a falling U.S. currency, the goal is to escape the falling house. The protection is to own investments in nondollar currencies. A simple and effective solution is to buy non-U.S. stocks and non-U.S. bonds.

There are two subtleties to this guidance. First, a company's exposure to the dollar is not determined by the location of its corporate headquarters. For example, Toyota may have more exposure to the U.S. dollar than does Microsoft. Toyota sells a lot of cars in the United States, and Microsoft sells lots of software outside the United States. So the definition of a non-U.S. stock depends on the location of sales.

Second, a declining dollar puts pressure on foreign companies. For example, the weakening dollar has made German goods less attractive and consequently fewer German workers have jobs. Remember that the U.S. current account shrinks when Americans stop buying Italian handbags and German cars. That means the companies who make Italian handbags and German cars need fewer workers. The savvy investor has to escape the effects of the falling dollar both within the United States and in other countries.

How much should be invested in nondollar assets? My advice for the average investor is 15% of net worth. To minimize risk of currency fluctuations, I suggest that people align their investments with their buying behavior. For example, the average American spends about 15% of her or his income on foreign goods. Thus, a completely reasonable, and low-risk strategy suggests that 15% of an investor's net worth be invested in nondollar assets. Those who want to speculate with me on a further dollar decline, and those with a taste for foreign goods, could allocate even more to foreign investments.

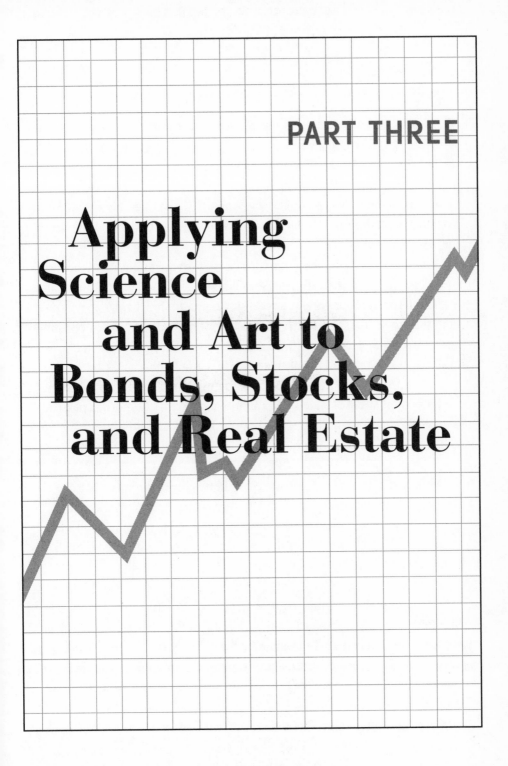

PART THREE

Applying Science and Art to Bonds, Stocks, and Real Estate

n Part Three, we evaluate the prospects for bonds, stocks, and real estate. In Part One, we learned that markets are far from rational. Thus, we cannot rely upon the world to ensure prices are fair. In Part Two we examined the macroeconomic forces driving investments.

In this section, we evaluate investments using the science of irrationality, including our understanding of the lizard brain, and the art of macroeconomics.

With these two complementary tools, we turn our attention to the most important financial investments. In Chapter 7, we examine bonds, and ask if interest rates are going to rise substantially. In Chapter 8, we evaluate the stock market. Has the bull market in stocks returned, or is the early twenty-first century stock market rally a trap? In Chapter 9, we evaluate real estate and ask if there is a housing bubble.

In *The Meaning of Life,* the Monty Python comedians start by asking, "What's it all about?" In answer, the movie provides humorous perspectives on ponderous subjects including birth, conflict, old age, and death, and concludes with:

> Well, that's the end of the film. Now, here's the meaning of life. . . . Well, it's nothing very special. Uh, try and be nice to people, avoid eating fat, read a good book every now and then, get some walking in, and try and live together in peace and harmony with people of all creeds and nations.

After a tumultuous film, "be nice to people" might seem a bit obvious. Similarly, the "sell long-term bonds" advice in this section might appear modest. After brain scans, chimpanzee productivity, and seashell arbitrage, can't the new science of irrationality say more? Absolutely. The final two chapters of this book provide novel and surprising advice on how to outsmart the lizard brain. This innovative "logic of the lizard" approach builds on the clear evaluations of bonds, stocks, and houses of this section.

chapter seven

BONDS
Are They Only for Wimps?

U.S. History Has Favored the Bold

"Bonds are for wimps!" So declared Harvard Professor Greg Mankiw in 1993 when I was a Ph.D. student in his macroeconomics class. Professor Mankiw is not only a world-class researcher, but also a great communicator. I found him to be an excellent teacher, and his ability to make economics interesting has allowed him to write several best-selling textbooks.

When Professor Mankiw said, "Bonds are for wimps," I don't think he was making an investment recommendation. Rather he was being a great teacher by using colorful phrasing instead of using the technical term "the equity premium puzzle."[1]

The academic research on the equity premium puzzle examines the money that has been made in U.S. stocks and U.S bonds. What was the conclusion of this research as of 1993? Bond investing had provided safe, but unspectacular, returns. Over the history of the United States, those investors willing to take a flyer on risky stocks would have made much more money than bond investors, even when adjusting for the more volatile nature of stocks. With the benefit of hindsight, therefore, only the extremely timid (a.k.a. the wimps) ought to have chosen U.S. bonds over U.S. stocks.[2]

Warning: Past performance is no guarantee of future returns. Every mutual fund has such a disclaimer. All of the research summarized by Professor Mankiw examined the past. In 1993, it was true that through-out the past, U.S. bonds had been worse investments than U.S. stocks.

Obviously, investors ought to care about the future not the past. Accordingly, this chapter analyzes the outlook for bonds, not just past performance.

Before starting on our bond journey, a few preliminaries are required. First, we're going to look at only U.S. government bonds. The bond universe encompasses many other bonds including junk bonds, municipal bonds, and many more. Why do we only cover government bonds? Because of the story of the goat.

Two men go to a car junkyard looking for spare parts for a classic vehicle. The junkyard is large, so the owner suggests that the men look around to see if they can find a junked car with the needed parts. Interestingly, the owner warns the men to look out for his pet goat.

During their walk through the junkyard, the men pass a hole in the ground. One of them kicks a pebble into the hole and both are surprised that they do not hear the pebble hit bottom.

As might be predicted, the men forget their spare parts mission and begin throwing larger and larger items into the apparently bottomless hole. After some minutes, and still unable to hear anything hit bottom, they heave a transmission into the hole. Soon afterwards, a goat runs up to the side of the hole, pauses, and then jumps into the hole. Shaken by the goat's apparent suicide, the men return to the junkyard owner.

"Did you find your parts?" the owner inquires. Without mentioning the items they had thrown in the hole, the men tell the owner about the goat that jumped to its death. The owner says, "That's funny, but it couldn't have been my goat, as mine was securely tethered to a transmission."

In the bond world, U.S. government bonds are like the car transmission while all other bonds are the goat. If U.S. government bonds sink in value, they will drag all other bonds down with them. There might be some delay while the other bonds teeter on the edge, and some goats may have longer ropes than others. Nevertheless, if U.S. government bonds decline in value, so will all other U.S. bonds.

What about the possibility that bond prices will soar? As we will see, that is not possible. In the current environment, bond prices can either fall or perhaps rise modestly. The first message in this chapter is: U.S. government bonds will measure the speed and length of any decline in the bond market. Thus, we keep our eye fixed on these bonds.

The second message is: Bond prices move in the opposite direction of interest rates. In other words, rising interest rates are bad for bond owners.

Why are rising interest rates bad for bondholders? This can be confusing, and the reason for the confusion is as follows. Is it better to earn 4% or 8% on a bond? The answer is obvious; the 8% bond is better. So rising interest rates might seem good for bondholders. The answer is exactly the opposite: Rising interest rates are bad for bond owners. Falling interest rates are good for bond owners.

The potential confusion is resolved by clearly separating today's bond prices from future returns on bonds. My friend Chris (the MIT rocket scientist we met earlier) and I recently had a similar revelation in a nonfinancial situation. Chris is a great athlete and better than I at every sporting activity we have played, at least until recently. A frigid Boston winter forced us indoors, and we decided to begin playing racquetball. Because I had played a lot of racquetball previously, I soundly beat Chris during our first match.

After the drubbing, Chris was a bit morose, especially given his history of outrunning and outplaying me in a variety of sports. I said, "Losing badly was the best possible outcome for you." When he asked me to explain, I said that he had nowhere to go but up. As we continued to play each other in a series of matches, Chris performed steadily better. Our first match was a short-term defeat for Chris, but set him up for months of steady progress. The worse he did in the initial match, the better his prospects for improvement.

A similar situation exists for bonds, especially government bonds. The lower a government bond's current value, the more it will grow until maturity. An old joke asks, what's the difference between men and bonds? The answer is that bonds eventually mature. Not only do all U.S. government bonds mature, they mature exactly on schedule and at a price of exactly $100. Thus, the lower the current price of a U.S. government bond, the more gains to the eventual price at maturity of $100. Lower bond prices mean higher future returns. Similarly, higher bond prices mean lower future returns.

When interest rates go up, bond prices go down. When interest rates go down, bond prices go up.

Another way to look at bonds is to divide current owners from possible buyers in the future. If, for example, home prices were to plummet, that would be bad for current homeowners but good for future buyers. Similarly, a drop in bond prices is bad for current bond owners, but good for future bond buyers.

The decision to invest in bonds rests upon a prediction about the direction of interest rates. Buyers of bonds are betting that interest rates will remain stable or decline. Those who believe interest rates will rise should avoid owning bonds. Accordingly, the mission of this chapter is to examine the future of U.S. interest rates.

Revenge of the Bond Wimps

In 1993, Professor Mankiw said bonds were for wimps because the economic research suggested that brave investors ought buy stocks.

While bonds may be for wimps, those wimps who bought bonds in 1993 had very good outcomes—perhaps better than if they had bought stocks. In the time since the "bonds are for wimps" statement, the total amount earned from buying U.S. Treasury bonds has been almost the same as from buying stocks. Furthermore, those who bought bonds knew that the U.S. federal government would pay them back. Stock owners took big risks, which included two consecutive years of serious stock market declines.

In recent decades, bonds have been the profitable tortoises to the profligate hares of the stock market. In fact, the good years to have bought bonds started in the early 1980s, more than 10 years before Professor Mankiw said bonds were for wimps. Interest rates over the last 20-plus years have seen a persistent and powerful decline (see Figure 7.1). Accordingly, bond owners have been handsomely rewarded for more than 20 years.

I remember reading a magazine article in the early 1980s that suggested buying what it labeled the Reagan bonds. These were long-term U.S. government bonds with interest rates significantly above 10%. I took note of the argument neither because I believed it nor because I was going to buy the Reagan bonds. I took note because the article seemed so ridiculous.

Consistent with the theme of this book, bonds were a great buy at precisely the time they were hated. In the late 1970s and early 1980s, the hot investment themes were real assets, including gold, jewels, land, and impressionist paintings. In a time of inflation, everyone knew that bonds were for idiots (and probably wimpy idiots at that).

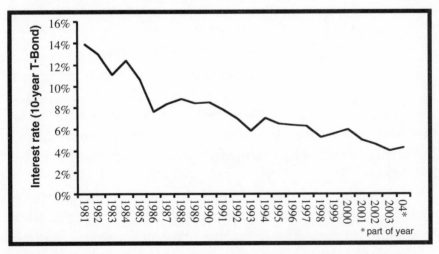

FIGURE 7.1   20+ Years of Declining Interest Rates and Rising Bond Prices
Source: Federal Reserve

Over the last 20 years—since the time that bonds were hated—bond investors have had the best of all imaginable investment worlds. They have enjoyed high returns and low risk. Fantastic. Is this trend likely to continue?

The Mother of All Deficits: Eating Up the World's Savings?

In an episode of *The Simpsons* our hero Homer Simpson is sent to hell. His somewhat innovative torture is to be forced to eat donuts until it becomes excruciating. Accordingly, the devil's workers collect all the donuts in the world, which they stuff one after another into Homer's mouth. Far from being unhappy, however, Homer eats every donut in the world and still wants more.

There is a similar specter haunting the bond market; it is the voracious U.S. federal budget deficit. If, like Homer Simpson, the U.S. government eats up all the available credit, what will be left for homeowners and businesses? If there is not enough money to be borrowed at low interest rates, then large budget deficits might cause interest rates to rise.

There are indeed reasons to be afraid of the U.S. budget deficit as it is forcing the U.S. government to borrow an additional billion and half dollars a day. Former U.S. Senator Dirksen (who died in 1969) is reported to have said: "A billion here, a billion there, and pretty soon you're talking real money." While there is no written evidence that the senator actually made this statement, $1.5 billion a day (including weekends) is definitely real money.

The problem with large deficits is that they eat up the supply of credit or "crowd out" private investments. Here's how James Tobin, Yale professor and winner of the Nobel Prize in Economics, described the problem:

The key issue is "crowding out." Funding the Federal debt and paying interest on it absorbs private saving that otherwise could be
channeled to investments that will benefit Americans in the future—
homes; new plants and modern equipment; education and research;
schools, sewers, roads provided by state and local governments;
and income-earning properties in foreign nations.[3]

How much will budget deficits crowd out private investments? Figure
7.2 shows budget projections as calculated by the congressional budget
office (CBO). We are so accustomed to deficits that most economists
chart the size of the overspending. Thus the "deficit" that is a negative
number is usually shown as a positive.

I think the CBO assumptions are somewhat optimistic, particularly with
regard to future spending. Nevertheless, the CBO picture of the future is
about as accurate as is available. It estimates that the U.S. federal government deficit will be large and will not shrink for many years to come.

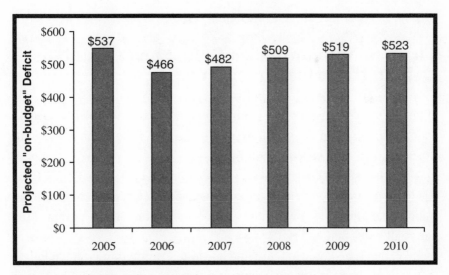

FIGURE 7.2 $500 Billion Deficits for as Far as the Eye Can See
Source: Congressional Budget Office

Whenever you read deficit projections, you should ask, "how do these projections account for social security?" During the 2000 presidential campaign, Vice President Al Gore talked about putting the social security savings into a "lockbox."[4] This was such a theme of his campaign that he was mocked for his lockbox on *Saturday Night Live*. While the lockbox comedy skit was funny, the topic is deadly serious. When President Bush predicts that the deficit will be cut in half by 2008, he is using social security surpluses to cover other expenses.

Because social security currently has a surplus, combining it with other accounts makes the deficit look smaller. Since the social security funds will be spent in future years, I prefer to work with the "on-budget" figures. In other words, Figure 7.2 shows the deficit as if the social security funds were in a lockbox.

Given that the federal government is likely to be running large deficits indefinitely, these large deficits will put upward pressure on interest rates. To understand how much, we need to put these figures into the proper perspective.

The U.S. Annual Budget Deficit and Cumulative Debt in Historical Perspective

While the U.S. budget deficit seems likely to be large for the foreseeable future, the situation doesn't look particularly grim in comparison with other times in U.S. history.

There is a story of a snail who was walking through New York's Central Park. A tortoise attacked the poor snail and stole his money. When the police asked the victim what had happened, he said, "I don't know, officer, it all happened so fast."

Like the speed of slow-moving creatures, most things are relative. Accordingly, the U.S. financial position should be compared with the size of the overall economy (GDP). Using this comparison, the current fiscal position is not as bad as at previous extremes in U.S. history. Figure 7.3

shows total U.S. federal government debt as a percentage of the overall size of the economy for a few selected years.

The three years shown in Figure 7.3 are the extreme points of their eras. During World War II, the United States ran up enormous debts. By 1946, just after the end of World War II, the U.S. federal debt had risen to 122% of the overall economy. Using the current projections, the most extreme figure over the next decade will occur in 2011 when the U.S. federal debt is projected to reach 74% of the size of the overall economy. Not only is this figure far below World War II levels, it is not substantially different from where we stood in 1996.

When we move from the cumulative federal debt to the annual budget deficit, the current projections look even better. While $600 billion is an enormous sum, when scaled against the size of the economy, our current deficits are tiny compared with those during World War II. Figure 7.4 shows the annual deficit as a percentage of the overall size of the economy for a few selected years.

In 1943, the government's one-year deficit exceeded 30% of the

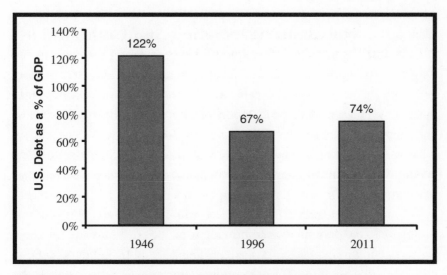

FIGURE 7.3   The U.S.'s Cumulative Debt Is Below Historical Highs
Sources: Office of Management and Budget, Congressional Budget Office

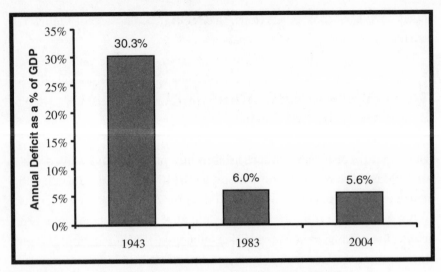

FIGURE 7.4   The U.S. Annual Deficit Is below Historical Highs
Sources: Office of Management and Budget, Congressional Budget Office

overall economy! The CBO projects that over the next decade, 2004 will have the largest deficit when measured against the size of the economy. The projected 2004 figure of 5.6% of GDP is smaller than the 6.0% of GDP figure that occurred in 1983 (the largest of the Reagan era deficits).

Is it possible to have $500 billion deficits as far as the eye can see without harming the economy? The answer appears to be a resounding yes. In fact, throughout the early 1980s, the United States ran large deficits every year while the economy prospered. Specifically, in spite of large deficits, interest rates fell during the 1980s. While we can't know what would have happened in the 1980s with smaller deficits, the U.S. economy seems able to handle deficits in the range of 5% of the size of its economy.

So what is the likely effect of deficits on interest rates? With current projections, the deficits look to provide some upward pressure on interest rates but with no cause for panic. The projected U.S. federal deficits and debt are well within historic ranges. The key will be to watch as the deficit and debt figures change. If annual deficits and cumulative debt swell beyond current projections, they could cause interest rates to rise substantially.

Three Ways to Lose Money in Ultra-Safe U.S. Government Bonds

The federal government deficit, as currently projected, does not seem to spell doom for bonds. Those who argue that the deficit will cause problems have been making their bearish case for decades. In fact, Professor Tobin's quote regarding the crowding out effect was made in 1986. Eighteen years later, Alan Greenspan said, "One issue that concerns most analysts, especially in the context of a widening structural federal deficit, is inadequate national saving."[5] Those who fear that the large U.S. federal deficits will eat up all the available savings might eventually be proven right, but there is no evidence of a problem yet.

Even though U.S. government bonds are among the safest investments in the world and there is no imminent risk from deficits, there are three ways investors can lose money: (1) You never get your money back, (2) you get worthless money back, or (3) you get much less money back than alternative investments.

Bond Risk #1: Government Default

The most extreme risk is that the U.S. government defaults on its bonds. Many corporations and other countries have defaulted on their bonds. It is almost impossible to imagine the U.S. federal government defaulting. In the most extreme circumstances, annual U.S. government deficits could reach trillions of dollars. Even in such circumstances, the government has unlimited ability to create dollars so there is essentially no risk of default.

A U.S. government default is almost impossible. Those who worry about such a default ought to be investing heavily in items such as guns and food. I am not saying that it is impossible for the U.S. government to default on its bonds, just that this is extremely unlikely, and if it happens we will have much more to worry about than our investments.

Bond Risk #2: Inflation

The second risk to bondholders is that they will be repaid but that the dollars they are repaid with might be able to buy very little. On this subject, the science fiction legend Robert Heinlein (author of *Starship Troopers, Stranger in a Strange Land,* and many other classics) wrote, "$100 placed at 7 percent interest compounded quarterly for 200 years will increase to more than $100,000,000—by which time it will be worth nothing."

We already covered the risk of repayment with worthless dollars in the inflation discussion. As of right now, there is no sign of dangerous levels of inflation in the United States. Nevertheless, the risk exists and is one of the most serious risks for bondholders.

In most circumstances the interest rate on government bonds exceeds the inflation rate. While this has almost always been the case in the United States, the amount of cushion—the difference between interest rates and inflation—has varied dramatically. Figure 7.5 shows the interest rate on the 10-year U.S. Treasury bond minus the rate of inflation.

The extra return on bonds above inflation has been decreasing for the last 20 years. The 1983 bond investor received 7% above inflation while the 2003 investor received only 1% above inflation.

In comparison to current inflation, bond buyers today are getting the worst deal they have had in decades.

Bond Risk #3: Opportunity Cost

In 1989, I was the chief financial officer of Progenics Pharmaceuticals, a start-up biotech company (now publicly traded with the stock symbol PGNX). For no good reason related to my job, I wrote an analysis of the RJR-Nabisco leveraged buyout. The *Wall Street Journal* published a short version of my analysis as an editorial.[6]

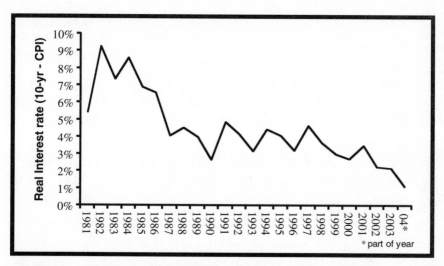

FIGURE 7.5   Interest Rates Adjusted for Inflation Are Extremely Low
Source: Federal Reserve, Bureau of Labor Statistics

One of the consequences of this article was an invitation to give my first lecture at Harvard. I was honored by the request so I flew to Cambridge to present my analysis. How did my first Harvard lecture go? The short answer is that it went amazingly poorly. Early in the lecture, I asserted that RJR-Nabisco bondholders had lost $1 billion because of the leveraged buyout. My calculation simply added up the loss on all RJR-Nabisco bonds as quoted on bond markets on the day the deal was announced. (These bonds traded actively so it was easy to get an accurate measure of how much the price dropped because of the buyout announcement.)

A student objected by saying that the bondholders had lost nothing. She argued that the RJR-Nabisco bondholders were still going to get all their money back. Accordingly, she said that the current price of the bonds was irrelevant. I tried to argue against this view, but it was shared by most of the students. After about 20 minutes of incoherent verbal flailing, the professor had to intervene and say, "Please, let's just assume that

Terry is right and move on." This intervention allowed the lecture to continue, but obviously I had lost all credibility.

Let's view this issue in the context of a $1,000 dollar investment into a 10-year U.S. Treasury bond. Assume that the bond is bought with an interest rate of 4%. The purchaser gives the government $1,000. In return the government promises to pay $40 a year for 10 years, plus return the original $1,000 at the end of the tenth year.

Now let's consider what would happen if, soon after the purchase, interest rates on 10-year treasuries jumped from 4% to 6%. What would happen to our investor? The investor owns a bond that still promises to pay $40 a year for 10 years and to return the $1,000 upon maturity. From this perspective, the bondholder doesn't appear to have lost any money (this is the student's argument from my lecture). On the other hand, the rise in interest rates means that the market price of the bond would have dropped by $150.

So how much money would our bondholder lose? Is it $0 or $150 or something else?

The economist's answer is that the bondholder would lose the full $150 even if the government makes all the payments as promised. Where does the loss come from? The loss is caused by the change in the "opportunity cost." By investing at 4%, the bondholder has lost the opportunity to earn 6% on the $1,000. And these are not simply losses on paper, these are real dollars that the investor could have in his pocket but never will.

In my first Harvard lecture, and many since then, I have learned that opportunity cost is a difficult concept to grasp. Even highly trained people who understand the idea tend to overlook opportunity costs.

While the opportunity cost in financial terms is often misunderstood, in other areas of life it is clear. A famous—and almost certainly fake—wedding toast goes as follows: "Sometimes at rare moments in human history, two people meet who are meant to be together forever. When such romantic lightening strikes, I hope that the bride and groom have the strength to say, 'I am sorry, I'm already married.' "

For those who are unwilling to divorce, the opportunity cost of marriage is the forgone opportunities with other potential mates. A similar theme is revealed in stories of a mythical culture where women were allowed to have up to three husbands, but where divorce was banned. It was said that women in this culture almost never had a third husband, and when they did, he tended to be extremely handsome. By some calculations, the third husband has the highest opportunity cost in this marriage system because he rules out all future possibilities.

So the bondholder who locks in a 4% interest rate for 10 years loses when the world changes to provide opportunities for 6% investments.

How Low Can Interest Rates Go?

U.S. bonds have had a 20-year run. When will interest rates begin to rise thus ending the bull market in bonds?

Predictions, particularly of the future, are tough. (Economists have a nearly unblemished record for predicting the past.) The most famous wrong prediction of an economist is probably Yale Professor Irving Fisher's quote that, "Stocks have reached what looks like a permanently high plateau." Professor Fisher made this sanguine statement in October 1929 just before the stock market collapsed by 90% and the Great Depression began.

Professor Fisher was, by some accounts, the world's most famous economist and he made his remarks at precisely the wrong time. This is amazing, but not too different from the record of many economists.

One of my neighbors is a meteorologist (and don't call her a weather lady) for one of the Boston TV networks. She's a bit of a celebrity in the area. I see her from time to time in our building's elevator, and my running joke with her has two themes (neither of them are at all funny). First, I blame her for bad weather and thank her for the occasional nice day. Second, I tease her for forecasts that often miss the mark. Actually, I used to tease her; once she found out that I am an economist, the teasing had to end.

Although their failures are usually less spectacular than those of Professor Fisher, many seers in many fields have missed the mark by similarly wide amounts. Some decades ago I read an article arguing against immigration into the United States. The article said, look we're all immigrants here in the United States (even Native Americans arrived only 15,000 years ago), but enough is enough. The country is finite and filling up. It's just common sense that the United States can no longer accept huddled masses upon its teeming shore.

The punch line was that this anti-immigration piece had been written hundreds of years ago when the country was empty by modern standards. By reprinting the article the newspaper was arguing in favor of immigration.

There are two ways to be wrong in making predictions. Irving Fisher was wrong to predict no end to the trend that prevailed in the roaring stock market of the 1920s. In my experience, it is even harder to predict turning points in powerful trends. This was the mistake of the original author of the anti-immigration piece who thought America was overpopulated hundreds of years ago.

When will the bull market in bonds end? In spite of the hazards of predicting market turns, I have a clear answer: The bull market in bonds will end soon, maybe not today, maybe not tomorrow, but soon and for the rest of your life. Actually that's Humphrey Bogart's line as Rick near the end of *Casablanca*. While prospects are not quite so bleak for bonds, the bull market has largely run its course.

How low can interest rates go? The historical answer is that interest rates can move substantially lower. In the Great Depression, the interest rate on some U.S. Treasury debt fell to 2 basis points (that's 0.02%!). At this rate, a year's interest on $100 is two cents! At around the same time, the interest rate on 3 to 5 year Treasury notes was under 1%.[7] Similarly, Japan has had interest rates below 1% on some of its government debt in recent years.

Even the current low interest rate on U.S. treasuries isn't the lowest possible. Rates can go significantly lower. They cannot, however, go below zero. That may seem obvious, but the proof is actually a bit subtle. Would you give the U.S. government $100 in order to receive $99 back in a year? The obvious answer is no. A far better alternative would be to put the $100 in a safety deposit box and thus still have $100 in a year.

The cost of storage is the key to understanding the lower bound on interest rates. In our society we can store money safely at very low cost. Thus, we can always get at least $100 back in the future for $100 stored away today.

Consider the very different storage world of a squirrel. Squirrels bury food in good times and hope to retrieve some of it in bad times. On their acorn investments, squirrels always accept negative interest rates. When a squirrel saves 100 acorns by burying them, it always receive fewer than 100 acorns back upon retrieval because some have decayed or been eaten by other animals. If a squirrel buries 100 acorns and later eats only 80, it has just accepted an interest rate of negative 20%. Squirrels must accept negative interest rates because they have no better storage options.

Modern industrial societies have highly secure, low-cost storage options for money. A safety deposit box that is rented for a few dollars a year can hold a lot of cash. Thus, unless one fears a breakdown of civilization, interest rates cannot go below zero. No one is going to accept a promise of less than $100 for an investment of $100. The fact that interest rates cannot go below zero means that the majority of the bull market in bonds has already occurred. To be precise, interest rates have gone from above 12% to below 4% in the last 20 years. That means we've already seen at least two-thirds of the entire bull market in bonds.

Buying Bonds at the Wrong Time

The bull market in bonds that began in the early 1980s has largely run its course. The majority of possible profits has already been made. This does not mean that bonds are bad investments now, but it does mean that they cannot be fantastic investments.

It is easy to calculate the maximum returns on bonds. Consider our $1,000 investment in a 10-year Treasury bond at 4% per year. How much can our bond buyer make? If interest rates went to their theoretical minimum of zero, the bond would jump in price from $1,000 to $1,400. So the absolute maximum gain on the 10-year Treasury bond is 40%.

Recall that in the early 1980s, I ignored the advice to buy the Reagan bonds. Other investors apparently shared my view. The data on investments into bond mutual funds reveal that investors really started loving bonds only when the stock market tanked in the last few years. In fact, bond mutual funds took in all-time record amounts in 2002.[8] This appears to be another example of investors being completely out of sync with investment opportunities. Bonds were an amazing opportunity in the early 1980s, but by the time investors got really excited about bonds, the majority of the bull market in bonds was over.

In the mockumentary *This Is Spinal Tap* Rob Reiner plays Marti DiBergi, a filmmaker touring with the world's loudest band. In perhaps the most famous scene of the movie, Nigel Tufnel (played by Christopher Guest) reveals the band's secret. Spinal Tap is the world's loudest band because their amplifier "goes to eleven" and not just to 10.

DiBergi asks, "Does that mean it's louder? Is it any louder?"

Nigel responds, "Well it's one louder. Isn't it? It's not 10. You see, most blokes are going to be playing at 10. You're on 10, here all the way up, all the way up, all the way up. You're on 10 on your guitar. Where can you go from there? Where? . . . Nowhere. Exactly. What we do, if we need that extra push over the cliff, you know what we do?"

DiBergi offers, "You put it up to 11?" to which Nigel responds, "Eleven, exactly, one louder." Puzzled, DiBergi asks, "Why don't you just make 10 louder and make 10 be the top number, and make that a little louder?" After a stunned silence, the scene ends with Nigel saying, "These go to 11."

The new version of the *Oxford English Dictionary* includes "goes to eleven" to mean to put to the maximum volume. The majority of the bull market in bonds is over because, metaphorically, bonds cannot go to eleven. Where can you go from a 4% interest rate on the 10-year Treasury bond? Nigel Tufnel would respond with "nowhere." So perhaps bonds in this environment are not for wimps, but rather for risk-takers.

Protecting Investments from Changing Interest Rates

What are the implications of this analysis for investors? The 20-year bull market in bonds has largely run its course. U.S. bond prices can fall, go sideways, or rise very modestly. The huge gains of the last two decades cannot continue. In addition, it is likely that the inflation adjusted (real) interest rate will rise.

This is a toxic environment for the backward-looking, pattern-seeking lizard brain. Bond prices have risen for the past 20 years, and the lizard brain is built to predict that the trend will continue. Yet we know that interest rates cannot go below zero. Thus, we have a pending collision between the assumption of the lizard brain and economic reality.

The implication is that most of us have too much riding on low interest rates. The lizard brain has been lulled into interest rate overconfidence by the unsustainable 20-year bull market of rising bond prices and falling interest rates. Thus, most people should adjust their financial position to have lower exposure to rising interest rates. There are three ways to protect ourselves from interest rate rises.

Tip #1: Borrow at Fixed Rates

Borrowing at fixed interest rates reduces risk. If interest rates rise then it will be great to continue to enjoy today's low rates. If interest rates fall substantially, then it is always possible to refinance. Thus, fixed-rate debt is lower risk than adjustable or floating rate debt.

Tip #2: Lend Short-Term

If you own bonds, you are a lender. The shorter the term of your loan, the less risk you face from interest rate changes. If you own U.S. government bonds, for example, those that mature soon are less risky than those that mature later.

Tip #3: Borrow Less

If the inflation-adjusted interest rate rises, then the burden of debt will increase. One obvious way to decrease the burden of rising rates is to reduce the amount of borrowing. For those with nonmortgage debts, one route is to sell some stocks or other assets and pay off some debt. Those with mortgage debt can prepay a chunk of the principal. (Some mortgages do not allow or reward partial prepayment, but these mortgages can be refinanced if necessary.)

Acting on these tips will reduce risk and position the investor for profit. It is possible to benefit from rising interest rates. The financial media suggest that rising interest rates would hurt the economy with no benefits. This analysis suffers from two flaws.

First, if the economy is strong, interest rates will rise. One of the few ways to have continued low interest rates is to have a recession or worse. U.S. interest rates in the Great Depression were close to zero. Similarly, Japan has "enjoyed" low interest rates recently because it has suffered through 15 years of economic malaise.

Second, rising interest rates are great for savvy savers. Savers would prefer to get those superhigh interest rates of the early 1980s rather than today's puny returns. In order to profit from a rise in rates, however, it is important to buy bonds *after* the rates have risen. Thus, implementing the previous tips will position an investor to benefit from rising rates.

Making money in this interest rate environment requires overruling the lizard brain. The correct course now is likely to be the opposite of what has worked for the last generation. The lizard brain has been fooled by 20 golden years of falling interest rates and rising bonds prices.

chapter eight

STOCKS
For the Long Run or for Losers?

"If you had $1 million, what would you do with it?" My students in the spring of 2001 pondered this question. At the time, I was a visiting professor at my alma mater, the University of Michigan. My roommate from my undergraduate years, Peter Borish, had returned to give a short guest lecture to this class of about 150 college students, many of them majoring in economics.

Peter Borish is a famous and accomplished investor. Before posing this investing question, Peter's comments made it clear that he was extremely knowledgeable and sophisticated about the world of finance. Accordingly, the class was a bit tense as many students thought they knew the "right" answer, but were intimidated. After what seemed like a long time, Gayla, one of the students whom I knew well because she served as an academic liaison between the students and me, broke the silence.

"I'd buy stocks, I would diversify and try to minimize transaction costs. Accordingly, I would probably not try to pick individual stocks, but rather invest through mutual funds. My mutual funds would focus on companies of all sizes and include some that buy international stocks," answered Gayla.

Gayla was a great student, and her answer was textbook. In fact, her answer is nearly identical to that given by finance guru Professor Jeremy Siegel of the Wharton School of the University of Pennsylvania. Professor Siegel's book *Stocks for the Long Run* is a comprehensive analysis of investing. This book has played an important role in changing the way that Americans invest.

We will review the main statistical findings of *Stocks for the Long Run,* but before we do, let's pose the same question to Professor Siegel. "If you had $1 million, what would you do with it?" In the last chapter of his book, Professor Siegel provides his answer.[1] In the 1998 edition Professor Siegel told investors: "1. Stocks should constitute the overwhelming proportion of all long-term financial portfolios. . . 2. Invest the largest percentage—the *core holding* of your stock portfolio—in highly diversified mutual funds with very low expense ratios. . . 3. Place up to one-quarter of your stocks in mid- and small-sized stock funds. . . 4. Allocate about one-quarter of your stock portfolio to international equities."

The 20-year old college student gave the same answer as Professor Siegel. Buy stocks, diversify, and keep expenses low. This is the main message to investors from many sources.

Conventional wisdom says that if you want to be rich, stocks are the best investment. In fact, this message has become so ubiquitous that it is almost a mantra: Stocks are the best investment. Stocks are the best investment. Stocks are the best investment.

Gayla came through with flying colors and gave the exact same answer as professionals who make their living advising others on what to do. How did Peter Borish respond to this answer? He asked, "Do you drive your car by looking in the rearview mirror?"

When it comes to stocks, Peter's question is fundamental. U.S. stocks have had an undeniably bright past. Unfortunately, we are not able to go back in time and buy stocks in 1982 or even 1802 (the beginning of Professor Siegel's analysis). What is relevant to us is not the past, but the future. To understand the prospects for stocks, we have to dissect the past and see if the sources of past success are likely to continue into the future.

The Big Pile of Stock Market Cash Visible in the Rearview Mirror

It is not a coincidence that Gayla gave the same answer as *Stocks for the Long Run*. Professor Siegel has played a major role in promoting stock ownership. So much so that it is worth summarizing his main findings. This section uses the analysis of the second edition of *Stocks for the Long Run*, which was published in 1998. This is important for understanding the cycle of irrationality. This 1998 edition was the one that existed at the height of the technology bubble. From 1802 through the publication of the second edition there was one key to making good investments. It was: To make money as an investor, the correct strategy throughout U.S. history was to buy U.S. stocks.

Professor Siegel's work shows the following.

1. Over the course of history in the United States, stocks provided the best return.
2. For investors with a suitably long-run view, stocks were the best investment in *every* period.
3. While buying stocks when they were low (after a crash) would obviously have been the best strategy, even buying stocks when they were high (even right before a crash) was a fine strategy.

Let's look at each of these extraordinary facts (and they are facts) in detail. Table 8.1 shows that U.S. stocks have left other investments in the dust.

A $1,000 investment in stocks in 1802 would have been worth over $7 billion by 1997! This calculation assumes that all proceeds from owning the stocks including dividends were used to purchase more stocks. Thus, stocks were by far the best choice for the 1802 investor.

In contrast, from 1802 to 1997 gold did not even keep pace with

TABLE 8.1   For 200 Years, U.S. Stocks Have Been Great Investments

Investment of $1000 in 1802	*1997 value*
U.S. Consumer Price Index	$13,370
Gold	$11,170
U.S. Government Bonds	$10,744,000
U.S. Stocks	$7,470,000,000

Source: Stocks for the Long Run, *Second edition, p 6*

inflation. The investor who exchanged 10 loaves of bread for gold in 1802 would have been able to buy fewer than 10 loaves of bread with that same gold in 1997. Those who invested in U.S. government bonds could feel smart compared to the gold bugs. Overall, however, the stock investor would have been rewarded with close to 1,000 times more wealth in 1997 than the bond investor.

If you had a time machine and could travel back to 1802, your course of action would be clear. Buy stocks. This is Professor Siegel's first point—stocks have been the best investment. His second finding addresses the following questions: What if your time machine dropped you off at some other point in time other than 1802? Should you, for example, have bought U.S. stocks in 1861, 1914, or 1929?

The answer is that at almost every time in U.S. history the correct answer is stocks. Obviously, U.S. stocks have declined in many individual years so some multiyear period is required for a fair comparison. Professor Siegel does the calculation for 30-year time periods. This can be thought of as an appropriate time frame for a person saving for retirement who begins investing relatively early in his or her career.

The stunning finding: In *every* 30-year time period, except for 1831 to 1861, stocks performed better than bonds. Stocks were the right decision in every 30-year time period for more than a century. Amazing!

Professor Siegel's third point addresses the issue of timing (bad timing, to be specific). Years ago, I remember a somewhat cruel TV interview of one investor with extremely bad timing. The unlucky chap had made a major purchase in the stock of Braniff Airlines on the day before it filed for bankruptcy. Braniff never reemerged from bankruptcy; the company was liquidated and stockholders lost every penny.

The reporter asked the investor, "What were you thinking when you invested tens of thousands of dollars into Braniff hours before they went out of business?" The investor (and he was a professional) responded with, "I bought the stock because I thought it would go up in price."

Whenever I make an investment decision, I wonder if I am going to suffer the fate of the Braniff buyer. Will my purchase be at exactly the wrong time? For these fears, Professor Siegel has a response—relax. So far in U.S. history it has been impossible to buy at the wrong time. In fact, even if you bought on the day before a market crash, stocks have outperformed other investments over the following 30-year period.

The Dow Jones Industrial Average, for example, lost an amazing 89% of its value during the Great Depression.[2] To understand this, you have to imagine a modern stock market crash taking the Dow down to about 1,000. So some investors bought stocks in the late 1920s and watched their wealth evaporate. For those who were patient, however, buying stocks on the worst day of a lifetime was still better than buying bonds.

Yes, even the unlucky investor who bought stocks on September 3, 1929—the high water point before the crash—did better than the investor who bought bonds. Professor Siegel calculates the 30-year return on a $100 investment at the 1929 peak as follows: bonds $141, stocks $565. He makes similar calculations for all other market peaks. (Stocks have not yet recouped their losses since the 2000 peak, but we will not know the "long-run" payoff of late 1990s' investments for many more years.)

The history of U.S. investing is clear. Always and everywhere the best course for the patient investor is to buy U.S. stocks.

In *The Paper Chase* Harvard law professor Charles Kingsfield grills a student about a case. The student is unable to provide any useful analysis. After some verbal flailing, the student blurts out "I have a photographic memory." To which Professor Kingsfield responds, "That will do you no good at all."

Similarly, the fact that stocks look good when we look at pictures of yesterday does no good at all to those of us who want to make money now and tomorrow. To determine if stocks are a good investment now and in the future, we need to go beyond *Stocks for the Long Run* and look at more than the past return of stocks.

Why Jeremy Siegel Does Not Play Professional Basketball or Live in East Germany

"Better lucky than good," summarizes the feelings of many toward performance. This view suggests that winning is more important than having deserved to win. When it comes to U.S. stocks since 1802, they have indeed won. To decide how much to invest in U.S. stocks today, however, we have to try to divide the past success of U.S. stocks into luck and skill. If U.S. stocks did well because of skill, they are more likely to be good investments now than if their strong performance was simply lucky.

As in many areas of finance, if we are to determine whether U.S. stocks have been lucky or good, we have to confront one of our human shortcomings: our tendency to place too much faith in actual outcomes. One aspect of this problem is called "survivorship bias" and was illustrated in the documentary *Hoop Dreams* that chronicles the lives of two talented young basketball players in their quest to play professional basketball.

One message of the movie (and there are many) is that these two young men make their decisions based on overly optimistic expectations about playing in the NBA. They devote their lives to basketball in the hopes that they can become rich and famous. One of the causes of overoptimism is the fact that all of us see only the winners in the competition to become NBA players. This bias toward seeing only the survivors causes us to overestimate the chances of success. It causes many people to devote their lives to a quest that is unlikely to succeed.

Being fooled by survivorship bias is almost unavoidable when we watch professional sports. Our arenas and TV screens are filled with professional athletes who have made it to the big time. Even on their bad days we know that these professional athletes live exciting lives filled with cash, cars, beautiful women and homes (often chronicled in MTV's show 'cribs'). All of these athletes are the winners in a competitive athletic world that begins before high school. Except for news reports and documentaries, we do not see the players who have worked just as hard and never earned a penny from athletics.

Because we almost always see only those who survive, and therefore win athletic competitions, we tend to overestimate the ease of becoming a professional athlete. In *Hoop Dreams* the odds of making it from U.S. high school basketball into the NBA is estimated to be 1 in 7,600. The film shows that young basketball players are far too confident of their chances. Consequently, they make life decisions that are different (and presumably worse) than if they acted upon the true odds.

Survivorship bias is present in many areas of life other than professional sports. We generally only see the winners in politics, modeling, acting, and entertainment. The trouble comes when we make decisions based on our overoptimistic estimates of success. Survivorship bias pushes us toward investing time and money in prospects that appear alluring, but would not be exciting if the true odds were known and understood.

As a kid, my friend Jay was fooled by survivorship bias. The credits of every movie that he saw included "Completion guaranteed by The Completion Bond Company." This is a form of insurance that pays off if a film isn't completed. When he grew up Jay planned to start his own completion bond company since every movie that he saw had clearly been made and so insuring them seemed like a sure thing.

The survivorship bias argument against stocks for the long run is that U.S. stocks have done well, but many other stock markets have done terribly. Consider an investor in East Germany who patiently invested his or her money into stocks.

Our East German stock investor would have lost every penny when the communists took over East Germany after World War II. For an East German, stocks for the long run would have meant a complete loss.

Consequently, there are no Jeremy Siegels promoting East German stock investments.

U.S. stocks are the Michael Jordan's of the investing world. No sane person would decide how much time to practice basketball with the assumption that she or he could be the next Michael Jordan. Similarly, no one should decide how much to invest in stocks based solely on the history of U.S. stocks.

Thus, in addition to the U.S. stock market performance, we should consider the outcome of other markets. Consider some of the debacles that faced equity investors in major markets around the world just in the last century. Russia, China, and much of Eastern Europe became communist with state ownership of much or all business. Germany suffered through hyperinflation and destruction in World War II. The allies in World War II similarly destroyed Japan. By some measures Argentina was richer than France a century ago yet has had severe economic struggles since then.

Some people argue that the poor performance of stocks in countries like East Germany is irrelevant. The argument goes something like, "Equity investments in a place and time where property rights are not respected (or are so heavily taxed) will always be a poor bet. Communist markets of any kind by their nature have to be inherently fictional—a government made-up number."

So is it fair to include East Germany? The answer depends on the time period you analyze. No sane investor would have wanted to own East German assets after the country was taken over by the Soviet Union. The investor back in 1802, however, had no idea that part of the world would become communist (Karl Marx was born in 1818) and part of the communist world would be called East Germany. So the part of the world that ended up becoming East Germany belongs in the analysis of the stock returns from 1802 (the beginning of Professor Siegel's U.S. data), and excluding it would be committing an error of survivorship bias.

Interestingly, one doesn't have to go all the way to communist countries to see that just looking at the United States is a form of survivorship bias. *In Triumph of the Optimists: 101 Years of Global Investment Returns,* Elroy Dimson, Paul Marsh, and Mike Staunton argue that most analyses of stock market returns are overly optimistic.[3] Most studies, the authors argue, ignore places or time periods where stocks did very poorly. The authors study 16 major countries (the United States plus 15 others including the U.K.) and write that standard analysis "has provided investors with a misleadingly favorable impression of long-term equity performance."

The argument of survivorship bias has also been performed rigorously in academic papers. These results suggest that part, but not all, of the advantage of U.S. equities is a result of survivorship bias.[4] U.S. stocks have been both lucky and good. It would be naïve to expect the future of U.S. stocks to be as bright as the past.

Why Jeremy Siegel Does Not Live in Nuclear Winter without Electricity

Our examination of survivorship bias is worthwhile but incomplete. Students of Eastern philosophy are told, "The Zen that can be taught cannot be real Zen." Similarly, the survivorship bias that can be measured cannot be the real survivorship bias. To understand the profound problem in measuring survivorship bias, we can gain perspective from the field of cosmology. This field studies such deep issues as the formation of the universe.

The analysis of survivorship bias in cosmology is motivated by the following observation: Our universe is built with certain basic properties including the speed of light and other parameters that most of us have never heard of such as Planck's constant. Everything in the universe is affected by these parameters. The amazing thing is that scientists have determined that if these basic aspects were even slightly different, then life would be impossible.

Stephen Hawking summarizes this in *A Brief History of Time:* "The remarkable fact is that the values of these numbers seem to have been finely adjusted to make possible the development of life."[5] One obvious explanation for our good fortune is that God or another intelligent force designed the universe. Scientists have developed the "anthropic principle" either as an alternative to intelligent design or in order to understand the details of intelligent design. The anthropic principle comes in a weak form and a strong form. Stephen Hawking describes the two versions of the anthropic principle:

> The weak anthropic principle states that in a universe that is large or infinite in space and/or time, the conditions necessary for the development of intelligent life will be met only in certain regions that are limited in space and time. The intelligent being in these regions should therefore not be surprised if they observe that their locality in the universe satisfies the conditions that are necessary for their existence. It is a bit like a rich person living in a wealthy neighborhood not seeing any poverty.[6]

According to the strong anthropic principle,

> there are either many different universes or many different regions of a single universe, each with its own initial configuration and, perhaps, with its own set of laws of science. In most of these universes the conditions would not be right for the development of complicated organisms; only in the few universes that are like ours would intelligent beings develop and ask the question, "why is the universe the way we see it?" The answer is then simple: if it had been different, we would not be here![7]

Most efforts to estimate survivorship bias in stocks ask the equivalent of the weak form of the anthropic principle. They test the outcome of an average stock investment around the world, not just the United States. In the case of *Hoop Dreams* this weak form of survivorship bias requires us to look at all 7,600 high school basketball players for each one who makes it to the NBA.

The strong form of survivorship bias is much more fundamental. It asks us to consider not just stock markets in other countries, but also other possible global histories. This sort of question is most often investigated in movies, particularly those that involve time travel. In *Back to the Future,* Marty McFly (played by Michael J. Fox) travels back to the time when his parents were in high school.

In his effort to get back to the future, Marty changes the outcome and jeopardizes his family. As Marty looks at a family snapshot that he carries in his wallet, he sees the image of his siblings—and then of himself— begin to dissolve as his actions in the past change the future. By the end of the movie, of course, the happy outcome includes a different, improved outcome for the modern McFlys.

With regard to U.S. stock returns, the strong form of survivorship bias suggests that not only has the United States been the luckiest of all countries, but also that the whole world has been extremely lucky. Just as small actions by the time-traveling Marty McFly had big effects on the future, "small" events that did not happen in the history of this world could have destroyed the value of stocks.

Among the most obvious bad thing that didn't happen is nuclear war between the United States and the Soviet Union. This avoidance of war seems to have happened with a large dose of luck. Recently released documents from both sides during the Cuban Missile Crisis reveal just how close we came to global nuclear war. During one confrontation between U.S. and Soviet ships, two soviet commanders gave orders to launch nuclear weapons.

This near nuclear miss is described by Noam Chomsky as follows:

We learned that the world was saved from nuclear devastation by one Russian submarine captain, Vasily Arkhipov, who blocked an order to fire nuclear missiles when Russian submarines were attacked by US destroyers near Kennedy's "quarantine" line. Had

Arkhipov agreed, the nuclear launch would have almost certainly set off an interchange that could have "destroyed the Northern hemisphere," as Eisenhower had warned.[8]

How much have U.S. stocks benefited by global luck? This is extremely difficult to ascertain because it requires assigning probabilities to events that didn't happen. Furthermore, such analysis should include all possible alternative scenarios including those that would have exceeded the actual outcome.

Presumably humans could have had an even better outcome than we realized. For example, we could live in a world without holes in the ozone layer, where Princess Diana is still alive and married to Prince Charles, and where there are no nuclear weapons that can be hijacked and used to hold the world hostage.

How can we quantify these alternate possible histories? The mathematical tool of Monte Carlo simulations allows one to run the calculation, but still depends on the assumptions. Some of the best efforts to generalize this stronger form of survivorship bias have been done by Nassim Nicholas Taleb and are contained in academic papers, his first book *Fooled by Randomness,* and his forthcoming book *The Black Swan.*[9]

Taleb concludes it is likely that all of the excess return of U.S. stocks is due to luck, not skill. While we can't know the answer for sure, I lean toward believing that things have turned out better than we could have expected.

Putting both weak and strong forms of survivorship bias into the analysis of U.S. stocks requires adding some lines to Professor Siegel's table. The amended data might look something like what we see in Table 8.2.

So where do we stand on assessing the elements of luck and skill in historical U.S. stock market performance? U.S. stocks have done better than stocks in other countries. Furthermore, it seems likely that the world has been lucky in avoiding any global wars, nuclear or otherwise, since 1945. Both of these suggest that luck played a significant, and perhaps dominant, role in the fantastic performance of U.S. stocks.

TABLE 8.2   U.S. Stocks Have Benefited from Good Luck

Investment of $1000 in 1802	1997 value
U.S. Consumer Price Index	$13,370
Gold	$11,370
U.S. Government Bonds	$10,750,000
U.S. Stocks	$7,470,000,000
East German Stocks	$0
U.S. Stocks had there been a nuclear war	$0

Source: Stocks for the Long Run, Second edition

U.S. Stocks Have Survived. Are They Expensive Today?

The historical survivorship analysis suggests that the amazing performance of U.S. stocks is unlikely to be repeated. Buying stocks today is not the easy choice that it would be if we had a time machine and could go back into U.S. history.

My father is a physician of the old school. He likes to mock modern-day physicians and their reliance on technology. He jokes, "If all else fails, let's look at the patient." His meaning is, of course, that we ought to start by looking at the patient. Similarly we are several pages into a discussion of stocks without actually looking at any stocks. Let's look at the financial patient and analyze some stocks.

We begin with Microsoft and then move to the entire S&P 500. Microsoft is one of the most profitable companies in the world and consequently one with among the highest stock market value. It is also part of all the major financial indices including the Dow Jones Industrial Average, the S&P 500, and the NASDAQ 100. Beyond financial strength, Microsoft generates strong emotions in many people, ranging from frustration with Windows glitches to the joys of a beautiful Excel spreadsheet.

When it comes to investing, we put aside our feelings and look at the numbers. Perhaps the most common analysis uses the so-called "Fed model" that compares a stock to the 10-year Treasury bond. The 10-year Treasury bond is a safe alternative to risky stock investments. Figure 8.1 shows the projected return on a $100 investment in the next year for Microsoft stock and for the 10-year Treasury bond.

Investing $100 in a Treasury bond earns $4.40 in interest per year (at current rates of 4.4%). The person who puts $100 into Microsoft stock (at $28) will receive a dividend of $1.14. In addition, $100 of Microsoft stock buys ownership in additional profits that will be retained by the company. This figure for 2005 at Microsoft is expected (by Wall Street analysts) to be $3.43 for every $100 investment.

So is Microsoft stock a good investment? The answer is that it depends on your optimism about the future. The T-Bond is going to pay $4.40 a year for 10 years and then you will get back the $100 investment. Microsoft stock could be much better or much worse. The payoff to Microsoft is the fact that it could grow substantially. Microsoft is far riskier, however, than the government bond and even big companies can go bankrupt. While the bond investor can be pretty confident of getting

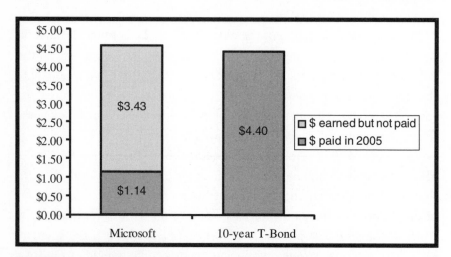

FIGURE 8.1   Microsoft vs. 10-Year T-Bond (1-Year Return on $100 Investment)
Sources: Federal Reserve, Microsoft, The Wall Street Journal

back the original $100, the stock investment contains an element of spec-ulation.

Is the risk of stock investing worth the reward? Before addressing this question, Figure 8.2 shows the same calculation for the S&P 500.

A $100 investment in the S&P 500 is estimated to return $5.92 in expected 2005 profits versus $4.57 in Microsoft profits. So the stock market places a premium valuation on Microsoft profits, presumably reflecting the superior value of the company's franchise. Beyond this dif-ference, an investment in the S&P 500 also yields more money today in dividends than a similar investment in Microsoft.

This Fed model framework provides an easy summary of optimistic and pessimistic views on U.S. stocks.

The pessimistic view of stocks (Figure 8.3) is that earnings will be (or actually are) lower than projected. The negative view on earnings includes both a pessimistic view on the economy as well as the way in which earnings are calculated. Accounting rules still allow for earnings games related to issues including stock options and pensions. In addition,

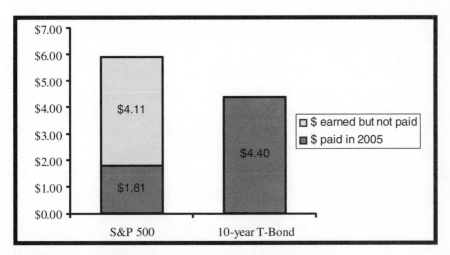

**FIGURE 8.2   S&P 500 vs. 10-Year T-Bond (1-Year Return on
                $100 Investment)**
Sources: Federal Reserve, Standard & Poor's, Goldman, Sachs & Co.

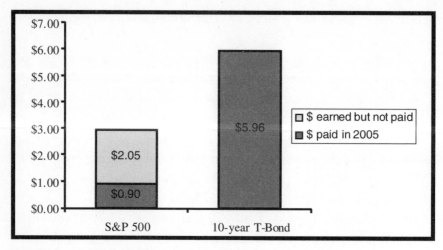

FIGURE 8.3 A Pessimistic View of Stock Prices (Return on $100)
Sources: Federal Reserve, Standard & Poor's

most pessimistic stock analyses include an expectation of higher interest rates. Thus, the pessimist contrasts lower stock returns to higher bond interest rates and concludes that stock prices are too high.

The optimistic view centers on the growth in earnings. The optimistic chart (Figure 8.4) assumes that the economy will grow modestly and that corporate profits will grow at the same rate as the economy. As we'll see, profits have had a good run where they have done better than the economy, but even with the more conservative assumptions, it is easy to build a positive case for stocks. (Figure 8.4 assumes 7% annual growth in the economy, which could come from 3% growth in productivity, 3% inflation, and a 1% growth in the population.)

Even though this Fed model view of stocks avoids many of the details, we can already draw some conclusions about stock valuations.

Stock Prices Do Not Look Ridiculously High

Stock and bond returns are about equal. Good arguments can be made to suggest that stocks are expensive or cheap. This balance of possible reward and risk is characteristic of fair value.

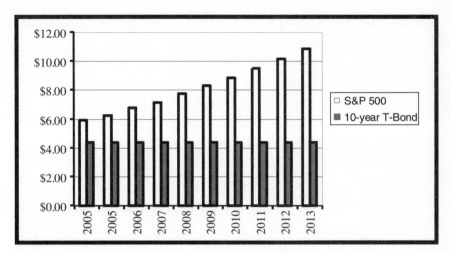

FIGURE 8.4   An Optimistic View of Stock Prices (Return on $100)
Sources: Federal Reserve, Standard & Poor's

Stock Prices Are Not Cheap

While stocks do not look terribly expensive, by most measures they are priced above historical averages and far above the valuation levels that existed at true market bottoms. So stocks appear to be either fairly valued from a current perspective, or richly valued from a historical perspective. It is hard to characterize stocks as really cheap.

Growth Rate Is Crucial to Determining Stock Valuations

The expected growth rate is enormously important to valuations. In the case of Microsoft, a $100 investment earns less today than the same investment in a 10-year Treasury bond. Furthermore, investors in Microsoft stock risk losing part or all of their money. To make the risk worth the reward, Microsoft earnings must rise over time to be substantially above the payoff to the ultra-safe Treasury bond. This question of earnings growth is so crucial that we will examine it further.

Beyond simple valuation calculations, emotional mood swings play a major role in stock prices. In some periods, investors are willing to take risk and predict good futures. In other periods, investors are skeptical and want cash now to compensate for risk. In *The Great Crash,* John Kenneth Galbraith uses the word "bezzle" to describe an aspect of this mood swing. Bezzle is derived from embezzle, and Galbraith describes the ability of people to siphon funds out of companies and the world more generally. In good times, investors (and perhaps regulators) are optimistic and lax. Therefore the bezzle increases. In contrast, Galbraith writes, "In [economic] depression, all this is reversed. Money is watched with a narrow, suspicious eye. The man who handles it is assumed to be dishonest until he proves himself otherwise. Audits are penetrating and meticulous. Commercial morality is enormously improved. The bezzle shrinks."[10]

The overall pattern of optimism and pessimism is a recurring theme in investments. When everyone is optimistic about stocks, they tend to be worse investments. Doom and gloom generally predict good stock market returns. These emotions get reflected in stock prices. Consider that the S&P 500 investor today accepts about $1.81 in dividends and foregoes $4.40 in sure interest. Why accept a lower return? The lower return today is accepted because investors are optimistic about the growth of dividends. In other periods, stock investors have been so skeptical as to require that dividends exceed bond interest.

In the modern market, such skepticism is reserved only for those companies that are perceived as particularly risky. For example, a $100 investment today in Altria (formerly Phillip Morris) yields $5.50 in dividends.[11] An investor earns more today from Altria dividends than from the interest on a 10-year Treasury bond. Because investors fear that smoking-related lawsuits might bankrupt Altria, they price the stock so that they are paid to take risk. While this skepticism exists for Altria, for the market as a whole, investors are willing to accept lower dividends.

Currently, optimistic investors accept low dividend yields in the hopes of future gains. Even without any change in stock market fundamentals, any move that clamps down the bezzle and general optimism would be reflected in lower stock prices.

Where do we stand on stock valuations? Based on the Fed model that compares stocks to 10-year Treasury bonds, stocks appear to be reasonably valued. Based purely on the Fed model, optimists can buy in the hopes of strong profit growth and pessimists can sell on the expectation of profit disappointments and interest rate rises. Beyond the Fed model, however, valuations are dependent on growth rates and emotional swings.

Natural Limits to Earnings Growth

Some years ago, I watched Arnold Schwarzenegger being interviewed about the appeal of bodybuilding. He was asked, why are some people obsessed with physical size? Arnold replied, "You don't go to the zoo to see the mice." His claim was that humans are naturally built to care about size. (In *Pumping Iron* Arnold seeks to make his opponent Lou Ferrigno feel bad about himself. Accordingly, he hits Lou with the worst insult possible to a bodybuilder, "Lou, you're looking very small today.")

Stock market pundits are obsessed not only with the size of corporate profits, but also with their growth rate. You can imagine investors in fast-growing companies making Arnold-like comments of, "You don't buy stocks for their book value." The obsession with growth is appropriate given the fact that stocks are risky and pay less today than safe Treasury bonds. The main reason to accept the risk of stock market losses is the promise of a growing profit stream. Thus, investors are correctly obsessed with growth.

What are the prospects for corporate profits growth? Here, there is a clear answer. It is that profit growth, and consequently stock prices, cannot continue their historical performance.

Before getting to the reasoning for the limits on profit growth, it is nice to point out that this is one of the few questions that have an unambiguous answer within the investing world. This rarity of clarity is the subject of an entire subset of the jokes about economics (also known as the "dismal science"). For example, if you laid all the economists in the world end to end they still wouldn't reach a conclusion. Or, more cruelly, if you laid all the economists in the world end to end that would be a good thing. To counter this, let's make the clear statement and then explain the reasoning.

Fact: Corporate profits have been growing above their natural speed limit for a long time. The future for stocks cannot be as bright as the past.

On the road to this conclusion we start at the basics—with bacteria. Almost every biology textbook contains a section that describes bacterial growth rates in terms of something like this: Some bacteria can divide every two hours. If this replication pace were sustained for several weeks, the offspring of one bacterium would weigh more than the universe.

Continuing our Arnold theme, bacteria could mock Internet companies by saying, "Yahoo!, you're growing very slowly today." Left unconstrained, one bacterium would become 4,096 in one day, over 16 million in two days, over 60 billion in 3 days, and enough to weigh more than the earth in a couple of weeks.

So bacteria can grow really fast. Over the long run, what has been the growth rate of bacteria? The surprising answer: zero. Bacteria have been around for a really long time. Doing the simple mathematical calculation of the annual growth rate over their history, bacterial growth rates are infinitesimally greater than zero.

An unavoidable mathematical law causes the contrast between doubling every two hours and a long-term growth rate of zero. At least for the last several billion years, the earth itself has not changed significantly in weight. The long-run rate of growth of the earth has therefore been zero. Thus, anything that is a subset of the earth, including bacteria, must have a long-run growth rate of no more than zero.

This is a mathematical truism. A part of a system cannot sustain a higher growth rate than the system for an indefinite time.

Just as bacteria are part of the earth, any single company is part of the global economy. Thus, over the long run, no company can grow faster than the world's economy. For example, Figure 8.5 shows the growth in

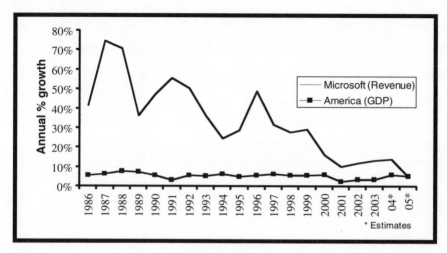

FIGURE 8.5   Microsoft's Growth Rate Has Slowed toward That of the U.S. Economy

Sources: Microsoft, U.S. Department of Commerce, Congressional Budget Office

Microsoft's revenues from its public début until today as compared with the growth of the U.S. economy. (The best graph would use global economy growth; the chart uses the United States because the story is the same and the U.S. statistics are more reliable.)

When Microsoft was a young company, its growth rate was spectacular. Over the years, however, that growth rate has slowed and now is much closer to that of the entire country. Over the long run Microsoft cannot grow faster than the economy. In fact, the gap is projected to disappear in 2005 (Figure 8.5).[12]

Whenever a company, or a set of companies, is growing faster than the economy, that growth rate is unsustainable. The relevant question is not if growth will slow to the natural speed limit but when growth will slow.

Both corporate revenue and profits are subject to the same natural speed limit. Neither revenue nor profits can grow faster than the economy indefinitely. Figure 8.6 shows, however, that U.S. corporate profits have been growing faster than the economy.

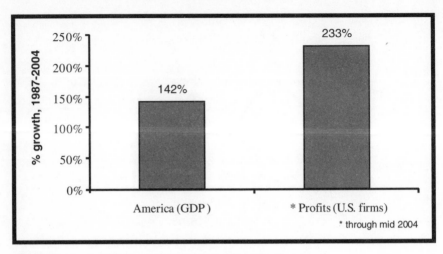

FIGURE 8.6   Profits Have Grown More Than the Economy
Sources: Bureau of Economic Analysis, U.S. Dept. of Commerce, Congressional Budget Office

Looking at the data from the same period as the Microsoft chart, U.S. corporate profits grew faster than the economy. This growth in profits—that is above the natural speed limit—is unsustainable. While there is no obvious time for this above-average growth to end, it must eventually end. The logic is as inescapable as death and taxes.

Buying the Hype at Precisely the Wrong Time

Profits of U.S. firms have been growing faster than the economy. What does this imply for stock prices? When something is doing better than average, it probably pays to be a bit cautious. If an athlete, for example, has a fantastic year, it would be prudent to expect the next year to be less fantastic.

As investors, it seems that we are built to feel exactly the opposite. We tend to overweight recent events. This leads us to be most optimistic at exactly the wrong time. Consider the case of Sun Microsystems. In the late 1990s Sun was riding a boom caused by Y2K and the Internet bubble. Sun's revenues and profits were shooting up at rates approaching 100% a year.[13]

What should a rational investor have done when evaluating Sun's performance in the late 1990s? The answer is that, rationally, 100% growth rates are unsustainable. Thus, a prudent investor would have given a lower weight to Sun's current performance. Historically, investors have priced stocks at somewhere between 10 and 20 times a firm's current profits. Prudence in the late 1990s might have argued that Sun deserved something toward the low end of this range.

Did investors realize that Sun's performance in the late 1990s was unsustainable? Quite to the contrary, their lizard brains caused them to bid Sun's price stock up until they were paying close to 100 times current earnings! Precisely at the moment when Sun's profits were growing at the most unsustainable pace, investors valued those profits at the highest level. The result was financial devastation for Sun shareholders as the stock lost more than 90% of its value.[14]

Figure 8.7 suggests a potential problem for stock prices. It shows that stock prices have risen even more than corporate profits in the years since 1987.

The diagram takes the most conservative estimate of stock market appreciation. As a starting point, it takes the highest level of the Dow Jones Industrial Average before the 1987 crash.[15] Any other starting point would yield an even higher growth rate. Furthermore, the calculation ignores dividends, which would again serve to dramatically increase stock market returns.

We end up with two layers of unsustainable growth. Corporate profits are growing at an unsustainable pace relative to the economy, and the stock market's valuation of those profits is growing even faster. If profit growth is going to slow toward its natural limit, then current profits might be reasonably valued at prudent multiples. Quite to the contrary, investors have bid up stock prices so that they are paying more now for every dollar of profits than before.

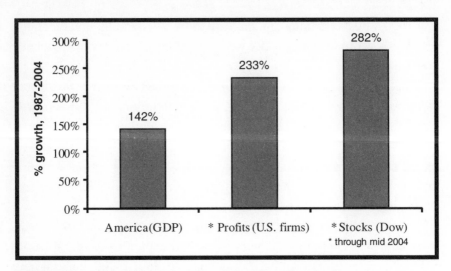

FIGURE 8.7   Stock Prices Have Risen Even More Than Profits
Sources: Bureau of Economic Analysis, U.S. Dept. of Commerce, Congressional Budget Office

When will corporate profits and stock prices slow down to their natural speed limit? I was pondering this one night while watching a Tonight Show visit by Phil McGraw ("Dr. Phil") who was promoting his book *The Ultimate Weight Solution.* Jay Leno was making fun of the author's weight, and Dr. Phil responded by saying, "Are you saying I'm too fat to write a diet book?"

Leno responded by saying that he wouldn't be making the joke except that the title of the book is the "ultimate" weight loss solution. Less extreme adjectives, Leno suggested, would have been more appropriate for a man of Dr. Phil's size. Presumably, "a pretty good weight loss solution" or "moderate weight loss for fatties" would not have drawn Leno's wit.

Professor Siegel does not make a similar mistake in his work promoting stocks. His book is called the *Stocks for the Long Run,* not "Stocks for the Super, Super Long Run" or "Jurassic Investing Secrets." Over the truly long run, Professor Siegel's argument cannot be right. Stocks cannot be the ultimate investment because over the long run, they can only be average.

No one knows when the natural speed limit will hit corporate profits and stock prices. John Maynard Keynes famously quipped, "In the long run we are all dead." His point is that arguments about the truly long run have little meaning to people whose horizons stretch out just a few years. Just as Microsoft grew very rapidly for more than a decade, there is no reason to expect an imminent slowdown in the growth of stock prices. Nevertheless, such a slowdown is inevitable.

Buying Stocks with the Wall Street Bulls

Our fundamental analysis so far has made two conclusions. With current profit projections and interest rates, stock prices look to be close to fairly valued. There is some hint of trouble in the fact that both profits and the valuation of the profits are increasing at unsustainable rates. The next piece of the valuation puzzle is an attempt to gauge investors' moods. The universal investing rule is that popular investments are unprofitable and vice versa. Where do we stand in the cycle of excessive optimism and pessimism toward stock ownership?

We can look at Wall Street gurus for clues. The big financial firms employ market strategists who make both predictions and investment recommendations. Richard Bernstein is one such strategist who works for Merrill Lynch & Co. In 2003, Mr. Bernstein was criticized for being too negative on stocks.[16] Bernstein fretted about a number of problems including the U.S. trade deficit and the possibility of rising interest rates.

Compared to his brethren Mr. Bernstein has been quite negative on U.S. stocks for years. In 2003, however, stocks prices soared. Investors who listened to Mr. Bernstein made less money than if they had listened to his competitors. Not surprisingly, Mr. Bernstein was under fire for his ursine outlook.

How bearish was Mr. Bernstein? The amazing fact is that for all his "bearishness" Mr. Bernstein suggested that people invest almost half their total financial wealth in the risky stock market. How can this be considered too bearish? The answer is that we live in an investing climate dominated by Professor Siegel's view that stocks are the best investment, so almost any portion not in stocks is viewed as "bearish."

Putting almost half your money at risk seems to be quite a bold suggestion. Nevertheless, Mr. Bernstein was conservative compared to his peers. Table 8.3 shows the recommendations of a set of leading Wall Street firms highlighted by the *Dow Jones Newswires* at the time that Mr. Bernstein was under fire for being bearish.

This is not a list of the Wall Street bulls; this was the entire list selected by the *Dow Jones Newswires!* It shows that Mr. Bernstein was more pessimistic about stocks than all of his peers on this list.

This suggests that there is more pain ahead for stocks. While Mr. Bernstein has been getting less flack of late, Wall Street is still extremely bullish on stocks. Investments are profitable when they are hated. Recall

TABLE 8.3   In an Optimistic Environment, Caution Is Labeled Pessimistic

Firm	*Strategist*	*% into Stocks*
A.G. Edwards	Mark Keller	70%
Banc of America	Tom McManus	70%
Bear Stearns & Co.	Francois Trahan	60%
CIBC World Markets	Subodh Kumar	70%
Goldman Sachs & Co.	Abby Joseph Cohen	75%
Legg Mason	Richard Cripps	60%
Lehman Brothers	Chip Dickson	70%
Merrill Lynch & Co.	**Richard Bernstein (the "bear")**	**45%**
Morgan Stanley	Steve Galbraith	65%
Raymond James	Jeffrey Saut	65%
Salomon Smith Barney	Bill Helman	55%
Wachovia	Ken Liu	78%

Source: Dow Jones Newswires[17]

that 1982 was the best time to buy U.S. stocks in a lifetime. At that point, stocks were universally hated and essentially ignored.

Reasons to Own Stocks Even If They Are Only Average Investments

When I was a teenager, I spent some time at the local roller skating rink. In addition to enjoying the huge bell-bottoms and other clothes from the 1970s (the decade that taste forgot), I was puzzled by one of the establishment's rules. As an unskilled but thrill-seeking skater, I was constantly getting in trouble with the staff for skating too fast.

While I am sure that I did skate too fast, the rules made no sense. "No skating faster than average" was the law posted around the skating club. I spent many hours grappling with the logic. If even one person skates slower than the average, then by pure mathematics, someone else (and maybe many people) must be skating faster than the average. So the rule made no sense. The skating rink's employees were unimpressed with my logic, but I learned the mathematics of averages.

When it comes to investments, the logic of averages is unavoidable. No investment class can be above average indefinitely. Stocks have had a long run and are not cheap. So I don't recommend buying stocks in the hopes that they will have higher returns than other assets.

Even if stocks are only average, however, there are some good reasons to buy them. First, stocks provide protection against inflation and deflation. By buying stocks, and therefore the real assets that they represent, you are locking in purchases at today's prices. This means that if inflation rates rise, the value of those underlying assets should also rise. Similarly, if prices fall, the assets controlled by the corporation will also fall. So stocks provide protection in the event that the United States' long run of almost perfect inflation rates ends.

Second, stocks provide protection against currency swings. Because many U.S. companies derive substantial revenue from international sales, stock prices are buffered against changes in the value of the dollar.

In 2003, for example, the U.S. dollar lost about 20% of its value against the euro, and lost substantial ground against most other currencies.[18]

The decline of the dollar made most Americans poorer. When we go to buy a bottle of French wine or a car made in Japan, our dollars buy less. However, the earnings of many U.S. companies were helped by the decline in the dollar. Continuing our Microsoft theme, a piece of software that sold for 100 euros brought in over 120 dollars at the end of 2003 versus about 100 dollars at the start of the year. By selling the exact same product at the exact same price in foreign currency Microsoft reaped higher returns.

Stocks can be bought for risk-reducing reasons even if they are going to be only average investments. This is an interesting turn of events. Stocks are often thought of as the high-risk, potentially high-reward investments. It may be that stocks have become average investments with some risk-lowering features.

Another reason to buy stocks is the ability to avoid taxes legally. Both capital gains and dividends are subject to low tax rates. In addition, it is possible to build your own tax-advantaged mutual fund. The technique is to own a lot of stocks and to make sure that before the year ends, you sell enough of the losers so that your tax bill is zero. This feature of stocks has always existed, but until recently it was not feasible for most people because of high trading commissions. The online brokerage revolution has made it possible to legally defer paying taxes on stock market gains indefinitely.

Just as a family loves all its children, even the ones who are not superstars, there are good reasons to own stocks even if they are going to be only average investments.

Even If You Do Not Buy Any Stocks, You Own a Lot of Stock

The final chapter of this book contains a summary of my recommendations for investing. For most people, my suggestion for stock investing will be lower than that advocated by Wall Street. Imagine for a moment that you follow my advice, or decide for other reasons to invest a modest amount in stocks. Now fast-forward 30 years to learn that stocks have done fantastically over that time. In 2035 you are looking back at your current financing decisions.

Many investors that I know have fantasies of having made huge bets at just the right moment. One of my friends correctly predicted the surge in biotech stocks in the late 1990s. He made some money on his investments, but missed much of the opportunity (some of the stocks he followed went from $5 to over $100 in a year). Almost every conversation with him includes discussing his fantasy of borrowing every dime possible and buying those biotech stocks for the entire ride. Many other investors speak of similar dreams—betting against stocks during the bubble days, buying after the terrorist attacks in 2001, and more.

Imagine our prudent stock investor who looks back on 30 years of stock market gains. The fantasy will be that she or he had invested every penny in stocks and made a ton of money. Even better, if time travel is invented, perhaps our investor in 2035 can travel back in time and change the investments. Wouldn't it be great to look in your retirement account some years from now to find that magically your financial decisions had been altered so that you had made the perfect set of decisions?

In *Back to the Future,* Marty McFly also wishes that he could change the world. Near the beginning of the film, he sees his mentor, the crazy professor, shot down by terrorists. Wouldn't it be great if he could go back in time and change events so that the professor is prepared for the attack? That is exactly what McFly does by warning the professor when he is time traveling. Armed with this knowledge, the professor still gets shot, but a bulletproof vest protects him.

So if U.S. stocks continue their 200-year run, we'll wish we could go back in time to adjust our financial decisions accordingly. The funny thing is that when it comes to stocks, even if you don't buy any stocks, you will most likely participate in any continued stock market rally. I've been making this point to my buddy Doug for years.

Doug was a college roommate who now runs a number of entrepreneurial businesses in Southern California (and has become quite a surfer). He made a ton of money during the bubble years, in part by a huge investment in Qualcomm. At one point during those euphoric days Doug owned 8,000 shares of Qualcomm. He went out surfing one day and came back to learn that during his two-hour surfing trip, the stock had surged by over $70 a share. So in a morning of surfing, Doug's investment in one stock increased by over half a million dollars! Not bad.

Even after the bubble broke, Doug was still ahead on his stock purchases. During 2001 and early 2002, I constantly urged him to trim his stock holdings. "Do you think that stocks are going to decline further?" Doug asked. I responded by saying that my advice was not based on a prediction of the stock market. Frustrated, Doug said, "Why should I sell stocks if they are going to go up?"

I had Doug then draw up a list of his assets. He was a rich guy worth millions. This money was divided between California real estate, the value of his businesses, and his stock holdings. I then asked him to describe a scenario in which his businesses were in trouble. The answer was that his businesses would suffer serious decline in a recession. The final question was to ask Doug about the value of his stock and his real estate in this scenario. The answer was that if the economic conditions went south, all three of his major sources of wealth would decline together.

The conclusion was that even if Doug owned no stocks, his wealth would go up along with a stock market rise. Doug participates in any stock market boom even if he owns no stocks. His real estate and his businesses are worth more in the good economic times that foster stock market gains.

Similarly, most of us effectively own stocks even if we haven't bought any. Most importantly our job prospects probably go up and down with the stock market. If we put most of our financial eggs into stocks then precisely when we might need those resources because of problems in our lives, they are likely to be less valuable.

Most of us need not fear missing a stock market rally. If events turn out rosy, when we look back from the perspective of 2035, it will be as if we had stuffed our portfolios full of stocks. In a stock market boom, we are likely to enjoy high salaries and rising real estate values. If things turn out less perfectly, we will likely need the money that we have and be glad if it isn't all invested in risky stocks.

Our Love Affair with the Stock Market Continues

Stocks seem to be close to fairly valued. It is easy to construct scenarios that make stocks look cheap and similarly easy to imagine worlds where they are expensive. This balancing of risk and reward is the definition of fair value.

My worries about investing in U.S. stocks come not from such fundamental analysis but rather from a perspective on emotional cycles. When financial manias reach the magnitude that we saw in the late 1990s, the recovery generally requires a period of extreme pessimism. While we had a significant bear market after the bubble burst, it seems that we never reached the requisite depths.

The final piece of evidence in this argument is that almost no one believes it. In fact, I find it hard to believe myself. I began serious stock purchases in the early 1980s. You could buy fantastic, rapid-growth companies with single-digit PEs. I used to walk around my San Diego apartment hitting the *Wall Street Journal* with excitement and muttering to myself, "It is a historic time to buy stocks." I knew that stocks were cheap.

Throughout my investing life, stocks have been the best investment. So much so that I have earned far more from stocks than from wages. All of my training suggests that stocks cannot be as good an investment now as they have been throughout my life. Nevertheless, I don't really believe it. Or more precisely, my backward-looking lizard brain simply can't get over the fact that stocks have made me a lot of money.

For those of us who have made money for decades by plowing money into stocks, it is extremely tough to kick the habit. The argument against being completely bullish on U.S. stocks is an argument of cognition against experience. My lizard brain still tells me to invest everything in stocks even though my analyses suggest otherwise. With my rational side, I am able to control my investments, but I can't stop my lizard brain from loving stocks.

Love affairs, whether of the wallet or the heart, share common elements. In *Shakespeare in Love* the young playwright falls in love with cross-dressing Viola de Lesseps (played by Gwyneth Paltrow in her Academy-Award-winning role). Along their romantic road to an eventual happy ending, Shakespeare and his love must endure a set of challenges, including a very public engagement between Viola and Phillip Henslowe (played by Geoffrey Rush).

Because Viola's fiancé is a lord, the whole gang ends up before Queen Elizabeth. Another lord in the audience asks the Queen how the story will end. She replies, "As stories must when love's denied: with tears and a journey."

While we have had some tears in our love affair with stocks, Figure 8.8 shows that there has been no journey away from stocks. Over the 10 years spanning 1994 to 2003, investors have placed an additional $1.5 trillion in long-term equity mutual funds. In the post-bubble world, the rhetoric surrounding stocks is somewhat tempered but there has been no movement away from stocks as an investment class. Before stocks represent outstanding value, I predict there will be many years during which investors are taking money out of stocks.

It is the 1998 edition of Professor Siegel's *Stocks for the Long Run,* that proclaims, "Stocks are actually *safer than bank deposits!*" Of course, two years after this edition was published, the S&P 500 lost half its value, and the NASDAQ lost 70% of its value. In the post-bubble, 2002 edition of *Stocks for the Long Run* the dust-jacket promotion of stocks being safer than bank deposits has been removed. Nevertheless, the message remains the same. In fact, Professor Siegel's advice on investment allo-

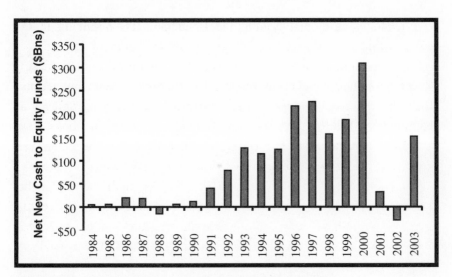

FIGURE 8.8   America's Love Affair with Stocks Is Not Over
Source: Investment Company Institute, 2004 Fact Book, Table 13

cation is worded identically in both pre- and post-bubble editions, "Stocks should constitute the overwhelming proportion of all long-term financial portfolios."[19]

Stocks for the long run is still the conventional wisdom. In their 2004 retirement planner, The Motley Fool website says, *"Fools opt for stocks above all else as our vehicle of choice for growth over the long term."* (Devotees of the Motley Fool call themselves "fools" as a compliment.)

We've seen that Wall Street still recommends that about two-thirds of all investments should be in stocks. Furthermore, Americans own historically high levels of stocks. In a Shakespearean sense, we've had the tears of a bear market, but we have not had the voyage away from stocks that generally marks the end of an investment era.

U.S. stocks are still the most loved of all investments. If the most loved investment proves to be the most profitable, it will be the first time in investing history. I conclude, in answer to Peter Borish's question, that buying stocks is indeed driving the financial car by looking in the rearview mirror.

I still recommend a significant investment in stocks, not because I expect them to have higher returns than all other investments, but because stocks have tax advantages and generally unrecognized advantages as risk reducers. While I advocate a substantial investment in stocks, I am far more sanguine about their prospects than Professor Siegel or Wall Street.

chapter nine

REAL ESTATE
Live in Your Home; Make Your Money at Work

Can We Continue to Make Lots of Money on Our Homes?

In the late 1980s my friends Peter and Julie paid more than $1 million for an apartment on Manhattan's Central Park West. Their beautiful 4,000+ square foot residence is in a prestigious building and has a view of Central Park.

Peter bought the property even though he held negative views on the economy. Accordingly, I asked, "If you think the economy is in trouble, doesn't that mean that housing prices will fall? Doesn't your doom and gloom view mean that you will lose money on your home?"

"Make your money at work and live in your home." That was Peter's response to my query. He explained that he expected to continue to make good money at work, and that he didn't really care what happened to real estate prices. He intended to live in his apartment indefinitely, thus the ups and downs in valuation were irrelevant.

Peter's "don't expect to make money on real estate" philosophy seemed reasonable for three reasons.

First, housing appreciation will have its ups and downs. For every buyer of a house, there must be a seller. Unless sellers are idiots, they should sell only if the price is fair. Since housing prices sometimes go up a lot, "fair" requires that housing prices should sometimes go down. Houses are risky investments and should not be expected to increase continuously. There should be bear markets in houses. This is predicted by both the rational (efficient markets hypothesis) and irrational views of markets.

Second, throughout most of history land and home prices have, in fact, gone up and down. The most obvious U.S. example of a real estate bust is the dustbowl of the 1930s. But it does not take a depression to hurt land prices. From 1992 through 2004, for example, Japanese land prices fell every year and lost almost half their value.[1] This severe decline took place even though Japan remains one of the richest countries in the world and did not suffer an economic depression.

Third, the theory of comparative advantage—one of the most important theories in economics—suggests that most people should make their money at work and not in real estate. According to an oft-told story, Professor Paul Samuelson, winner of the 1970 Nobel Prize in Economics, was once asked by a physicist to name one idea in economics that is true and nontrivial. Without hesitation, Professor Samuelson answered "comparative advantage." What is this theory, and why does it validate Peter's cautious view of real estate prices?

Comparative advantage, first articulated by David Ricardo in the nineteenth century, suggests that we (both as a country and as individuals) can make the most money by focusing on what we do best.[2] In his famous economics textbook, Professor Greg Mankiw (whom we have met before and will again in a minute) asks whether Tiger Woods should mow his own lawn.[3] The theory of comparative advantage says that even if Tiger Woods has an *absolute advantage*—meaning that he is better than all others—in lawn cutting, he should spend his time with a golf club in his hands and not grass clippers.

My favorite example of a failure to understand comparative advantage comes from a 1979 article written by James Fallows about President Jimmy Carter. Mr. Fallows worked at the White House and would ask for time on the private tennis courts through President Carter's secretary. Mr. Fallows claims that President Carter himself would schedule the White House tennis courts. On his request for court time Fallows writes, "I always provided spaces where he [President Carter] could check Yes or No; Carter would make his decision and send the note back, initialed J."[4] (President Carter has denied this.)

Comparative advantage and common sense suggest that even though President Carter was in a unique position to schedule the courts, his time would have been better spent elsewhere.

What does comparative advantage have to do with real estate prices? Most people are not experts in real estate, but are experts at something else—often the work they do for a living. Is it more likely that you will make money by doing what you have trained for all your life, or in something you spend a few hours on a year?

The answer seems as clear as the fact that Tiger Woods should not mow his own lawn and Jimmy Carter should not schedule tennis courts. Those of us who are not real estate specialists should expect to make our money in the area where we are experts—at work. This provides the connection between Peter's enigmatic comment and economic theory. We should expect to make our money where we have a comparative advantage (in our jobs) and not where we are comparative neophytes (in our home purchases).

So how did Peter do in his work and with his real estate investment? His outcome was exactly the opposite of that predicted by the theory of comparative advantage. Peter has done fine at work, but even better in his home. Peter's real estate investment has soared in value and has increased his net worth by millions of dollars. So Peter actually lived in his home and made his money in his home!

Both economic theory and historical experience suggest that Peter was right to seek shelter in his home and profits in his paycheck. His actual outcome—making more money in real estate than in income—is similar to that of many Americans.

In fact, Americans have come to rely on the housing market for financial gain. While the stock market has gone nowhere for almost half a decade, housing prices have steadily increased. Accordingly, U.S. real estate values are at all-time highs both in pure dollar terms and also as a percentage of our wealth.[5]

Can we continue to both live in and profit from our homes? Can we continue to make our money where we don't have a comparative advantage? Alternatively, is it likely that home prices will stabilize or even decline?

The Harvard Economist versus the Gutsy Immigrant

With the 2005 version of *King Kong* (starring Jack Black, but not as the monster) coming to theaters can it be long before we have more super monster battles on the big screen? In 1962 King Kong fought Godzilla, who in turn has fought many other beasts. Perhaps the most surprising was the defeat of Godzilla by the caterpillar children of Mothra ("Mosura" in the original Japanese).

When it comes to housing prices, there was an interesting—albeit unknown—superbattle that took place in Massachusetts back in the late 1980s. On the one side stood world-famous Harvard economics professor Greg Mankiw. In opposition was Fatima Melo, a Portuguese immigrant with no college education. In the battle to predict housing prices whom would you bet on?

In 1989, Professor Mankiw and David Weil (who was a graduate student at the time, and is now a professor) published an article entitled, "The Baby Boom, the Baby Bust, and the Housing Market."[6] In it, these two esteemed academics concluded, "real housing prices will fall by 47% by the year 2007." They went on to write, "indeed, real housing prices may well reach lower levels than those experienced at any time in the past forty years."

The academic duo speculated on the spillover effects of their predicted housing bust. They write, "Even if the fall in housing prices is only one-half what our equation predicts, it will likely be one of the major economic events over the next two decades." These professionals predicted that housing prices would decline substantially and seriously harm the economy.

Not too far away from Harvard University, our young immigrant was facing a decision. Should Fatima and her husband buy a small house or a much larger one? Their family was growing and faced the decision of buying a house for their current needs, or something a bit roomier (and more expensive) to expand into. Fatima urged her husband to buy the biggest house they could afford.

Fatima anticipated that housing prices would rise (she was fortunate to never have taken an economics course). If prices were to rise, the bigger the investment in real estate, the more profits. Fatima advocated taking a risk, and she convinced her husband to swing for the fences. Accordingly, the young couple took their savings and borrowed as much money as the bank would lend them. They bet big in anticipation that a rising real estate market would make them money.

So who was right about housing prices? Was it the book-smart academics with their complex mathematical equations, or was it street-smart and gutsy Fatima putting her family fortune on the line? Figure 9.1 shows the answer. U.S. housing prices have soared. The price index is calculated by using repeat sales of the same property. This is a perfect measure as it compares apples to apples and exactly tracks changes in housing prices.

The professors predicted a 47% fall in housing prices after adjustment for inflation. In reality, housing prices—even after adjusting for inflation—have risen dramatically.

The professors were exactly wrong.

Furthermore, the professors predicted that the decline in housing

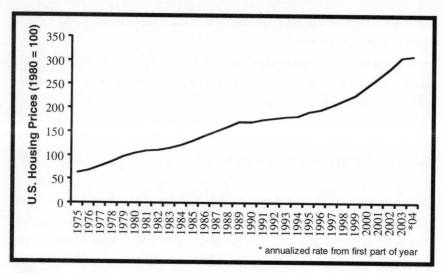

FIGURE 9.1 U.S. Housing Prices Have Surged
Source: Office of Federal Housing Enterprise Oversight

prices would put a drag on the economy. Exactly the opposite has occurred with rising housing values contributing to rising wealth and supporting the economy during a period when stocks have not risen.

The U.S. housing boom has been nothing short of amazing. Not only have prices risen dramatically since the professors issued their dire predictions, prices have been rising continuously since World War II. Furthermore, U.S. housing prices rose in every single year since at least 1975—no down years for three decades! That is absolutely stunning.

How did our dueling pair of forecasters perform? Fatima has parlayed her real estate investments into some serious wealth. She put $5,000 down on her first house and borrowed $90,000. She sold the house for $358,000. With the profits, Fatima and her husband bought a house that was three times larger. The new house has appreciated considerably so the couple has accumulated household equity in excess of half a million dollars. In spite of their modest incomes ("jobs that pay shit," in their words), Fatima and her husband have become rich by aggressively buying real estate.

Professor Mankiw has also prospered. He became a tenured member of the Harvard economics department at a young age. He has written several economics textbooks and has earned millions from their sale. Professor Mankiw is currently the chairman of President Bush's Council of Economic Advisors.

Is Your Home Overvalued?

Housing has had a great run in the United States for more than 50 years. Is it likely to continue? This question can be answered in three parts: (1) Determine a price to earnings ratio (P/E) of your home, (2) estimate a fair P/E for a home, and (3) salt to taste (adjust for local market dynamics).

What Is the P/E of Your Home?

A first step is to determine the "fair" value of a property. As with stocks and bonds this is impossible to do precisely, but easy to approximate. The calculation of fair value relies upon calculating a price to earnings (P/E) ratio.

A stock's P/E is calculated by dividing the price of the stock by the earnings for the stock. In the stocks chapter, for example, we looked at Microsoft. The current price of Microsoft (July 2004) is $28, and the predicted earnings for 2004 are $1.27 per share. Thus, Microsoft's P/E is 22.

To calculate the P/E of a house or other piece of property, we divide the price of the property by the income it produces. This is easy for a rental property (as long as we are careful to adjust for taxes). For a property that is occupied by the owner, however, there is no rent. In this case, the "earnings" are the estimated rental payments if someone else occupied the property.

For example, I live with my wife and our new baby in a condominium near Harvard University and Harvard Square. As our place has filled up with cribs and baby toys it has become obvious that we will need to move. Accordingly, I have been getting some estimates for the value of our place. The market price for our condominium is something like $650,000.

What is the value of our property? Because I don't assume the market price will stay constant, and I'm not sure when we will sell, I estimate the value independent of the current price. The key is the going rental price for the property. Even though we aren't currently earning anything on our property, I will use the market rental rate as the "earnings" for my P/E calculation.

The going rental rate for our apartment is about $2,800 a month. To calculate the P/E we need to factor in all costs including taxes. After our costs, we could generate about $2,000 a month in rental income from our property. So we could earn $24,000 a year in rent, after expenses. So the P/E for our condominium is the price ($650,000) divided by the earnings ($24,000). The P/E for our apartment is 27.

What Is a Fair P/E for a Home?

What is the fair P/E for a home? One way to answer this is to compare the P/E of a house to that of stocks and bonds. Table 9.1 makes this comparison and summarizes some key attributes of the different investments.

The U.S. stock market as measured by the S&P 500 has a P/E of about 18; this calculation uses the estimates for 2004 earnings ($61.50) and the current figure of the S&P 500 (1101).[7] The 10-year Treasury bond currently yields 4.4%. This converts to a P/E of 23.

TABLE 9.1 Key Investment Characteristics of Stocks, Bonds, and Real Estate

	Stocks *S&P 500*	*Bonds* *10-yr Treasury*	*Real Estate* *Your House*
Risky or Safe?	Risky	Safe	Risky
Potential for gain	$$	$	$$$
Tax treatment	Favorable	Neutral	Very favorable
Inflation protected?	Yes	No	Yes
P/E	18	23	??

How does a house compare with these two major alternatives? Table 9.1 lists four important investment characteristics and then analyzes the trade-offs between stocks, bonds, and real estate. When comparing two investments, the more favorable the investment attributes, the higher the fair value and the higher the P/E that can be justified. For example, if two investments are identical except for tax treatment, then the investment with the lower tax rate deserves a higher P/E.

Attribute #1, Risk: An investor in U.S. Treasury bonds is sure to get the original investment returned. Those who own stocks or houses risk losing their investment.

Attribute #2, Potential for Gain: The U.S. Treasury bond investor can make modest capital gains (if interest rates fall). Both the stock market investor and the home buyer have the potential for substantial gains. Because houses can be bought with very modest down payments, however, they have the highest potential for gain.

For example, Fatima's $5,000 investment in real estate became more than $250,000 in just a few years. An investor who bought the Dow Jones Industrial Average in 1927 would have achieved the same 50-fold increase if she or he had held the stocks until 2004.[8] So a few years' investment in housing can provide a lifetime's worth of gains in the stock market.

Attribute #3, Tax Treatment: Stocks are treated more favorably than bonds. Both dividends and long-term capital gains have lower tax rates than interest payments on bonds. Houses have the most favorable tax treatment. This ranges from the tax-deductibility of interest payments to the exemption of taxes on substantial capital gains from sales.

Attribute #4, Inflation Protection: Normal U.S. Treasury bonds are not protected against inflation (though some bonds do have such protection). Both stocks and housing are protected against inflation.

How, then, do housing investments compare with stocks and bonds?

The answer is that houses share many characteristics with stocks. Houses offer more potential for gain and better tax treatment than stocks. While the higher potential gain in houses should come with more risk, this has not been the case over the last decades.

So what is the right P/E for housing? Based on the characteristics of risk, return, taxes, and inflation protection, housing investments look similar or better than stocks. In addition, the finite supply of land might argue for a bit of a premium. Based on this analysis, housing could command a fair P/E as high as 30. Housing P/E's are categorized in Table 9.2.

Salt to Taste

As we all learned in elementary school, the three keys to real estate are location, location, location. While there is a single market for IBM stock, there are many, many different markets for real estate. While we have just made some general conclusions about "fair value" for a house, those P/E categories should obviously be adjusted for local circumstances.

When people look at real estate at a local level they tend to analyze by city and region. We can read that housing prices have gone up by 15% in Phoenix, but declined in Buffalo. In reality, however, "location" is a much more fined-grained notion than an entire city.

My friend Jon, who lives in Charlotte, North Carolina, learned the

TABLE 9.2   Is Your Home Overvalued?

House Price to Earnings Ratio	*Value Category*
More than 30	Expensive
Between 20 and 30	Premium
Between 10 and 20	Solid Value
Less than 10	Cheap

importance of location (and timing) over the last several decades. He sent me an e-mail summarizing his real estate experiences. The e-mail entitled, "financial frustration" said:

> I bought a condo in 1985, when I was single, two blocks from my office [in downtown Charlotte] for convenience for $60,000. The property lost value for years while houses two miles away gained in value. I sold the condo in 1993 after getting married in 1992 for $84,000 and bought a home for $180,000. Seven years and two children later, I sold this home for a small loss after significant improvements. Finally, I bought my current house for $360,000 just as the economy was slowing (June 2001). My original condo is now worth more than $200,000!

Jon has owned real estate since 1985 in a booming market. Nevertheless, due to family changes he has almost magically missed out on making money; his timing and movements missed the micro trends within his area. So there is much more to location than a city or region. In my own building, for example, the properties on different floors and on different sides of the building have performed differently.

Accordingly, our valuation ranges should be combined with knowledge of local conditions. Just as an above-average P/E may be appropriate for the stock of a super rapidly growing company, a property in the right location can justify high valuations.

Is There a Housing Bubble?

A glance through a bookstore can produce some serious fears about housing prices. Titles such as *The Coming Crash in the Housing Market* and *How to Profit from the Coming Real Estate Bust* are likely to get any homeowner's pulse racing. Are we experiencing a housing bubble and, if so, will the bubble crash?

There are some compelling clues that allow us to make a judgment as to the existence of a housing bubble.

Clue #1: Housing Prices Have Risen Far Faster Than Rents

There is no nationwide housing P/E. While we don't know the absolute value of the P/E we know that it has risen by 43% since 1982. Figure 9.2 graphs the rate of increase in housing prices divided by the rate of increase in rents.

Since 1982, housing prices have risen 43% more than rents. My wife and I have had a similar experience with our property. The market price of our condominium has almost doubled in just the last 5 years. In the same period, rents in our building have increased by about 20%.

So housing prices have risen faster than rents. Does this mean that current housing prices are too high? No. It could be that housing prices were too low back in 1982. What is unavoidable, however, is that relative to rents, real estate is less attractive today than it has been at any time over the last several decades.

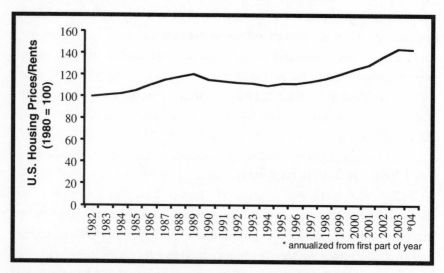

FIGURE 9.2   U.S. Housing Prices Have Risen Faster Than Rents
Source: Office of Federal Housing Enterprise Oversight, Bureau of Labor Statistics

Clue #2: Housing Supply Has Grown Faster
Than Housing Demand

Economists are odd people in many ways. In addition to using the words supply and demand far more frequently than normal humans, we also spend a lot of time thinking about elasticity. As I found out in college, the abstract concept of elasticity can make the difference between wealth and poverty.

Once a house has been built, it is not particularly easy to convert it to something else. Thus the supply of real estate is relatively *inelastic*. That means that the supply of housing changes only slowly. In contrast, something that is elastic can respond quickly to changes.

What about housing demand? Barring some sort of tragedy, the number of people who need housing is also unlikely to change quickly. Does this mean that the demand for housing is also inelastic? No. Housing demand fluctuates far more rapidly than population.

In tough times, people are remarkably flexible in their living arrangements. A recent college graduate, for example, with a good job can't imagine living at home. If unemployed, however, the same person becomes much more tolerant of her or his parents. In good times, therefore, demand for housing rises far more than population growth, and in bad times, people find ways to economize.

Thus the housing market is characterized by inelastic supply and relatively elastic demand. So what? These sorts of markets have the interesting characteristic that price can change very rapidly.

I learned this lesson when I was in college at the University of Michigan. Doug, the millionaire surfer, made a good living each Saturday scalping tickets at football games. My friend Scott and I decided to get some of this easy money. We hit upon the following strategy. Go to the student dormitories farthest from the stadium. Find students groggy from Friday night drinking and offer to buy their tickets for $1. Then ride our bicycles down to the stadium, sell the tickets for more, and collect our profits.

We did this one bright Saturday morning and managed to make about $100 in a couple of hours. I remember our first sale. A couple was walking away from a BMW. I approached the man and asked if he needed tickets. He asked, "How much?" Scott responded with "face value" of $12. The man instantly agreed, and we had $22 in profit!

The following Saturday, Scott and I were up early aggressively buying tickets. Buoyed by our success, we purchased more than 60 tickets, each for $1. As we rode our bikes to the stadium, however, we saw people offering to sell huge batches of tickets. We soon began selling tickets as fast as possible. The going prices started low and then plummeted. One buyer wanted six tickets. I offered six for $0.25 each. A competing scalper undercut me by offering all six tickets for a total of $1. Scott and I lost almost all of our investment.

What happened? We learned that like housing, football games have inelastic supply and elastic demand. While both games that we worked were against similar quality opponents, the forecast predicted rain on the second Saturday. The supply of tickets was a constant of just more than 100,000 seats (the University of Michigan's stadium is known as the "big house"), but demand was slightly lower the second week.

In markets with inelastic supply and elastic demand, prices can move very rapidly. As game time approaches there are either more buyers or more sellers. A relatively small shift in demand makes the difference between too many buyers and too few. This translates into the difference between high ticket prices and almost free tickets. On our second weekend of ticket scalping, Scott and I ended up throwing away dozens of tickets.

The housing market has inelastic supply and relatively elastic demand. There is no equivalent of kickoff time when supply becomes worthless so the rental effects are not as extreme. Nevertheless, the real estate market is subject to relatively large changes in rents for relatively small changes in demand.

Importantly, the supply of U.S. housing has been growing far more rapidly than the population. Figure 9.3 shows the relative growth between the 1970 and 2000 census.

Over the last three decades, the growth in housing units in the United States has exceeded the growth in population. As discussed, this does not imply disaster. Over this time period, the United States has become far richer. As we have become richer, it is reasonable to expect that we would have more houses. Nevertheless, the fact that supply has grown so much more than population is a clue. If times get tougher, it is possible that demand for housing could drop enough to put significant pressure on prices.

Clue #3: Vacancies Are on the Rise

For the next clue, Figure 9.4 shows the U.S. rental vacancy rate.

The U.S. residential rental vacancy rate is at the highest level on record. This is obviously good news for renters who have more power in their negotiations with landlords. On the other hand it is unambiguously

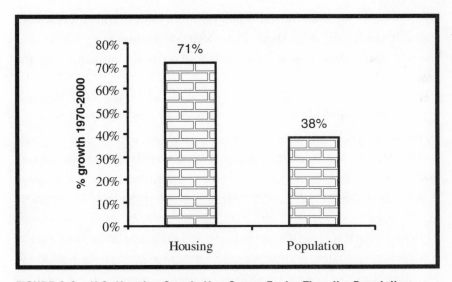

FIGURE 9.3   U.S. Housing Supply Has Grown Faster Than the Population
Source: U.S. Census Bureau

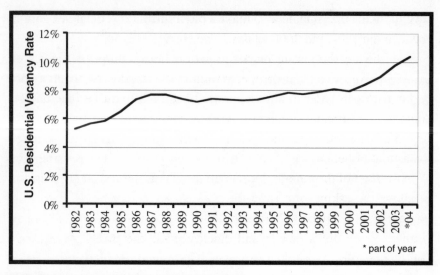

FIGURE 9.4 U.S. Vacancy Rate Is Climbing
Source: U.S. Census Bureau

bad news for landlords. It is also bad for homeowners who are not land-lords. Potential buyers of homes are constantly evaluating the alterna-tives of buy or rent, thus the prices of all homes are influenced by the rental market.

Clue #4: Mania-Like Behavior in Some Areas

Irrational markets are at least as much psychological as they are eco-nomic. The real estate market shows at least two signs of mania beyond the statistics. First, many markets show frenzied buying that accompa-nies bubbles. Second, there is a widespread belief that real estate prices cannot fall.

My friends Tom and Florentien just bought a house in the Boston met-ropolitan area. I ran into Tom one evening and I asked how he was doing. He said, "I'm exhausted. I had to get up at 5 a.m. and take a one-day business trip. Now I've got to go make a bid on a house." I inquired further about the pressing need to make a bid immediately. Couldn't Tom go home and make a bid the next day? The answer was no.

The Boston real estate market is—as of July 2004—still in a total mania. In Tom's case, the property went on the market on Saturday and he knew that in order to have a chance he needed to bid by Tuesday. As soon as a reasonable property comes on the market, multiple potential buyers flock to make aggressive bids. The winning bid generally is above the asking price.

In the case of the condominium adjacent to ours, the winning bid came in above the asking price and the deal closed within hours of the unit coming on the market! Through some inside connection, the buyers learned of the hot property and quickly made the owner an offer she couldn't refuse.

This behavior is crazy. Buyers are forced to make huge decisions with very little time for consideration. The mania is not nationwide as many markets are more subdued. Nevertheless, there are many places where this buying frenzy is common. Such behavior is typical of bubbles.

The second sign of mania is the belief that real estate prices cannot fall. When people envisage bad times in real estate, they imagine a plateau for some period of time. It seems impossible that real estate prices could actually decline. In Chapter 3, we met the trustees of my condominium who thought buying more property was a "can't lose proposition."

This belief in housing price rises is shared by professional analysts. Dr. John Krainer is an economist who works for the Federal Reserve. He wrote an excellent article entitled "Housing Price Bubbles."[9] In his conclusion, he writes, "Following the observation that declines in nominal house prices are unusual, I hold the house price fixed at its current level." Dr. Krainer does go on to analyze the possibility that housing prices could decline. Nevertheless, it is telling that he begins by assuming that prices will not fall. When markets are at their irrational tops, people consider declines to be impossible.

If it looks like a mania and feels like a mania, it's probably not a duck. The housing market shows the psychological signs of overvaluation.

Is There a Housing Bubble?

No.

I do not believe there is a bubble in U.S. housing prices. However, there are substantial risks to housing prices and they may fall substantially.

If housing prices could decline a lot, why is this not a bubble? In a true bubble, prices become so far out of line that it would be impossible for them not to fall. In the tulip mania, for example, it was possible to buy a house for the price of a single tulip bulb.[10] Because tulip bulbs can be produced in massive quantities with a bit of sunshine and water, it is impossible for bulbs to continue to sell for the price of a house.

Similarly, U.S. tech stocks in the late 1990s reached impossible levels. Cisco, for example, had a P/E in excess of 100, a figure that could not be justified by fundamentals. While irrationality can last a long time, Cisco's stock simply had to fall. I went on record with, "if Cisco's stock price does not decline, I will tear up my Harvard Ph.D. in business economics, because a continued high stock price would disprove everything I have learned." (Many other people went on record as well.)

So a bubble is such a degree of irrational pricing that only one outcome is possible. There are warning signs in U.S. housing prices: It is true that housing prices cannot grow faster than rents indefinitely, and it is also true that the long-run growth in housing cannot exceed the growth in population. Thus, the boom times in housing will end. The valuation levels, however, do not justify the label of a bubble. It is possible, therefore, that a decline in housing prices may be avoided.

U.S. housing is expensive but not so high as to ensure a collapse. In addition to the unsustainable trends and the bullish psychology already covered, however, there are additional risks to the housing market.

Risk #1: Rising Interest Rates

In June 2003, the interest rate on the 10-year Treasury was 3.11%. One year later, in June 2004, it was 4.82%. This stunning increase of more than 50% in just one year shows how rapidly rates can rise. How far will interest rates rise? What will the effect be on housing prices?

First, how far will interest rates rise? We learned two key facts in the discussion on bonds that are worth repeating. First, as compared to the last 20 years, interest rates are extremely low. Second, this is especially true when interest rates are adjusted for inflation. Figure 9.5 shows the real—inflation-adjusted—interest rate on 10-year Treasury bonds. This is calculated by subtracting the inflation rate from the interest rate.

Unless the economic world has changed completely, real interest rates will rise. This can occur via a decrease in inflation or an increase in interest rates. If inflation does not fall from current levels, how far will interest rates rise? Over the previous 10 years, the real interest rate (the premium over the inflation rate) has averaged 3.3%. Consumer price

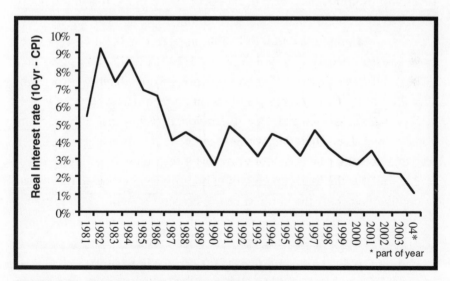

FIGURE 9.5   Real Interest Rates Are Extremely Low
Source: U.S. Federal Reserve, Bureau of Labor Statistics

inflation is heating up a bit. The annualized rise so far in 2004 is 3.3%. A different method of estimating inflation that looks at year over year changes in prices registers a slightly more benign 3.1%.

Thus, if the real interest rate returns to the average of the previous decade, the interest rate on the 10-year Treasury will rise from 4.8% to somewhere between 6.4% and 6.6%.

The interest rate on the 10-year Treasury bond could therefore easily rise to above 6%. In fact, such a rise could be said to restore interest rates to normal levels. The 3.11% rate of June 2003 looks like an irrationally low interest rate, and the subsequent rise a return to a level with more appropriate compensation for inflation.

What would the effect of a 6% interest rate rise be on home values? The exact answer is difficult because it relies on so many factors. However, a simple approximation is made by assuming that home buyers will make a mortgage payment that is a fixed percentage of their paycheck. This assumes, for example, that a buyer who can afford a $1,000 monthly

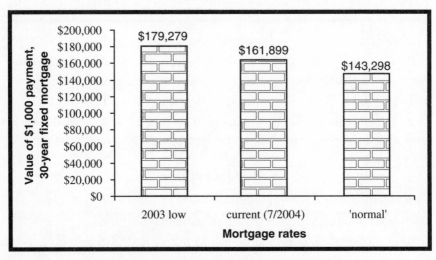

FIGURE 9.6   Rising Interest Rates Would Hurt Housing Prices
Source: U.S. Federal Reserve

mortgage payment today would be willing to make the same payment in a higher interest rate environment. Let's see the effect of interest rates with this assumption and then adjust the answer.

The analysis looks at the amount a person can borrow with a 30-year, fixed-rate mortgage and a monthly payment of $1,000. At the low mortgage rates of 2003, this hypothetical buyer could have borrowed $179,000. At the current rate, the figure drops to $162,000, and if real rates return to "normal," our buyer could only borrow $143,000 (see Figure 9.6). Thus, for a buyer who allocates a fixed percentage of her or his income to a mortgage payment, a return to historical real interest rates would decrease the feasible home purchase price by 20%.

This view suggests that a return to a more "normal" real interest rate could push home prices down as much as 20%. Of course, the decline could be far less as sellers are reluctant to cut prices even in soft markets, and buyers might be willing to stretch budgets. On the other hand, interest rates could swing from their 2003 irrational low to rates significantly above 6%.

Two conclusions seem obvious: Interest rates are historically low by almost any measure, and so rising interest rates are likely; and, they will put downward pressure on housing prices.

It is said that the snake that bites is rarely the snake that is visible. Almost everyone is aware of the risks that rising interest rates create for housing prices. By contrarian logic, therefore, rising interest rates are unlikely to topple the housing market. If there is to be a big bad wolf in housing it is likely to come in the form of some less discussed risks.

Risk #2: Leverage

I first learned about leverage during my high school physics class. My teacher got the biggest, strongest football player in the class to compete against a scrawny boy. The battle was to push a door that was half open; the football player was given the task of trying to close the door, while the scrawny nerd tried to force it open even further.

The twist was that the football player had to push right next to the hinges, while the skinny kid got to push on the edge farthest from the hinge. The scrawny boy won easily! The reason was leverage; being farther from the hinge provided an enormous advantage.

Housing has been the road to riches for two reasons. First, U.S. housing prices have been rising relentlessly since World War II. Second, because people are able to buy houses with relatively small down payments they can have tremendous leverage.

Recall Fatima Melo's home purchase that we discussed earlier. The young couple bought a house for $95,000, which they sold for $358,000. So they bought a house that increased in value by 277%. So how much did they earn on their investment? They invested $5,000 and borrowed $90,000. After selling the house and paying off the mortgage this $5,000 had swelled to $268,000! Now that's leverage! Figure 9.7 shows the return on this investment in reality (with leverage) and how it would have performed without leverage.

Financial leverage is great in bull markets. To make the most money the rule is simple: The lower the down payment, the greater the return on

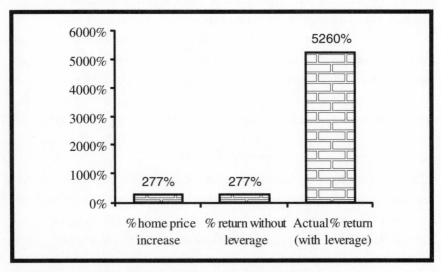

FIGURE 9.7   **Leverage Boosts Returns in a Rising Market**

investment. Alternatively, for any fixed down payment, the bigger the house, the more profits. The road to riches in the U.S. housing market has been to buy as much property as possible and borrow as much as possible to leverage profits. It has truly been an astounding way to make money.

There are two risks to leverage. One is individual, and the second is the spillover effect on others.

Groucho Marx learned the individual consequences of leverage in the 1929 stock market crash.[11] Groucho was opposed to gambling but had nevertheless invested his life savings into stocks. And he bought stocks on margin. In the 1920s the customary margin requirement was 10%. This allowed a speculator (or investor) to buy $1,000 worth of stock with $100 of cash. A 10% margin requirement allows for 10 to 1 leverage.

What are the effects of buying stocks on margin? With maximum leverage, any movement in the stock is magnified 10-fold. So a 1% rise in stock would produce a 10% return on investment. Throughout the bubbly 1920s people focused on the ability of leverage to *increase* returns.

Groucho found out that leverage works to dramatically *decrease* returns in a down market. A 1% decline in a fully margined account leads to a 10% loss on investment. More important, a mere 10% decline leads to total wipeout—a 100% loss.

As Groucho's stocks declined in 1929 he did what he could to avoid selling into a dropping market. He put up additional cash, and he borrowed money to provide margin for his stocks. In the end, he lost every penny.

Leverage was financial disaster for Groucho Marx (fortunately for him, he was able to recover through making successful movies after he went bankrupt). Groucho's decision to margin stocks also hurt other investors. At the market top, Marx owned a lot of stock. Once he was bankrupted he owned none—he was forced to liquidate his holdings as the market declined.

In a leveraged market, price declines put owners in financial distress as they are forced to liquidate. The liquidation puts further selling pressure on prices, and the further declines then cause more financial distress and more forced selling.

Margin calls were widely attributed as a major cause of the 1929 crash. The Securities Exchange Act of 1934 was enacted to curb the excesses of the 1920s. Section 7 of the Act addresses margin lending, beginning:

> For the purpose of preventing the excessive use of credit for the purchase or carrying of securities, the Board of Governors of the Federal Reserve System shall . . . prescribe rules and regulations with respect to the amount of credit that may be initially extended and subsequently maintained on any security.[12]

Under this law, the Federal Reserve sets stock margin rates. They have maintained the required level at 50% for several decades.

A dollar today can buy two dollars' worth of stock. The same dollar can buy many, many dollars of real estate. It is relatively easy to borrow $20 for every $1 of down payment. Furthermore there are a large number of ways to avoid putting any money down to buy real estate (and these go far beyond "no money down" techniques so common on infomercials). Small down payments create massive leverage. The greater the leverage, the greater the possible gains—and possible losses.

Mortgage debt is now at all-time highs, and home equity as a percentage of home values is at an all-time low.[13] Investors are increasing their leverage.[14] Presumably, they hope to hit a home run like Fatima's. The negative potential, however, is that leverage in the real estate market will lead not to riches but to an outcome more like Groucho's.

Risk #3: Adjustable Rate Mortgages

My nephew Brent attended the University of Montana and immediately after graduation began work as a real estate agent in his hometown of Ann Arbor. Early in his career he had a great chance to buy some bargain real estate.

A development project created a number of condominiums. A city ordinance required that some of the units be sold at cut-rate prices to low-income people. Business is generally slow for new real estate agents so, freshly minted Brent met the low-income guidelines. He was able to buy a condominium for about $20,000 below market price (the law prevents him from reselling for two years).

When it came to financing, Brent wanted a mortgage with the lowest monthly payment. Accordingly, he picked an adjustable-rate mortgage (ARM). After three years, Brent's interest rate will change. Brent's ARM produces a low payment. It also produces risk for my nephew. With interest rates near both theoretical and historical lows, those who have ARMs face the risk that their payments may rise substantially.

I asked Brent if he feared rising interest, and he replied by saying "if my mortgage interest rate is adjusted upwards, I'll just sell my condo." Sound reasonable? It may, but it is not for the same reason that the Dow Jones Industrial Average lost 500 points in one day in 1987. The problem with Brent's strategy is that he's not the only one with that strategy. Many people with ARMs may think they will sell prior to big mortgage payment increases, which is the functional equivalent of an elephant stampede trying to get through a small door opening—all at the same time.

To understand this risk it is necessary to understand the systematic effects of everyone's strategy. Sometimes it pays to do the same thing as everyone else. In the United States, for example, it is obviously good to drive on the right side of the road. Similarly, it is easier to swap word processor files around if we all use the same programs (nowadays that program is Microsoft Word). As we have learned, however, finance is a game where it often pays to avoid the herd.

The 1987 stock market crash was made more severe by the common use of portfolio insurance. The stock market was soaring in the early part of 1987, and people wanted to get rich. Some people were also worried that stock prices were too high. They could have reduced risk by selling some of their stocks, or by a whole host of financial strategies such as selling short or buying puts. The trouble with all of these techniques for reducing risk is that they also reduce the gains. What was a greedy but scared investor to do?

So-called "portfolio insurance" provided the answer. With it, the buyer could enjoy all the benefits of owning stock and also be protected against losses—or so the argument claimed. Here's how portfolio insurance worked. Stuff the portfolio with stocks. This provides the fuel for fat returns if stocks rise. The "insurance" on the portfolio was a plan to sell stocks if they declined. As stocks would sink, the investor would rapidly shift out of stocks and into safe bonds.

In theory, portfolio insurance had all the benefits of stock ownership without the risk. If stocks began to decline the investor would magically be shifted out of stocks. This seemed like such a great idea that firms sold this insurance and many investors bought it.

What happened to those who bought portfolio insurance? They got massacred in the 1987 stock market crash.[15] And they almost destroyed everyone else, too. In the second half of 1987, the stock market began to decline. As stocks declined, those who owned portfolio insurance sold stocks, which in turn caused prices to fall further. This selling culminated in the Dow Jones Industrial Average losing over 20% of its value in one day. The decline in the 1987 crash in percentage terms was almost twice as large as the 1929 crash.[16]

Investors' portfolios turned out not to be protected from the 1987 crash. The theoretical analysis of portfolio insurance assumed that markets would move gradually. In the real world, prices did not move gradually, but rather took huge steps down. Investors who thought they would exit stocks after small declines found themselves selling at precisely the wrong time.

If only one person had used portfolio insurance it might have worked fine. Because the strategy was common, however, the system built upon itself to create a selling frenzy. Those with portfolio insurance made the worst mistake possible in mean markets; they bought at the top, and put themselves in a position where they had to sell at the bottom.

Similarly, if Brent were the only person with a "sell if rates rise" strategy, it might work fine. However the truth is exactly the opposite. One-third of new mortgages are adjustable-rate mortgages, which is near an all-time high.[17] The prevalence of adjustable-rate mortgages makes the "sell my place if interest rates rise" strategy risky. If interest rates continue to rise, then millions of homeowners will be looking to sell when their mortgages adjust. This is unlikely to be a profitable time to be a seller.

When bad things happen they often appear unavoidable. In reality, however, the required steps to avoid ruin need to be taken much earlier. This is something that investors need to know, and also something that would have helped a man named Robert Brecheen.

At around 9 p.m. on August 10, 1995, Robert Brecheen tried to commit suicide by overdosing on pain pills. Mr. Brecheen was rushed to the hospital and revived by the administration of powerful drugs. At 1:55 on August 11, just five hours later, Mr. Brecheen was executed by lethal injection in the Oklahoma State Penitentiary.[18]

Mr. Brecheen was sentenced to death for committing murder in the first degree. After years on death row, all of his appeals had been denied and his execution loomed. Rather than let the state kill him, Mr. Brecheen decided that he would control the time and manner of his own death by committing suicide. Even in this, he failed. Mr. Brecheen got into a situation where he had zero control over his life. He was not able to even decide how or when to die.

Investors who are on the wrong side of mean markets face outcomes that are far less severe than execution but similarly inflexible. Those who buy at that top are often forced to sell at the bottom. A key to making money in mean markets is to retain control of the time of one's buying and selling.

Adjustable-rate mortgages remove control of when to sell a home. Those with adjustable-rate mortgages may be pressured to sell their properties at the same time as others. Thus, those who seek to profit from market craziness should avoid adjustable-rate mortgages.

Solution #1: Plan to Buy a Larger Home in the Future

The *Mean Markets and Lizard Brains* advice is to own some real estate but expect to move to a more expensive property in the future. If housing prices were a bubble, the correct strategy would be to own nothing and rent. Because housing prices are high, but not in a bubble, the suggestion is to own something less than your dream house. This strategy can be profitable regardless of whether housing prices fall or rise. How can this strategy win in all environments? Here's how a similar strategy worked in the stock market.

Near the top of the technology stock bubble, I found out that my older sister Sue had invested most of her retirement account in an aggressive technology mutual fund. I suggested that this was a very bad idea and that she sell. Some weeks after she agreed to sell her overvalued tech stocks, I asked if sister Sue had made the phone call to change her investment. "No," she said, " I haven't, I don't want to miss the rally."

To solve the problem we came up with the following strategy. Sister Sue sold one-quarter of her stocks. Now, I said, if stocks go up you will make a ton of money as you still have hundreds of thousands of dollars invested. If, however, stocks decline you'll have saved a lot of money by selling.

Technology stocks did decline, and Sue asked if she should buy back the stock. I said, no, now sell another quarter. If stocks rally, you will make money. If they fall, you will have saved more money. We continued this process until she completely exited her technology stocks. In the end she exited pretty close to the NASDAQ top of 5,000 and actually made money on her tech stock investments.

How can a decision to sell be good in both up and down markets? The answer is that it is a psychological trick. Obviously, the decision to sell stocks reduces profits if stocks rise afterwards. In the case of a stock market rally, I suggested that sister Sue savor the profits on the stocks she still owned, not the profits she hadn't earned on the stocks that she had just sold.

The win-win framing of selling stocks is a form of irrationality. Nevertheless, such tricks can help us precisely because we are not completely rational decision makers. Our financial plans are often hurt by our irrationality; it is great to use irrationality to our advantage.

Owning a relatively small house also allows for a win-win outcome with the appropriate psychological framing. As always, I follow my own advice. My wife and I live in a Cambridge condominium worth a bit more than $600,000. We hope to have more children, and when we look out five or 10 years, we'd like to live in a larger place. The current cost of the house we expect to own is more than a million dollars.

I can make myself believe that we will make money in either a housing boom or bust. If prices rise, we make an additional capital gain on our current property. If prices fall, our dream house will decline in price by more than our current home. Thus, we will be able to upgrade to our dream house for less than it would cost today.

So own some property, but expect to move up in the future.

Solution #2: Have a Fixed-Rate Mortgage

My advice on adjustable-rate mortgages is extreme. In *As Good As It Gets* when Jack Nicholson's neighbor (played by Greg Kinnear) swings by for a visit, Nicholson launches into a tirade:

> never, never again interrupt me. Okay? I mean, never. Not 30 years from now . . . not if there's fire. Not even if you hear a thud from inside my home and a week later there's a smell from in there that can only come from a decaying body and you have to hold a hanky against your face because the stench is so thick you think you're going to faint even then don't come knocking . . . don't knock . . . not on this door. Not for anything. Got me. Sweetheart?

I paraphrase Nicholson to say, don't get an adjustable-rate mortgage, not even if you are sure you will move in one year, not even if the adjustable-rate mortgage payment is much smaller than the payment for a fixed-rate mortgage. Not for anything.

There are actually at least three good reasons to have an adjustable-rate mortgage. First, real estate professionals may rationally want to take a gamble in the area where they are experts. This applies to my nephew Brent. If anyone is going to be able to get out at the top, it is likely to be a professional like Brent with his finger on the pulse of the market.

Second, adjustable-rate mortgages can be perfect for someone who knows she or he will sell soon. Consider, for example, a person who will move in two years and who has an adjustable-rate mortgage that is fixed for the next three years. For this person, an adjustable mortgage is almost as safe as a fixed-rate mortgage. (Even in this situation, adjustable rates are bit more risky because plans change and the fixed-rate mortgage provides more flexibility.)

Third, people who have lots of financial reserves can use adjustable-rate mortgages. A central problem with an adjustable mortgage is that a homeowner may be forced to sell into a down market. If the homeowner has plenty of money stashed away for such a day, then there cannot be a forced sale. So people who can afford fixed-rate mortgages can afford to bet against the pros and not risk too much.

It is said that banks are willing to lend to anyone who doesn't need the money. Similarly, adjustable-rate mortgages provide lower payments but should be used primarily by those who can most afford the higher payments of a fixed-rate mortgage.

So most, but not all, people should avoid adjustable-rate mortgages. My advice on this subject is precisely the opposite of that of Federal Reserve Chairman Alan Greenspan.[19] In a speech on February 23, 2004, Chairman Greenspan noted that in the decade prior to his speech, those with adjustable-rate mortgages paid far less than those with fixed-rate mortgages. He also pointed out that adjustable-rate mortgages are far more common in some other countries. He concluded, the "traditional fixed-rate mortgage may be an expensive method of financing a home."

I disagree with the chairman for two reasons. First, I believe that interest rates are likely to rise. Thus, when adjustable-rate mortgages come to their adjustments, I expect payments to increase.

Second, an adjustable-rate mortgage is a bet on interest rates. If rates increase by less than the market expects, you win with an adjustable rate. If rates increase by more than the market expects, you lose. Thus, those who choose adjustable-rate mortgages put their wealth at risk by betting on interest rates. Furthermore, that bet is taken against professionals.

My friend Greg used to bet against professionals of a different sort. He loved poker and used to test himself by playing against card sharks in Las Vegas. Because he was playing against pros, Greg expected to lose. He judged his ability by how long he could stay in the game before going broke. After one extremely successful evening, a pro took Greg aside and said, "You're an excellent young player, but when you have a strong hand, your left jaw muscle tightens." It was no surprise that Greg usually lost against such competent adversaries.

Competing against poker professionals was a losing game for Greg. Because he expected to lose, he never played for large stakes. He certainly would never have bet his house against professionals. Those who take adjustable-rate mortgages are betting their houses (or at least a substantial chunk of their wealth) against professionals.

Adjustable-rate mortgages are tempting because the payments can be so low. One day, while we were sitting in the Jacuzzi of our condominium, my neighbor Alec told me that he was moving out of Cambridge to a big house that he had purchased in the suburbs of Boston. As always, I asked, "fixed or adjustable mortgage?" Alec responded "adjustable." When I asked why an adjustable-rate mortgage, Alec replied, "If we had a fixed-rate mortgage, we couldn't afford the purchase."

I would recommend precisely the opposite strategy. If an adjustable-rate mortgage is needed to make payments affordable, I suggest purchasing a less expensive property.

Make Your Money at Work; Live in Your Home

Real estate has been the path to riches in America. Housing prices have risen relentlessly for decades. Furthermore, the magic of leverage has allowed people to make incredible rates of return. Millions of Americans have made the bulk of their wealth through real estate.

Unfortunately, the easy money has been made. The housing market is expensive and has a number of structural risks. The path ahead will be less rosy than the path behind. If we are lucky we can still have an expanding housing sector, albeit at a far more modest pace than in preceding decades. If we are unlucky, we may face persistently declining housing prices for some time.

Accordingly, I suggest that people return to Peter's advice regarding housing. Buy a home that you plan to live in. Expect to make your money in the area where you are an expert.

I also suggest putting yourself into a position where you can withstand some housing market turmoil. Even if the more optimistic scenario unfolds, it is likely that there will be some severe shocks to the system. When such shocks occur, those with the strong financial hand will be in a position to scoop up some values. Those with the weak financial hand are likely to be shaken out of the market at the wrong time.

There is value in strength in many areas. I learned a variant of this lesson when I was living in Uganda. I rode my motorcycle to Queen Elizabeth Park in western Uganda. In the park, I met with John, a man who worked for the Jane Goodall Institute helping chimpanzees. When John learned that I had ridden my motorcycle through the game park he became quite concerned. "Are you good with the bike?" he asked. I replied that I had just learned to ride. He looked concerned. He said, "There are three types of animals to fear as you drive out of the park, and I have specific advice for each type."

"First, stand your ground against elephants. They are more likely to give a mock charge than a real charge—of course be prepared to ride away as fast as possible if the charge gets too close. Second, never stand your ground against the buffalo. They never give mock charges, and it is better to be trampled than gored."

"Third, lions are the toughest." John became concerned at this point— "the trouble with lions is that by the time you see them it's too late." He went on to say, "never ever back down from a lion. Once they sense fear they are all over you. Furthermore, never turn your back on a lion—they don't like faces and when they eat people they tend to sit on the human's face. They pick on weak animals so when the road goes through thickets where the lions hide, go fast and be loud, act like a strong and powerful animal."

Act like a strong and powerful animal! I took John's advice. Near every thicket I accelerated and drove the motorcycle at top speed. I also tried to keep the gear lower so that I could make more noise. I kept thinking, lions drag down the sick and old animals in the herd. Act like a powerful animal, and they will leave me alone. On the drive, I saw an elephant (I stood my ground and he walked away) and I outran a buffalo. I did not see any lions; if they saw me from inside the thickets, apparently they were impressed with my vigor.

My advice with housing is the same as John's with lions. Be strong and powerful. Make sure that you can withstand some tough economic times. Those who can take the pain of a tough housing market put themselves in the position to profit from irrationality, not to become prey.

The *Mean Markets and Lizard Brains* advice with regard to housing is to do the opposite of what has worked—have a fixed-rate mortgage and own a smaller home than you plan to have in the future. Taking these steps is very hard because it requires overriding the lizard brain. For decades the best strategy has been to buy as much U.S. real estate as possible and ride the rocket ship to riches. Our backward-looking lizard brain prods us to do what has worked in the past. In order to position ourselves for trouble, however, we have to avoid the course of action that has worked for generations. Those who can accomplish this psychologically difficult task put themselves in a great position to profit.

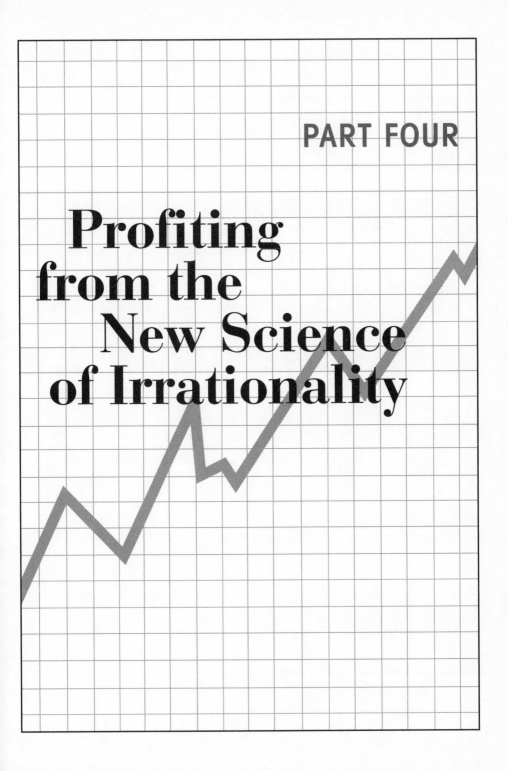

PART FOUR

Profiting from the New Science of Irrationality

T his final section provides investment advice. In Chapter 10, we learn more about the origins of the lizard brain and why it costs us money. While our instincts may have helped our ancestors, we find that financial markets are the most unnatural setting for our brains. An understanding of the lizard brain provides a timeless blueprint for effective and low-stress investing.

In Chapter 11, we return to the central question of *Mean Markets and Lizard Brains:* "Where should I invest my money?" In Part One we found that we are built to have systematic problems in markets. In Part Two we looked at macroeconomic drivers of financial performance. In Part Three we examined the prospects for bonds, stocks, and real estate. Now in the final section we summarize all of the findings. We discover that the current situation is particularly dangerous—kryptonite for the lizard brain. And then finally we come to a surprising answer to the question of where to invest.

chapter ten

TIMELESS ADVICE
How to Shackle the Lizard Brain

Timeless and Timely Tips

In *The Graduate,* a young Dustin Hoffman (playing the role of Benjamin Braddock) receives some succinct, and unsolicited, career advice from a friend of his parents, Mr. McGuire:

> "I just want to say one word to you . . . just one word."—McGuire
> "Yes, sir."—Ben
> "Are you listening?"—McGuire
> "Yes, sir. I am."—Ben
> "Plastics."—McGuire

I don't know if "plastics" was a good career choice in 1967 when *The Graduate* was released. I am sure, however, that there are better and worse times to work in particular fields. Similarly, the *Mean Markets* view is that there are good times and bad times to make particular investments. Gold, for example, was a great investment in the 1970s, and was a terrible investment in the 1980s and 1990s.

If markets were rational, then investing would be easy and stress-free. In the fairytale land of the efficient markets hypothesis, all investments are correctly priced at all times. Thus, in a hypothetical, rational investing world, it never pays to fret about possible mistakes; nor does it pay to seek bargains.

Out in the real world, however, markets are irrational and often mean. This creates both opportunity and risk. In a world where prices are often too low or too high, investors can find insanely good deals. We can also make insanely bad deals. Since the invisible hand has not built a world that is going to ensure our financial success, we have to do it ourselves.

Thus, the key to investing success—in the real world—is to be on the correct side of that irrationality. The *Mean Markets and Lizard Brains* advice for how to profit from manias and crashes is divided into two parts. First we'll seek to prevent our own lizard brain from ruining us (this chapter). Then we'll look for opportunities to make money from others' lizard brains (next chapter).

This division of tips for investing in crazy markets is somewhat akin to preparing for a sports competition. To win, it is always good to be strong, fast, and experienced. The best strategy on any given day, however, also depends on the competition.

In the late 1980s, for example, the Detroit Pistons won consecutive NBA championships. In each championship year, they had to defeat Michael Jordan's Chicago Bulls in the playoffs. To beat the Bulls, the Pistons relied upon excellent basketball skills (appropriate for any opponent), and they needed a specific strategy to contain Jordan. In this period of his career, Jordan was so dominant that opponents joked, "He can't be stopped, just contained."

To contain Jordan enough to win, the Pistons developed what became known as the "Jordan Rules." These included myriad defensive schemes, frequent double-teams, and a tough approach that made Jordan pay physically for any attempted slam dunks.

The Pistons' strategy was built on top of a talented roster that included Isiah Thomas, Joe Dumars, and Dennis Rodman. So the Pistons' victories over the Bulls came from two complementary approaches. First, they had great players with solid fundamentals appropriate for any basketball game. Second, they used a specific, situation-driven strategy.

Similarly, investing success in a financial world that is often crazy combines an approach that is timeless with opportunism driven by the current situation. This chapter contains timeless suggestions for mean markets, and the next chapter provides timely advice for this era.

Why Our Toughest Financial Battles Are with Our Irrational Selves

"We have met the enemy, and he is us." Walt Kelly coined this phrase in the comic strip Pogo on Earth Day 1971. Because people cause pollution, Kelly suggests that environmental progress must rely on modifying human behavior. Similarly, this chapter focuses on why we are so often our own worst financial enemies, and how to prevent this internal foe from bankrupting us.

In early chapters, we reviewed the evidence suggesting that mean markets stem from individuals who are far from rational. Furthermore, we found that the less-cognitive aspect of human mental abilities—the lizard brain—often causes our problems. To organize and utilize solutions to our financial shortcomings, it helps to understand why the lizard brain is built to bankrupt us.

Humans act irrationally in some financial situations because we are born without instincts that guide us to good solutions. In financial markets, we are fish out of water. The human financial situation is similar to that faced by other animals that live in unnatural, novel environments.

It is something we share with our closest genetic relatives, the chimpanzee.

Rational and Irrational Apes

Chimpanzees in the wild can demonstrate remarkable mental sophistication. I learned this directly in the summer of 1997, when I was living at a research station in the rainforest of western Uganda.

Harvard professor Richard Wrangham, who did some of his early work with Jane Goodall, founded the center in 1987. A central goal of the research was to follow and observe chimpanzees in their natural environment. When I arrived, the same group of chimpanzees (along with their offspring) had been observed and documented for 10 years.

In my stay with the chimpanzees, I grew to respect their intelligence. For example, one day I was following a group of wild chimpanzees when they entered an area of thick vegetation. My fellow human observers and I were unable to follow, and thus we lost contact with the animals.

Where could we find our chimpanzee group? My Ugandan companions suggested that we walk about two miles through the forest to a fig tree that was producing ripe fruit. Furthermore, the men suggested that we would arrive at the fig tree before the chimpanzees, and therefore we would be able to take a lunch break.

The Ugandans knew that the chimpanzees keep track of which trees are fruiting. Thus, the logical place to wait for them was at one of their tasty food sources. But how could we know when the chimpanzees would arrive? The answer is that the chimpanzees regulate their body temperature, and this provided an estimate for their arrival time.

When chimpanzees eat in these fig trees, they often climb high enough that they leave the shade of the forest floor and expose their dark and hairy coats to the sun. The chimpanzees don't like to overheat, so on sunny days, the chimpanzees tended to visit this particular tree in the cool morning. On cloudy days, like the one in question, however, the chimpanzees tended to arrive later.

We marched off to the fruiting fig tree, ate our lunch, and had a nap. The chimpanzees arrived right on schedule! I found this amazing. To get to the right tree at the right time, the chimpanzees used a mental map of the forest, they understood the seasonality of the fruiting, they understood the weather, and they knew how to find their way. They did it perfectly!

So chimpanzees can be really, really smart. The Ugandan men were able to navigate their way through the forest only because of years of experience. If I had been alone, I would have died in the forest long before I found any food (or chimpanzees). So these chimpanzees were able to solve this navigation problem better than most humans.

In contrast to savvy chimpanzees in the wild, those in zoos and research centers often look less intelligent. I learned this lesson in a humorous way from my friend Brian Hare, whom I met in Uganda that summer when he was a college student. He subsequently earned his doctorate from Harvard, and is now an accomplished primatologist.

Brian did some of his early work with chimpanzees at the Yerkes Primate Center in Atlanta. As an enthusiastic young scholar, Brian decided to see if he could get the chimpanzees to imitate him. Although one often hears the expression "monkey see, monkey do," there is very little evidence that monkeys or apes (chimpanzees are apes, not monkeys) learn through imitation.

Brian's test of chimpanzee imitation took the following form. Each day, he planned to do a headstand in front of the chimpanzees. Since chimpanzees do not normally perform headstands, any such behavior would be clear evidence of imitation. Brian explained his idea to the workers who cared for the animals. Their experience with captive chimpanzees had made them a bit cynical, and they laughed at Brian's youthful zest.

Undaunted, Brian proceeded to do a headstand in front of the captive chimpanzees. What happened? Within a few moments, the chimpanzees did respond, not by doing headstands, but by throwing their dung at Brian. (Their aim was pretty good, and they seemed to especially enjoy hitting him in the face.) He quickly abandoned his headstand project.

Captive chimpanzees exhibit lots of strange behaviors that seem very different from the sophisticated rainforest navigation that I had observed in Uganda. In their artificial settings, captive chimpanzees have little to do (their food is provided), they do not travel long distances, and they even weigh much more than their wild counterparts.

In short, captive chimpanzees sit around, eat too much, exercise too little, and are so bored that they throw dung for entertainment. (Sound like your boss?)

Are chimpanzees supersmart, or are they overweight, lazy, and bored? The answer is that they are capable of both types of behavior; what they do depends on their environment. When chimpanzees are in their natural environment, their instincts guide them to appropriate behavior. In contrast, when chimpanzees are in certain types of unnatural environments, such as zoos and research centers, those same instincts get them in serious trouble.

Humans as Zoo Primates

Humans can be thought of as self-domesticated apes or as zoo primates. Our not too distant ancestors lived in small groups and earned their food the old-fashioned way—by hunting animals and gathering plants.

Technological change, first in the form of agriculture, and later in the industrial and information revolutions, has changed our world fundamentally. A modern city is as unnatural an environment for a human as a zoo is for a chimpanzee. (A big difference, of course, is that we have built and moved into our own zoos, while people placed other animals in zoos.)

In recent years, scholars have shown that some of our individual irrationality can be explained by understanding the differences between the human ancestral environment and the current world in which we live. Just as zoo chimpanzees do crazy things, so do "zoo" humans.

This idea of a "mismatch" between human nature and industrialized living conditions has been explored quite thoroughly in nonfinancial areas.[1] Perhaps the problem shared by most people is that we enjoy the taste of foods that are bad for us. Why don't we derive pleasure from healthful foods? The answer, according to some theorists, is that our ancestors lived in a world where both calories and dietary fat were scarce.

For our ancestors, this theory suggests, the more calories they ate, and particularly the more dietary fat they consumed, the better. Ancestral humans who ate more of what we would term "junk food" were better able to survive and reproduce than their competitors.

Thus, our ancestors were built to love food, and to especially enjoy fatty foods. The world has changed, and saturated fats, for example, now cause heart disease. Nevertheless we are still built to feel joy at eating the foods that helped our ancestors, not the foods that would help us today. Professor William Irons of Northwestern University summarizes this hypothesis as follows in an important scientific paper:

> in ancestral environments, these preferences [towards different foods] motivated people to come as close as their circumstances allowed to optimal diets. However, in modern environments, the abundance of different types of foods is vastly different, and these preferences often motivate people to choose diets that are much less healthy than are possible in their [current] circumstances.[2]

Because we live in a different world from our ancestors, our very human nature pushes us toward food that is bad for us. In a famous scientific article, "The Past Explains the Present: Emotional Adaptations and the Structure of Ancestral Environments," Professors John Tooby and Leda Cosmides make the same argument about human logical abilities.[3] What was good for our ancestors can be bad for us living in a modern world.

Professors Cosmides and Tooby reason that it is simplistic—or downright wrong—to say people are irrational. Rather, our behavior depends on the context. In settings that were relevant to our ancestors, we are able to perform brilliantly. In novel settings, however, even with our big prefrontal cortexes, we look silly because we are fish out of water.

Using this logic, Professor Gerd Gigerenzer and colleagues are able to rephrase the Linda-the-bank-teller question that tripped us up at the beginning of this book in such a way that people behave rationally. Recall from Chapter 2 on individual irrationality that most people commit the "conjunction fallacy" by choosing answer (2) in the following problem instead of the correct answer (1).

Linda is 31 years old, single, outspoken, and very bright. She majored in philosophy. As a student she was deeply concerned with issues of discrimination and social justice, and also participated in antinuclear demonstrations.

Which of the following two alternatives is more probable?
1. Linda is a bank teller.
2. Linda is a bank teller and is active in the feminist movement.

Professor Gigerenzer changes the problem slightly to:

Linda is 31 years old, single, outspoken, and very bright. She majored in philosophy. As a student she was deeply concerned with issues of discrimination and social justice, and also participated in antinuclear demonstrations. (This part is identical to the other wording.)

There are 100 people who fit the description above. How many of them are:
Bank tellers?
Bank tellers and active in the feminist movement?

In this second version, the conjunction fallacy disappears as most people get the question right.[4] In a series of related experiments, Professor

Gigerenzer has shown that human brains work better when problems are described in frequencies (e.g., how many out of 100?) as opposed to probabilities (e.g., which is more probable?). Professor Gigerenzer argues that human brains are built to deal with frequencies.[5]

Why are humans better at frequencies than probabilities? No one knows for sure, but I always imagine humans in the ancestral environment thinking about outcomes in terms of frequencies. Something like, "Remember when it last rained like this, we caught those tasty antelopes on the west side of camp." I never picture them saying, "The probability of successful hunting increases by 7% during rains."

The conclusion of the work by Professors Cosmides, Tooby, Gigerenzer, and others is to reconsider how we should interpret human acts that appear to be irrational. This more nuanced perspective suggests that humans are not designed to be crazy, but rather that we can be pushed to crazy actions by certain situations.

There is an active debate within academia on the value of this ancestral perspective. Interestingly, many of the leading behavioral economists, including Professor Richard Thaler, see little value in considering how human nature was shaped in ancestral environments.[6] Others (including me) see the ancestral perspective as a primary organizing principle underlying all study of human nature, including its irrational aspects.

This idea that human problems stem from living in an unnatural environment helps to understand the deep cause of human irrationality, and it provides the basis for the practical advice in the rest of this book. The key hypothesis is that many of our financial difficulties stem from the fact that, like captive chimpanzees, humans are built for one world yet live in another. So humans are not built to make good financial decisions.

The lizard brain helped our ancestors achieve their goals, but in situations that were never experienced by our ancestors it often pushes us toward self-destructive or seemingly irrational acts. When it comes to financial decisions, the situation is far worse than a lack of natural talent. There are three sorts of decisions that we face. For some decisions the lizard brain's effects are neutral, for others the lizard brain guides us toward the correct solution, and for the third category the lizard brain is systematically out of sync. Financial markets are this third and worst of these settings.

Neutral Setting: The Lizard Brain Looks Silly in Las Vegas

In the 1980s, I lived in San Diego and took periodic road trips to Las Vegas with my buddy Jim. During one of those trips, I found him sitting at the roulette table using an "interesting" betting strategy. When the roulette ball landed on red he would place a bet on black for the next spin. Conversely, whenever the ball landed on black he would place his next bet on red. I asked Jim to explain his strategy, and he said, "Dude, isn't it unlikely that the ball will land on the same color twice in a row?"

Jim's analysis was not correct. As long as the roulette wheel is fair, it doesn't remember the previous spin. Thus, the bet on red has the same chance on every spin, even if, for example, it follows a streak of 10 red in a row.

Jim's logic reminds me of the misguided traveler who takes a bomb on a plane, not to blow it up, but rather for protection. When asked how a bomb (that he doesn't plan to explode) provides protection, the traveler responds with, "Dude, isn't it unlikely that there will be two bombs on the same plane?"

Although Jim's logic was not perfect, his betting strategy was fine. In fact, his alternating strategy has exactly the same probability of winning as other strategies, including bet red every time, or bet black every time, or even to bet black on sunny days. Any strategy that wagers on red or black has the same expected payoff.

In *Full Metal Jacket,* the Marine drill instructor says that he does not look down on anyone in particular. Rather than target some types of recruits for his abuse, he says, "Here, you are all equally worthless." Similarly, all betting strategies on the roulette wheel are equally worthless—they all cost the gambler money, and earn profits for the casino.

Recall that our lizard brain is built to find patterns, even when there are none. There is a study showing physiological surprise (as measured by electrical activity) when a pattern is broken. For example, when flipping coins, the more heads that occur the less surprised we are by another occurrence of heads. Even though the prefrontal cortex knows that the chance of heads is 50%, part of the brain uses the past to predict the future.[7] So if we sit and watch a roulette wheel long enough, our lizard brain will find a pattern, even if our prefrontal cortex knows that any pattern must be the result of randomness.

Fortunately, the roulette wheel is neutral with regard to the use of any strategy built on faulty pattern seeking. So in one sense our irrational pattern-seeking brain is harmless in memoryless settings like roulette. (Of course, the very fact that people enjoy betting on gambles that lose more often than they win is a costly exploitation of our lizard brains.)

Helpful Setting: The Lizard Brain Finds Food in the Kalahari Desert

Although our instincts seem silly in casinos, in other settings they help people make good decisions. In fact, many aspects of our brains, including the parts that see patterns when there are none, arose to help our ancestors.

Because our modern world is unnatural in so many ways, some of the best examples of instinctual problem solving come from the behavior of people living like our ancestors did, in small groups of foragers. Many of these foraging cultures, where people survive by hunting animals and gathering plants, existed just a few decades ago. Most such societies have disappeared (or been destroyed), but we have anthropological records of their foraging lifestyles.[8]

Until recently, for example, the !Kung San lived in the Kalahari Desert by gathering plants and hunting animals much as their ancestors had for ten thousand years or more. (The "!" is a "click" used in a few places around the world including the Khoisan language of these people, and !Kung San means "real people.")

In separate anthropological studies, Professor Richard Lee and Professor Irven DeVore lived among The !Kung San of the 1960s. They each report that these people were excellent at living in a very harsh environment.

Professor Lee writes that the !Kung San "are such superb trackers and make such accurate deduction from the faintest marks in the sand that at first their skill seems uncanny . . . Perhaps the most amazing skill is in the hunter's ability to figure out the number of minutes or hours elapsed since the animal went through."[9]

The ability to find and use patterns was a key survival skill of the !Kung San in the harsh desert. The !Kung San can read something extremely subtle in an animal's track, for example, and that allows them to obtain meat. Finding an animal thus relies precisely on the ability to find patterns in an uncertain world.

In natural settings our pattern-seeking brains can work beautifully. Unlike the casino, in the natural world it is usually good to look for patterns.

Until the invention of agriculture about ten thousand years ago, all humans foraged for a living. There is evidence that our brains today still reflect those ancestral foraging problems.[10] This suggestion comes from a variety of studies including some showing that men and women have different abilities that may have helped our ancestors find food.

In almost all foraging societies, there is a division of labor where women gather plants and men hunt animals. Without baby formula and plastic bottles, women must travel with infants so they can breast-feed. Thus, even if an ancestral society were equalitarian, it would be harder for women to hunt than for men. Thus, the need for women to feed babies directly through lactation pushed men and women toward different lifestyles, even in societies that were not sexist.

Among our foraging ancestors, men and women had different roles. In particular, the plant food that women sought did not move, while the animal food that men sought tended to move around a lot. This sexual division of labor caused researchers Irwin Silverman and Marion Eals to predict that woman would be better at remembering the location of objects.[11] Plants don't move, so it pays to remember where they are located. This type of memory is not very useful for hunting animals.

Experimentally, Silverman and Eals showed that women are significantly better at what they call "object location memory" tasks. This difference is so profound that it is easy to replicate even in small groups, and I like to test my students in class. After they have provided their answers, but before revealing their scores, I show my students the data from studies around the world. Out of a perfect score of 20, men average about 12 on this test, and women average about 14.

When running this task in my classes, I always disclose the men's score first. Harvard men are so good that they are even better than the average woman from around the world. So I get average male scores in the range of 16, which leads the Harvard men to think they will defeat the Harvard women. This is just a setup as Harvard women score almost perfect 20s and have always soundly defeated the men in my classes.

If Silverman and Eals are right, as this task suggests, not only are people built to solve ancestral problems, we are even adapted to solve certain types of problems. (A humorous strand of the research related to Silverman and Eals's work looks at differences in the way that men and women give directions. As far as I know, there is no scientific reason for the fact that men never *ask* for directions.)

So our natural instincts look pretty good in our natural environment. It's almost as though we were designed to be hunters and gatherers. As Richard Lee said of the !Kung San, we are almost "uncanny" in our abilities. We have brains that worked well to solve ancestral problems. Difficulties arise, however, when we take those ancestral instincts to unnatural environments. And there is no more unnatural environment for a human brain than a financial market.

Dangerous Setting: The Lizard Brain Loses Money on Wall Street

While the !Kung San can find reliable clues to make good decisions, investors face a very different situation. As we have discussed and shown repeatedly throughout this book, we tend to buy when we ought sell, and vice versa. By its very nature, investing requires us to be forward looking to anticipate future events. Our lizard brains, however, are designed to look backwards. Thus, the lizard brain causes us to be optimistic at market peaks (after rises) and to be pessimistic at market bottoms (after falls).

This backward-looking aspect of the lizard brain works well in natural tasks, even those that are very complex. For example, it is better to pick the closer of two identical animals. Thus, a !Kung San hunter should always pick the fresher of two identical trails. Furthermore, such a hunter can learn how to best use even extremely subtle signs that might lead to success.

In hunting, the relationship between information and success tends to be invariant. Precisely that which worked in the past is most likely to work in the future. Accordingly, the lizard brain is built to look for patterns in what worked in the past.

There are no similar rules in investing. Should we, for example, buy the stocks of fast-growing companies? Perhaps, unless too many other investors are also buying the stocks of fast-growing companies. If so, then the stock prices of these companies will be overvalued, and we'd be better off selling them.

Investing is fundamentally different from many ancestral tasks. Rather than do what worked best in the past, investing requires staying a step ahead of others. Thus, there can be no stable relationship between information and the correct course of action. This attempt to stay one step ahead of others, who are also trying to be one step ahead of you, leads to some strange statements.

Only in investing can you say, "As expected, Microsoft's earnings exceeded expectations by more than expected. In after-hours trading, the stock is falling because the earnings surprise was smaller than was widely anticipated."

For investing, the only rule is to predict what everyone else is doing, and move to profit from their behavior. Investors who do what comes naturally—or who use a fixed rule based on fundamental data—tend to become prey.

Investing is therefore the ultimate cognitive situation where we need precisely to restrain our instincts in order to make money. Unlike neutral games of chance, or ancestral problems like gathering and hunting, financial success means suppressing our "gut" response.

All of the irrational investing tips in this chapter are methods to prevent our less analytic parts from making our financial decisions. In short, to make money we need to shackle the lizard brain and throw away the key.

Shackle the Lizard Brain Investing Lesson #1: Don't Trade Emotionally, Unless You Are Tom Cruise

In a debriefing of his flying in *Top Gun,* Maverick (played by Tom Cruise) is criticized for risky flying. Civilian contractor Charlotte "Charlie" Blackwood (played by Kelly McGillis) says, "You perform a split S? That's the last thing you should do. The bandit is right on your tail— What were you thinking here, Maverick?" to which he replies:

You don't have time to think up there. If you think, you're dead.

Maverick is the ultimate instinctual pilot. Because he's got great natural skills he can win even with unconventional tactics. The analysis of Maverick's split S ends with, "Maverick makes an aggressive vertical move here, comes over the top and defeats the bandit with a missile shot. The encounter was a victory, but we've shown it as an example of what not to do."

Similarly, some people can make money almost by instinct. In January 1987, I was visiting the New York offices of the legendary trader Paul Tudor Jones II. He was not in the office, but rather was on a chartered jet flying out to the Super Bowl in California.

Paul called the office for a market update. In those days it was harder to stay current with market prices because the Internet was rudimentary and wireless technology was not well developed. Thus, when Paul called from the plane he didn't have any current information on the market.

Paul had started the day thinking that stocks would rise, and the previous day he had purchased what can be described as "a boatload" of S&P futures. So when he called to ask where the market stood, the higher the market, the more money he would have made. At the beginning of the call, Paul received some good news; the market was up a lot, and he had made some millions of dollars.

Just moments into the call, however, the stock market began to fall precipitously. As Paul heard the prices change, he asked to be patched through to the exchange floor in Chicago where the S&P futures trade. Shouting from his jet into the phone, patched through a noisy connection, I heard Paul sell all of his stock position—"get me out, now." In just a few moments the voice from Chicago told Paul that he was out. With a quick reaction to a fast-moving market, Paul exited his position for a hefty profit.

I was then surprised to hear Paul instruct Chicago to sell even more stock futures. Since he didn't own any, these additional sales created a short position where he would profit from a further market decline. In the space of just moments Paul had gone from a massive and profitable bet that stocks would go up to a massive bet that stocks would go down. Throughout the next few hours, stocks did, in fact, decline substantially and this earned Paul millions more.

"Gutsiest move I ever saw." Maverick's rival Slider whispers this about the risky and successful split S just after the official criticism of the maneuver. Paul Tudor Jones' instantaneous reversal—from betting on stocks to betting against stocks—qualifies as the gutsiest trading move that I ever saw.

In *Top Gun,* the instructors suggest that the other pilots learn not from the instinctual Maverick, but rather from the unemotional pilot Ice Man (played by Val Kilmer). Similarly, while we might all wish we could trade like Paul Tudor Jones, we probably should not attempt to mimic the instinctual nature of his trading.

Recall from Chapter 3 that Professor Odean finds typical investors tend to make precisely the wrong moves. The nonprofessionals in Odean's study tended to buy bad stocks and sell good ones. For these investors the instinctual split S moves tend to lead to losses not profits.

Professor Odean has published another study that confirms his earlier finding that trading is dangerous to most people's pocketbook. As with the previous work, this second study (coauthored with Professor Brad Barber) examined the brokerage accounts of thousands of individual investors. The goal was to look at the difference between men and women, and it has the provocative title of "Boys will be boys."[12]

In what way were boys being boys in this study? Professors Barber and Odean found that men in this study were worse investors than women. Per each dollar invested, men earned significantly less money than women. In investigating the reasons for the gender difference, it turned out that men traded 45% more frequently than women.

Every trade is costly so all other things being equal, the more an investor trades, the less money at the end of the year. All that extra trading definitely cost men. How about the actual stock selection? Were men or women better at picking winning stocks?

Professors Odean and Barber found that men and women are equally bad at picking stocks. On average, every trade cost the investors money as compared with not trading. Men did worse simply because they traded more. The study concludes, "Men lower their returns more than women because they trade more, not because their security selection is worse."

Conclusion: Never trade emotionally, and trade as little as possible. If you can trade like Paul Tudor Jones II or fly a jet like Maverick, then you don't need any advice.

Lesson #2: Never Trust Anyone, Not Even Yourself

During the technology bubble of the late 1990s, one of the best ways to make money was to get some stock at the initial public offering (IPO) of a company. The most famous of these IPOs was that of theglobe.com whose stock went up by more than 600% on the first day.

Of theglobe.com's stock at the offering price, $10,000 netted a profit of $60,000 in a matter of hours. Sure beats the day job! Dozens of other IPOs had enormous first-day rises.

How do we get our hands on some of that IPO stock? In *Glengarry Glen Ross* a group of real estate salespeople ask a similar question. In a tough environment where sales are lagging, Alec Baldwin is brought in to motivate the team.

Baldwin arranges a contest: Whoever sells the most in the next week will earn access to the coveted (and closely guarded) "Glengarry Glen Ross leads." These contain the names and contact information for people who are very likely to become buyers. With the promise of easy money, the salespeople do everything they can (legal and illegal) to get their hands on those golden leads.

In the bubble, people did all sorts of things to get into IPO stocks. I was never invited to participate in any of this, and I watched others with envy. On the day of the Etoys' IPO, for example, my friend Judith told me about an acquaintance who had made $20,000 "trading" the stock. When

I inquired further, I learned that this brilliant trade was caused by the grant of some of the IPO stock through a contact in the company. In the bubbly IPO environment of the time, this was simply a gift, not a trading success.

In late April 2000, my phone rang. It was Andy, my broker, offering me a chance to get in on an IPO. Was this Glengarry Glen Ross chance going to make me money? Hardly. The stock Andy was offering was in AT&T wireless, which trades under the stock symbol AWE. I could buy the stock at the IPO price of $29.50 per share. I did not buy.

Part of the reason that I did not buy was because of a story in the great investing book *Reminiscences of a Stock Operator*.[13] The book is filled with the trading exploits of a character based on the famous speculator Jesse Livermore. In one escapade, our hero receives a stock tip, listens carefully, and then makes money by doing exactly the opposite.

I thought of this story when Andy called with his AWE stock. Why was he calling me for this IPO when he had never called for any other stock offerings? I could think of many reasons for this unique offer, but none of them suggested that I would make money from buying this IPO. In fact, if I'd been a top gun trader, I would have bet against the stock by selling it short. Being a bit more cautious, however, I simply declined the offer to buy, and watched the stock carefully.

What happened to my only chance to play in the IPO game? The stock essentially went straight down. After a very brief and small rise above the offering price, the stock sank to under $5. (By the end of movie, the Glengarry Glen Ross leads are revealed to be worthless; so in some sense my opportunity did mirror that of the salespeople in the movie.)

One lesson from this experience is to not take tips from anyone. Interestingly, this extends to even taking tips from ourselves. How is it even possible to give ourselves a tip? And why should we be skeptical of our own tips?

Recall that it is useful to think of the brain not as one cohesive entity, but rather as a society of mind (to use MIT professor Marvin Minsky's phrase) having different, and sometimes competing goals. The more thoughtful, cognitive parts reside in the prefrontal cortex, while the lizard brain lives elsewhere. Recall also that recent studies in neuroscience implicate the lizard brain in some of the behaviors that tend to cost us money.

When we get an urge to make a trade, it may be the lizard brain providing us with a tip. While the lizard brain may have led our ancestors to big game, it is not likely to make us rich. So when we get a hot tip from ourselves in the form of a trading idea, we should treat it with suspicion. Is the idea based on good, unemotional analysis? Or does it arise magically from an unknown place?

Here's one clue that I have found useful to discovering the source. If I feel that there is a pressing need to trade now—that this is a fleeting and golden chance—then I suspect the lizard brain is at work. In all cases (whether the urge is strong or not), I wait at least one week between a trading idea and its implementation. Occasionally, this rule will cause me to miss a great trade, but it also prevents me from making a lot of bad decisions.

Conclusion: Never trade on other people's tips. Treat your own ideas for trades with some skepticism. Never trade impulsively, as you might be falling for a bad tip from the lizard brain. Always include a significant delay between an investment idea and an actual trade.

Lesson #3: Losers Average Losers

In Chapter 2 we discussed one of the two handwritten signs that I saw over Paul Tudor Jones II's desk in 1987. The second note said, "Losers average losers."

What does this mean? Let's analyze it in three steps. First, what is averaging? Second, what does it mean to average a loser? Third, why is it that losers average losers?

Averaging an investment means adding to an existing position. For example, I started buying Microsoft stock in the early 1990s. Taking into account all the stock splits, the price I paid was about $2/share. Over the next few years, I bought more of the stock at progressively higher prices (it eventually topped out at $60). As I bought more, the average price that I had paid for my Microsoft stock changed. In particular, my average price rose as I combined more expensive stock with the original buy at $2. Increasing the size of an existing investment is averaging.

Averaging losers is buying more of an investment that has gone down since the original purchase. If the price of Microsoft had dropped, and I had bought more at a lower price, then I would have been averaging my purchases on one of the "losers" in my portfolio.

"Losers average losers" means it is the bad investors (i.e., the losers) who buy more as an investment declines. Paul's note essentially means that adding to a losing investment is throwing good money after bad. This "losers average losers" is one of the most famous lessons in all trading. In fact, it is the number one lesson cited in *Reminiscences of a Stock Operator:*

> I did precisely the wrong thing. The cotton showed me a loss and I kept it. The wheat showed me a profit and I sold it out. Of all the speculative blunders there are few greater than trying to average a losing game. Always sell what shows you a loss and keep what shows you a profit.

The idea that losers average losers is not news (*Reminiscences* was first published in 1923). What is new is the link to the science of irrationality. Professor Kahneman has documented the irrational manner in which human psychology handles losses. As we saw in Chapter 2, our behavior becomes even more irrational when we are confronted with taking a loss. We become emotional risk takers, willing to bet the house in order to salvage our pride. This instinctual desire to avoid losses, paradoxically, tends to create even more losses.

Even experienced traders must fight the tendency to average losers. I recall a related incident when I was working at Goldman, Sachs & Co. The boss of the corporate bond area was visiting each trader to review buy and sell decisions. The partner became enraged when looking at one trader's list of buys and sells, and threw it in the garbage (nowadays this is all done on computer, but in 1987 there were paper copies). The partner said, "You've sold all your winners, and you've kept all of your losers. I want you to sell every one of these dogs before the day is over, or don't come in tomorrow."

Even great and experienced traders must fight the impulse to hang onto and average into losers. The Goldman, Sachs & Co. trader guilty of this cardinal sin was a veteran with about eight years' experience and was probably making more than a million dollars a year. In fact, the "losers average losers" sign above Paul Tudor Jones's desk suggests that even he felt the need for a reminder to avoid this mistake.

Conclusion: Never average losers. Buy more of an investment only when (and if) it increases in value.

Lesson #4: Do Not Dollar Cost Average

So losers average losers. Those who agree with this statement should not invest by "dollar-cost averaging." What is dollar-cost averaging, and why is it a form of averaging losers?

Here's how an article on the Motley Fool website describes dollar-cost averaging:

Dollar-cost averaging can be a good way to protect yourself from a volatile market. It's the practice of accumulating shares in a stock over time by investing a certain dollar amount regularly, through up and down periods . . . The beauty of this system is that when the stock slumps you're buying more, and when it's pricier you're buying less.

The conventional wisdom suggests that dollar-cost averaging is a great way to invest. It often takes the form of a payroll withdrawal that is invested into stocks. Such payroll purchases are a form of dollar-cost averaging because the same numbers of dollars are invested in each period.

Sound reasonable? In fact, dollar-cost averaging is a profitable strategy as long as the money is invested into something that goes up in price persistently. In bull markets, every drop in price is an opportunity, and as the Motley Fool suggests, the "beauty" is that the investor scoops up more shares during "pullbacks."

While dollar-cost averaging works in bull markets, it is not profitable in long-term declines. Imagine, for example, what would have happened to an investor whose dollar-cost averaged into Etoys stock. Each month, as the stock price of Etoys fell, the investor would be buying more shares for the same dollar amount.

As the Motley Fool piece suggests, it is true that "when the stock slumps you're buying more." That's great except for the fact that Etoys filed for bankruptcy; at which point the shares became worth zero.

Dollar-cost averaging doesn't work well for declining investments. The Japanese Nikkei peaked over 40,000 in 1989, and 15 years later it sits at around 12,000. So an investor who "yen-cost averaged" into Japanese stocks over the last 15 years would have been averaging losers; that is, owning more and more of a declining investment.

Even if you are optimistic that Japanese stocks will rise from current levels, you would be better off buying now. You could buy today at a much lower price than you would have paid by averaging, and you could have avoided 15 depressing, losing years.

Averaging into a declining market is a form of throwing good money after bad. If this is true, why is dollar-cost averaging so popular? The answer is that a lizard brain that has lived its entire life in a bull market loves dollar-cost averaging. In fact, the backward-looking lizard brain loves whatever has worked in the past.

In the United States, dollar-cost averaging into stocks has always paid off in the "long-run." That is because throughout history U.S. stocks have always eventually recovered and gone on to new highs. In what has been a 200-year bull market in U.S. stocks, marked by some extreme pull-backs, dollar-cost averaging has worked well. It will not be profitable, however, if stocks enter a persistent decline. Price declines in secular bear markets are not pullbacks, they are just setbacks on the way to more declines.

Dollar-cost averaging is a bull market strategy. It is the equivalent of being loaded for squirrel. As long as there are no vicious bears, then being loaded for squirrel is perfect. Thus, dollar-cost averaging into U.S. stocks is a form of investing by looking in the rearview mirror. It has been a great strategy throughout U.S. history, but that does not mean that it will be a profitable strategy in the future.

Conclusion: Do not dollar-cost average. Unless you have some secret knowledge that we are not in a bear market, dollar-cost averaging can be a form of averaging losers. Remember: Losers average losers.

Lesson #5: Do Not Open Your Mutual Fund Statements

In the closing credits of *Austin Powers,* Mike Myers in the title role is seen taking pictures of minx-like Vanessa (played by Elizabeth Hurley). As he takes photo after photo, Powers snaps his fingers while saying, "ignore this, ignore this, ignore me doing this." The joke is that it is even harder to ignore his snapping fingers when instructed to do so. In the context of photography, this little trick helps keep the model at ease and looking natural.

When it comes to investing, our inability to ignore extraneous information costs us money. With modern media and technology it is possible to get almost instantaneous information. Financial networks in the form of CNBC and Bloomberg TV allow everyone to keep up with breaking news. It is even possible for individual investors to listen in on some companies' earnings calls, right along with Wall Street professionals.

In earlier eras it took a long time for information to reach investors. Consider, for example, the effect of the battle of Waterloo on British financial markets in 1815. Early reports of the battle suggested that Napoleon was winning, and this caused the British markets to fall precipitously.

While the market was plummeting and sellers were panicking, Nathan Meyer Rothschild was calmly buying. Several days later, the news of Napoleon's defeat reached London and markets soared. This netted Rothschild some handy gains.[14]

What made Rothschild buy when others sold? He had advance information provided via the unlikely route of trained carrier pigeons that flew across the English Channel. Thus Rothschild got word of the French defeat several days ahead of others and was able to make a financial killing.

Can we all be Rothschilds by watching CNBC and listening in on earnings calls? The answer for most people is no. In spite of regulations making it harder for firms to release information selectively, by the time news is available to most people, it is too late to make profitable trades.

"Wake up will you, pal? If you're not inside, you're outside." So says Gordon Gekko (played by Michael Douglas) to Bud Fox (Charlie Sheen's character) in *Wall Street*. Only those on the inside can trade profitably on news; if you are not sure if you are on the inside, then you are not.

The worst thing people can do is try to trade on news. Perhaps the second worst thing we can do is to even listen to that news. People find it difficult to ignore information.

A famous experiment by Professors Kahneman and Tversky shows the effect of useless information on analysis. In the experiment, people were asked to estimate the percentage of African countries in the United Nations. Before their guess, a random number was generated—in front of the participants—by the spin of a roulette-like wheel. If people were rational, the useless information from a random spin of a wheel would not alter their analysis. In fact, the people in this study were not able to ignore the information. Those people who saw a high number on the wheel had higher guesses for the percentage of African countries in the U.N. than those who saw low numbers on the wheel.[15]

We are influenced by irrelevant information. This "anchoring" effect has been demonstrated in many different experiments. Anchoring, for example, is one good reason to make the first offer in a negotiation. No matter how absurd that first number, it often influences the final outcome.

Have you ever made a losing trade because of some talking head on TV, even when you disagreed with the analysis? If so, you know how hard it is to ignore a message, and how costly listening can be.

Ignoring the news on the TV is one solid suggestion. It might even be useful to not open your own mutual fund statements. There is evidence that the more frequently people look at their investing performance, the worse they do.[16] When we see losses, we tend to make emotional decisions to exit positions. As we've learned most trades are bad ideas, and emotional trades are the worst.

For those who can't ignore information, the answer is to avoid it. A simple rule is to align your rate of information acquisition with your trading horizon. If you are a day trader, then by all means have the TV on and watch streaming, real-time stock quotes. If, however, you are going to make a few, unemotional adjustments to your portfolio per year, then I suggest that you avoid as much information as possible.

I suspect that an investor, who just read annual reports, or even a farmer's almanac, would do better than one plugged into nightly conference calls of corporate earnings.

Conclusion: Keep your financial news flow consistent with your decision time frame. As much as possible, turn off the TV during the day, and don't look at your portfolio.

Lesson #6: Spin Control for Yourself

Nassim Nicholas Taleb, my friend, and the author of *Fooled by Randomness,* tells a story about one of his former clients. A Swiss firm hired Nassim's firm to put on a hedged position. The trade involved one Swiss investment paired with a non-Swiss investment.

The bet went on for some time, and it was very profitable. The clients, however, were not happy. They were making money overall, but the gain came by making more on the non-Swiss investment than they were losing on the Swiss investment. In cartoon terms, the payoff to the trade looked like:

Swiss investment	LOSS
Non-Swiss investment	GAIN
Total:	GAIN

Seeing the loss, particularly on the Swiss investment, ate away at the clients. Nassim tried to explain that the important thing was to make money overall. Nothing worked to assuage the clients until Nassim started just reporting the position as:

Total:	GAIN

Now the client didn't have to see that offensive "LOSS" and was happy. This may seem silly, but Professor Richard Thaler has shown that most people exhibit some form of this irrationality in what he calls mental accounting.[17] We might, for example, be willing to borrow money on our credit cards at 18% while keeping a savings account that earns 2%. A rational investor wouldn't keep such separate accounts, but rather would pay off the credit card debt with money in the savings account.

Even when there are no real accounts, people tend to keep separate mental accounts for their money, and this can create costly irrationalities. For example, I was out one evening shopping with Patricia. She found some costly cosmetic cream at the swanky store called Sephora. The cream cost $135 for a small tube.

"Are you going to buy the cream?" I asked. Patricia said yes, but then added "I've spent too much money today. I'll come back tomorrow morning and buy it." Patricia kept a mental account for each day's spending. This informal accounting system caused her to spend extra time, use extra gas, and pay an additional parking fee to acquire what she could have purchased immediately.

Like all people, I tend to maintain mental accounts, and it has hurt my investment performance. Beginning in early 2002, I started buying stock in some gold mining companies. I thought that the Federal Reserve's easy money policy might lead to a rise in gold prices, which in turn would increase the profits of gold mining companies. Accordingly, I invested a small amount in these stocks.

How did I do on my gold investment? Since my initial purchase, the price of gold has risen by more than 50%, and many gold mining stocks have doubled. So I was absolutely correct with my decision to buy gold. Unfortunately, I made absolutely zero on my investment.

Why did my trading so completely fail my analysis? The answer was that I was buying gold stocks in an account that had nothing else in it except for some inflation-protected bonds. Gold mining stocks can be pretty volatile. So whenever gold declined, I saw this account shrink dramatically in value. This made me feel like an idiot, and I tended to sell the stocks at exactly the wrong time.

I was suffering from a form of mental accounting. Gold is a hedge against inflation. Most of us will be far better off in a world where gold prices are low. So in periods when gold was dropping, my prospects were improving. When gold went down in price, my overall position looked like:

Gold investment	LOSS
Non-gold investments	GAIN
Total	GAIN

So I should have been happy when gold went down. The solution for me is the same as the solution for Nassim's clients. I now make sure that I look at my overall position. In the past, I had tended to look at each account separately. Now I force myself to use financial software to look at my total position.

So the lesson is we need to perform some "spin control" even for ourselves. We have to guard against goading our lizard brain to become active (and destructive). That means we should anticipate what sort of information would push us toward emotional decisions.

Conclusion: Look at your financial position in an aggregate fashion. In particular, be sure to combine any defensive positions with other investments that are being protected.

Lesson #7: When to Go "All In"

My buddy Chris, the MIT rocket scientist who we met a couple of times, is a world-class ultimate Frisbee player. This rapidly growing sport combines elements of soccer and American football.

Chris was a key member on the Boston-based team "Death or Glory" (a.k.a. "DoG") that had a dynastic hold over the sport both in the United States and internationally for many years. In the world championship in

1996 Chris scored eight goals as DoG defeated Sweden 21-13, with seven of these goals being almost full field passes; the equivalent of a "long bomb" in football.

How did Chris become one of the dominant offensive players in the world? Interestingly, although scoring requires outrunning the defender, Chris's success is not the result of speed. Although Chris is speedy, he often plays against others who are faster. Somehow he is able to score consistently on faster defenders and he dominates competitors with equal speed.

I asked Chris his secret. How do you outrun people who are faster than you? His answer, "I maintain the ability to make at least two different moves. When I get a slight advantage, I commit completely."

At almost all times, Chris is not running at full speed. Rather, he is jockeying for position, and carefully watching for an opening. This can come in some subtle form such as noting that the defender is leaning in such a way so as to be unable to react to a move in a certain direction. At that point, Chris is all in, sprinting at full speed.

In contrast, less experienced players are often running hard almost all the time. They look like they are doing well, but they do not score very often. These less successful players expend lots of effort and receive little reward.

There are some similar themes in investing. Many people tend to be all in, all the time. By this I mean that they have maximum capital at risk every day. In fact, the standard advice from Wall Street is to invest most money in stocks. An investor who follows this advice is fully committed to a risky course all the time.

In bull markets, being "all in" is very profitable, but problems surface when markets decline. Remember that Chris always maintains at least two options for his move. In contrast, investors who constantly put all their money at risk are not in a position to buy more at moments of irrationally low prices. By being fully committed all the time, investors remove the ability to buy more—they no longer have two viable options.

Being persistently "all in" financially has costs beyond just missing buying opportunities. In fact, it increases the likelihood that the lizard brain will activate precisely at the wrong time. This tends to lead to emotional "puke outs" where investors sell during buying opportunities.

This suggests that investors should maintain a financial reserve, and should only rarely and temporarily be "all in." Such an investing philosophy allows one to have the ability to buy or sell at any given time depending on the conditions.

There are some similar lessons to be drawn from competitive poker. The World Series of Poker has "no-limit" rules allowing players to go "all in" at any time. My observation is that there is a systematic difference between great players and good players related precisely to the decision of when to be fully committed. The great players tend to go all in with hands where they have a good chance to win. Other players seem to more often get trapped into going all in with worse chances to win.

A key to winning at poker is to know when to "lay down" a hand. That is to quit playing, even with a good hand rather than bet more money. The great players will sometimes lay down even solid hands. Better to lose a few dollars and stay in the game. Bad poker players get trapped going all in when they shouldn't.

Conclusion: Keep your investment position conservative enough so that you preserve both options of increased risk or decreased risk should others panic and present you with an opportunity. Choose the time to go "all in" carefully and scale down quickly.

Lesson #8: Do Not Get the Key to the Mini Bar

When I check into a hotel, I never get the key to the mini bar. Without the key, I don't need willpower to avoid any late-night temptation to devour junk food. I have found that most temptations are better avoided than resisted.

I've noticed that some hotels no longer have mini bars, but instead they lay the food out on top of a table. Thus, the "don't get the key" defense doesn't work. In such cases, I call down to the front desk and have them remove the food.

I once arrived at one such devious hotel so late at night that I wanted to go to sleep immediately and not wait for someone to remove the food. As a partial preventative measure, I put a towel over the chocolate bars and other treats. While I still knew the junk food was in my room, at least I couldn't see it.

As we have seen, our investing instincts are out of sync with market opportunity. The investments that feel good are precisely those that are most likely to cost us money, and vice versa. This leads to the paradoxical situation that we sometimes gain by having fewer options. Usually, having more options is better, but when our instincts lead us to bad choices— as with junk food in the mini bar or with emotional investing decisions—we can make ourselves better off precisely by limiting our alternatives.

This "less or more" insight into self-control has become closely associated with the story of Odysseus and the Sirens. On his way home from the Trojan War, Odysseus had to sail past the Island of Sirens. These maidens' song was so beautiful that sailors approached them and were killed as their ships crashed on the rocks surrounding the island.

The goddess Circe warns Odysseus of the danger and provides him with a solution in this passage of *The Odyssey:*

If any one unwarily draws in too close and hears the singing of the Sirens, his wife and children will never welcome him home again, for they sit in a green field and warble him to death with the sweetness of their song . . . but if you like you can listen yourself, for you may get the men to bind you as you stand upright on a cross-piece half way up the mast, and they must lash the rope's ends to the mast itself, that you may have the pleasure of listening. If you beg and pray the men to unloose you, then they must bind you faster.[18]

By following Circe's advice, Odysseus survives the Sirens. He has himself strapped to the mast, and he commands everyone else on the ship to put wax in their ears so that they cannot be tempted by the Sirens. Because Odysseus is unable to control his ship or his men, he hears the Sirens, but is unable to approach their deadly shore. He achieves his goal precisely because he has limited his options. By tying his hands, Odysseus gets what he wants.

Inspired by this story, "mast-strapping" is used in the scientific literature on self-control to explain how having fewer options can sometimes lead to a better outcome. If we didn't have self-control problems, then more options would always be better.

For many people, financial mast-strapping can be a valuable tool. One of the primary problems in investing is our own desire to trade too much. Almost everyone seems to suffer from this problem, and so do I. Even with all of my knowledge that trading on impulse is bad, I still feel the tug every time I watch a market.

Because I like to trade too much, I have done some mast-strapping to constrain my trading. The first thing I did was lock up the bulk of my family's financial assets in a full-service brokerage account that charges $100 a trade. Why pay $100 for something that can be bought for far less? For me, the answer is that $100 works to reduce my costly trading.

Originally, I also kept a small amount in a discount firm's account that charges $5 a trade. When the urge to trade struck me, I would indulge it, but only in this "small account" with the low commissions. This setup prevented me from overtrading most of our money. It was not, however, a perfect solution.

The Waco Kid (played by Gene Wilder) in *Blazing Saddles* had a similar problem to mine. While playing chess with the Sheriff Bart of Rock Ridge (played by Cleavon Little), Wilder says, "I used to be the Waco Kid." The sheriff asks, why "used to be"? In response, Wilder holds out his right hand, which is rock steady. The sheriff says, that looks fine, to which the Waco Kid raises his other arm which is uncontrollably shaky, and says, "yes, but I shoot with my left."

My first mast-strapping solution still had me doing the equivalent of shooting with my left. I did far too much trading in my "little" account. It didn't cost me any significant money, but I spent so much time on the account that I was probably making minimum wage for my efforts. After about a year of this experiment, I closed the smaller account. This more secure mast-strapping has, so far, been a total success. With no ability to trade cheaply, I haven't traded impulsively.

I suggest that almost everyone, except for the top guns of trading, structure their world so that they cannot trade impulsively. The exact setup will vary for each person. Many people would still trade even at a cost of $100 a trade, so the solution that works for me won't work for everyone.

A pervasive problem with our efforts to improve by mast-strapping is that there's usually someone who would profit from untying us. Just as hotels seek to profit by leaving candy bars on the counter, there will always be firms that are happy to help us trade. We need to be crafty to construct our finances so that we won't be tempted to make bad decisions.

I helped my friend Doug (the millionaire surfer) quit smoking. He agreed that if he smoked even one puff of a cigarette, he would have to pay me $100. Furthermore, immediately after that first puff, he would have to call me to acknowledge defeat. Our agreement was set up for one year, and Doug made it for the entire year without a smoke.

Why did this silly arrangement work to get Doug to quit? The answer is that it tapped into Doug's psyche in the right way. He and I were a bit competitive, and so the prospect of paying me even a nominal sum was loathsome. Furthermore, Doug is honest enough that he wouldn't cheat and lie about smoking. Finally, the need to call and immediately acknowledge defeat was a potent deterrent.

The right answer for everyone is to avoid emotional trades. The way to accomplish that is to make structural arrangements so that emotional trades are not possible. The details of the correct form of financial mast-strapping will vary for each individual.

Conclusion: Those who trade too much should arrange their finances so that impulsive trades are not possible. Remove temptation; do not expect to resist it.

Do Not Trade in the Red Zone

"Happy families are all alike; every unhappy family is unhappy in its own way." So begins Tolstoy's *Anna Karenina.* Similarly, successful traders avoid making self-destructive investment decisions. The specifics are idiosyncratic; the general lesson is to constrain the lizard brain that lurks within each of us.

All of the tips I've suggested can be understood as efforts to get control back to the investors' rational side and away from that lizard brain. While the lizard brain is great for lizard-like activities like finding food and shade, in financial markets, our instincts are the enemy.

My friend David the oil trader has learned how to avoid such mistakes on his way to a lucrative trading career. In Chapter 4 we heard one of David's secrets is that "he knows when the buying is real." I learned another of David's secrets one day in the 1980s. In order to profit from an anticipated rise in oil, I bought a single oil futures contract, which represented 1,000 barrels of oil. For every penny's rise in the price of oil, I stood to make $10.

Almost immediately after my purchase, however, the price of oil started to decline. My losses began to mount: $10, $30, $70, and more. This wasn't any fun at all. Furthermore, because I was a student, these amounts became a significant portion of my net worth at the time. I took the pain of my losing position for about 30 minutes, by which time the loss exceeded $200. I turned to David and said, "I've got to get out." He said, "I got you out a long time ago, I just wanted to see how much pain you could stand."

Over the years I've learned that David almost always exits his losing positions very quickly—just as he got me out of my trade almost immediately. He'd rather take a quick and small loss instead of letting the position eat away at him financially and emotionally. He summarizes his philosophy by saying, "I don't trade in the red zone." By that he means that losing trades (those in the red zone) are exited very quickly, while he's willing to ride his profits (trades that are in the black) for much longer.

Don't trade in the red zone.

While David interprets this strategy literally to exit losing positions, I interpret it more broadly. I suggest that people not trade in the emotional red zone. What's the definition of a psychologically defined zone? The answer can be drawn from the legal efforts to restrain pornography. In the 1964 Supreme Court case Jacobellis v. Ohio, Justice Potter Stewart wrote that, he could not define hard-core pornography, but stated "I know it when I see it."[19]

Similarly, there is no objective definition of the emotional red zone, but I think we know it when it happens to us. If an investment is eating away at us, we should consider exiting. (Such considerations should, of course, be done in an unemotional manner.) "Use the Force, Luke. Let go." The spirit of Obi Wan Kenobi suggests that Luke will know the right answer himself. Similarly, the specifics of avoiding the red zone are different for each person. The result, however, should be the same for all.

An investor who avoids the red zone, should, for example, be able to (i) go on vacation for weeks and not look at the markets, (ii) increase or decrease any position, (iii) take large price changes in all markets without having to buy or sell anything, and (iv) sleep without thinking about investments.

Those who can develop such a no-red-zone system can never be forced by their emotions nor by market dynamics to make a decision. The first step to making money is not "plastics" but to avoid letting the lizard brain make emotional and costly investment decisions. This is not easy because, like Michael Jordan, the lizard brain can't be stopped, "just contained." Those who contain the lizard brain will have taken the first step toward profiting from mean markets.

chapter eleven

TIMELY ADVICE
Investing in the Meanest of Markets

A Generation of Rewarding Risk

In the introduction we met Adam, my former Harvard Business School student who asked, "Where should I invest my money?" In the early 1980s, I grappled with the same question. At the time, I lived in southern California and did a lot of surfing with my buddy Gary. Surfers spend far more time bobbing around in the ocean waiting for waves than actually riding them. Gary and I filled our spare time with a debate about how to make money; I argued that stocks were the best investment, while Gary favored real estate.

I loved stocks in the early 1980s because they were amazingly cheap! The Dow Jones Industrial Average sat near 1,000, and fantastic companies had single digit price to earnings ratios. Gary's love of real estate was based on supply and demand. There is a limited supply of beach real estate and, over time, essentially an unlimited demand by people who want to soak up the sun.

Gary and I each acted upon our beliefs. I invested every dollar I had into stocks, while Gary developed an aggressive system of acquiring real estate. As soon as he could scrape together a down payment, he would buy a rental property. He would then squeeze every possible penny out of the rents and minimize costs (he even went so far as to do the weekly cleaning of his beach properties himself—I always pictured him in a wetsuit and a maid's outfit). As soon as he amassed enough cash for another down payment, Gary would buy another property to increase his empire.

So who was right, Terry or Gary? In the early 1980s, was it better to have invested in stocks or in southern California real estate? Stocks have gone up by more than 1,000% while land values have steadily increased, but at a slower rate. So does that mean I was right? No. As we discussed in Chapter 9, real estate allows much higher leverage than stocks. Thus, Gary's aggressive—buy as much as you can with borrowed money-strategy earned him a far higher rate of return than was possible in the stock market.

While Gary and I were both bored by bonds, they too provided very strong returns. In 1980, an investment in bonds, particularly a risky investment in long-term bonds, would also have been richly rewarded.

In the early 1980s, picking the right investment was easy. Stocks, bonds, and houses all soared. The only possible mistake, therefore, was to avoid financial risk. For an entire generation, risk was richly rewarded. The only way to lose, it turned out, was not to play. So if Adam were asking his question in 1980 the answer would be clear—borrow as much money as you can, take as much risk as you can stand, and rake in the cash. The conventional wisdom says that risk is still the right course for patient investors who seek high returns. But is it?

The Bull Market of a Lifetime?

The famous Chinese "curse" says "May you live in interesting times." The quirky aspect of human nature is that we are built to expect that our own idiosyncratically interesting times are simply normal. The international man of mystery, Austin Danger Powers, experienced a variant of this problem.

In 1967, Austin Powers (played by Mike Myers) was cryogenically frozen to prepare for the day that archvillain Dr. Evil (also frozen, and also played by Mike Myers) might once again threaten the world. Decades later, Austin was thawed when this threat materialized. Elizabeth Hurley, playing "minx"-like agent Kensington, became the partner of our recently defrosted superspy.

Agent Kensington introduces herself, "Mr. Powers, my job is to acclimatize you to the nineties. You know, a lot's changed since 1967."

Austin replies, "No doubt, love, but as long as people are still having promiscuous sex with many anonymous partners without protection while at the same time experimenting with mind-expanding drugs in a consequence-free environment, I'll be sound as a pound!"

The joke, of course, is that the norms of the 1960s regarding sex and drugs had become abnormal by the 1990s. This is not unique to the 1960s. Modern societies change very rapidly, and we are built to be perpetually behind the curve, thinking that this generation's fad is a permanent feature of human existence.

Like other aspects of human nature, our tendency to underestimate change may reflect our ancestral past. For tens of thousands of years, at least up until the invention of agriculture, our ancestors lived in a world where many important attributes never changed.

Our human tendency to expect that the future will be like the past may have helped our cavemen and cavewomen ancestors, but it does not work well in a rapidly changing modern society. It works even less well in financial markets where today's fad is likely to be tomorrow's loser. Recognition of the current situation is crucial as my friend Matt discovered.

A few years ago, Matt had a romantic dinner in Budapest overlooking the Danube River. A violinist approached the table while playing enthusiastically. After he completed the piece, the musician asked Matt if he had a request. Suave and confident in front of his date, Matt said, "How about the *Blue Danube?*" The violinist responded, "That was it."

Similarly, if we had the chance to request an investment climate, we might ask for a massive bull market in stocks, bonds, and real estate. We would love a setting where financial risk was rewarded almost without regard to the type of investment (even surfers could get rich in such an environment). To which the reply would have to be, "That was it."

We have just lived through an atypical and unsustainable financial period. In recent decades, stock prices have risen at almost three times their natural speed limit. Similarly, interest rates have fallen toward zero, fueling the real estate market with cheap mortgages. Finally, with our massive trade deficit we are racking up enough debts to make Uncle Sam an international beggar.

None of these trends are sustainable. By themselves, however, the required changes do not mean doom and gloom. Theoretically, stock prices can rise indefinitely (albeit at a slower pace), interest rates can remain low (even if they can't decline much further), and our adjustment to a trade surplus can lead to greater employment (even if this means lower real wages).

The danger lies not in the macroeconomic adjustments we face, but in our psychology. Just as the fleeting nature of the 1960s culture surprised a defrosted Austin Powers, we are not built to recognize the unsustainable facts about our world. It is an *economic* truth that the financial future must be different and worse than the fantasyland of the past generation. It is a *psychological* truth, however, that most of us will realize this change only after it has occurred and when it is too late to find profits.

The current financial environment is kryptonite for the lizard brain. Just as superman was really only vulnerable to kryptonite, the lizard brain gets us in particular trouble when powerful trends must end. The backward-looking lizard brain is literally surprised when patterns don't repeat. The golden generation of rewarding risk has set us up for financial losses. Because our lizard brains are set up to collide with economic necessity, these are the meanest of markets.

Is It Time to Take Less Financial Risk?

"When you have eliminated all which is impossible, then whatever remains, however improbable, must be the truth."—Sherlock Holmes

In answer to Adam's question, *Mean Markets* suggests that none of the big three investment alternatives—stocks, bonds, and real estate—is likely to provide great returns. Based on macroeconomic analysis these traditional investments range from fairly valued to expensive. Importantly, none of them appear to be cheap.

While none of these investment alternatives looks cheap, standard economic analysis doesn't find any of them to be wildly overpriced, either. Therefore, one might conclude that we will see a relatively benign investment world.

The science of irrationality, however, reaches more pessimistic conclusions. We are built to do that which has worked, and we have just lived through an extraordinary period that rewarded financial risk. Furthermore, the single best guide to future performance is to bet on that which is unloved. Wall Street, Main Street, and both neoclassical (the "rational" school) and behavioral economists (the "irrational" school) are betting that risk will be rewarded.

In *The Adventure of the Silver Blaze,* Sherlock Holmes solves the case in an unusual manner. Holmes's colleague, Inspector Gregory, asks, "Is there any other point to which you would wish to draw my attention?" Holmes responds, "To the curious incident of the dog in the night-time." Inspector Gregory protests, "The dog did nothing in the night-time." To which Holmes concludes, "That was the curious incident."

Sherlock Holmes solved the case because of the "dog that didn't bark." Similarly, the *Mean Markets* conclusion is that the best financial approach today might be to reduce risk. This is the opposite of the conventional wisdom. The very core of the efficient markets hypothesis is that investors who want high returns must accept high risk.

The "investment that doesn't pay today" may solve the current financial dilemma. Because markets are sometimes wildly irrational, the "reward only for taking risk" equation can be reversed. The analysis of this book suggests that now is one such time. Low-risk investments, even those that pay close to nothing today, may be the long-term road to wealth.

Financial success might require hunkering down in a low risk posture until markets become irrationally cheap. When the financial world is filled with pessimism and others are selling their risky assets, those savvy investors who are prepared will be able to scoop up bargains.

Thus, the *Mean Markets and Lizard Brains* answer to Adam's question is that each of us should reduce our financial risk to a level far below where we feel comfortable. Our lizard brains have been fooled by the last 20 years of unsustainable gains. Thus, it is likely that we are all walking around with overly optimistic views of the world. We are taking more financial risk than we think we are, and most of us are taking more risk than we would want if our lizard brains allowed us to see the world clearly.

For those who want to take the *Mean Markets and Lizard Brains* advice to reduce financial risk, here are eight steps that can be taken immediately.

Risk Reducer #1: Allocate More Money to Lower-Risk Assets

Sell some stocks. Shift some money from growth stocks to value stocks. Increase holdings of cash and short-term securities.

Risk Reducer #2: Buy Some Inflation and Deflation Protection

Buy inflation-protected bonds in the form of Treasury Inflation Protected Securities (TIPS) or Series I U.S. Savings bonds. Buy the stocks of companies that make the products that might go up in price (e.g., drug companies, oil companies).

Risk Reducer #3: Buy Short-Term Bonds

Buy bonds that mature soon, sell longer-term bonds.

Risk Reducer #4: Live in a Smaller House

Own a house that is less valuable than the one you plan to live in five years from now.

Risk Reducer #5: Have a Fixed Rate Mortgage

Variable-rate mortgages are risky.

Risk Reducer #6: Invest in Other Currencies

Buy bonds that pay European euros or Japanese yen. Buy stock in companies that make a lot of money outside the United States.

Risk Reducer #7: Pay Off Your Debts

Rewards go to those with strong financial structures able to withstand (and profit from) adversity. Reduce your debts to build a strong hand.

Risk Reducer #8: Seek a Secure Paycheck

Now might not be the best time to leave a boring but safe job in order to start a restaurant or work for a start-up company.

The Risk of Low-Risk Investing

The *Mean Markets* recommendation to reduce financial risk is grounded in three macroeconomics truths:

1. Stock prices cannot grow faster than the economy forever.
2. Interest rates cannot go below zero.
3. The United States cannot run a trade deficit forever.

While these three are facts, picking the correct investments to profit from these changes is an exercise in economic forecasting. As we all learned, economic forecasts often boldly go to incorrect conclusions.

In the *Foundation* series of science fiction books, Isaac Asimov tries something far more difficult than economic forecasting. Asimov suggests that the field of "psychohistory" can predict the future of society. Psychohistory is "that branch of mathematics which deals with the reactions of human conglomerates to fixed social and economic stimuli." Psychohistorians claim that while individual behavior is unpredictable, social trends can be forecast based on the laws of probability.

Asimov's fictional psychohistorian, Hari Seldon, correctly predicts events for hundreds of years. Long after his death, the great Seldon's pre-recorded comments are played to generations of leaders on a secret schedule, and his accuracy would make even Nostradamus envious. Then, directly in opposition to Seldon's predictions, the Foundation is conquered.

Even in a novel, forecasts tend to be wrong! How did Asimov's hero fail? The answer is that the Foundation's conqueror is a mutant called "the Mule." Based on probability, the chance of such a leader arising was so small that the laws of psychohistory could not anticipate such an unlikely turn of events.

Interestingly, wikipedia, an online encyclopedia, lists macroeconomics as a "see also" topic under the description of Asimov's psychohistory. Like psychohistory, economic forecasts are particularly bad at anticipating the effect of novel and unlikely events. If there is to be such a "mule"-like event within economics, it is the productivity increase that is possible because of information technology.

Everyone has been touched profoundly by information technology. My own personal stories stretch from "knowledge-work" to manufacturing. The Harvard Business School now uses an electronic course platform to coordinate all teaching activities and distribute materials to students. This has made my life as a professor vastly easier. All of my lectures are electronically uploaded to the web from my office and accessed in the classroom. Printed material is distributed to hundreds of students with the literal click of a button.

More concretely, my father-in-law Joel works for an American company that actually manufactures something—very high quality flashlights (some costing hundreds of dollars). I visited the flashlight factory and found a giant room with a bunch of intelligent machine tools and three people. The people maintain the machines and feed them raw materials. With the right tools, three people can make a huge number of flashlights.

Everybody has similar experiences, and many are more dramatic than mine. Day by day, and in countless ways, information technology is making it easier to produce goods and services. As foreseen by the great economist John Maynard Keynes, productivity increases driven by information technology hold the promise of allowing humans to combine leisure with material excess.

Productivity thus holds the potential to cure America's financial woes. Many of those most pessimistic about our financial future point to the massive debts we have both as individuals and through our government. For example, market seer Bill Gross of PIMCO is on record with his prediction that the Dow Jones Industrial Average will decline to 5,000.[1] One of the reasons that Mr. Gross cites for his pessimism is a total U.S. debt level that—measured against the size of the economy—is the largest in history, exceeding even the bubbly 1920s.

Similarly, Robert Prechter (of Elliot Wave fame) cites similar debt statistics in many of his works, including his 2003 book *Conquer the Crash.* Mr. Prechter sees the possibility for the Dow to return to 1,000 or lower, making Bill Gross seem optimistic.[2]

Debt levels are indeed high. Furthermore, many aspects of our indebtedness are relatively new. The first "plastic" money, for example, was invented only in 1950, and widespread use of credit cards didn't take off until the invention of the magnetic strip in the early 1970s.[3] Now that credit cards are ubiquitous, almost everyone drags around a hungry debt balance that requires constant feeding. We are acclimatized to think of such indebtedness as natural. Scholars of irrationality and cycles, however, point out that credit junkies can convert to frugality with chilling economic effects. Thus, the indebtedness of our society threatens our prosperity.

Just as a highly unlikely event surprised the laws of psychohistory, abnormally high levels of productivity can protect us from the seemingly inevitable consequences of our indebtedness.

Through a similar lucky event, I survived a bout of indebtedness some years ago. While I was a student getting my Ph.D., Progenics Pharmaceuticals—the company that I had helped start, and for which I had served as president and chief financial officer—prepared for its initial public offering (IPO). With this event, I would be able to sell my shares and switch from bicycle-riding student to millionaire.

Because I know that markets are fickle, I resolved not to count my chickens too soon. Or at least not to spend them. So my goal was to act as if I were still poor until the cash hit my bank account. This, of course, proved impossible. In almost every conceivable way my expenses crept up. I took cabs, bought extra appetizers at meals, and flew to New York instead of taking the train. These expenses added up to some thousands of dollars of debts. Not to worry, soon the money would roll in.

After some months of trying to sell the IPO without much interest, Progenics decided to abandon its public offering. I was left with my debts and stock that I could not sell. About a year later, and after some business successes, Progenics restarted the IPO process. Once again I resolved to remain frugal in the face of my impending wealth, and once again I failed. Fortunately, this time the company went public, and I was easily able to pay off my debts.

If productivity growth can continue at its abnormally high pace it may do for the country what Progenics' IPO did for me. If we are all going to be much, much richer because of information technology, then it makes sense to spend some of our windfall in advance. The high levels of debt in our society, and even the high level of our trade deficit, can be seen as the logical pre-spending of our future wealth.

The negative alternative, however, is that productivity growth will recede toward historical averages. If so, then we may be stuck with the debts we have, and the attendant consequences. Therefore, high productivity growth appears to be necessary if we are to escape our debts.

With high enough productivity, financial assets can continue to prosper. This is possible even though stocks cannot outgrow the economy, interest rates cannot continue to decline, and the United States will stop consuming more than we produce. Thus, productivity is the single fundamental indicator that I will watch most closely in coming years.

The risk of being a conservative investor (owning low-risk investments) is missing out on a productivity-led boom. If financial markets continue to climb, then the low-risk investing strategy will earn lower returns than a higher-risk strategy.

The Pain of Low-Risk Investments

A Harvard faculty colleague of mine ends his course on decision making by giving two bits of advice. First, if you smoke, quit. Second, try to be less envious. Of these two suggestions, quitting smoking might be the easier one. Those who shift to a lower risk strategy must face the possibility that the risky investments they sell will continue to soar.

Very few people succeed without setbacks. Early in the life of my biotech startup, Progenics, I met with Paul Tudor Jones II, a lead investor. He asked how things were going, and I responded fine. He was seated and I was standing up on the opposite side of his desk. Paul rose, walked to my side of the desk and sort of backed me up against the wall. He said, "You must anticipate being pressed to your limits—and that's if you succeed."

Paul was prescient and along the way to Progenics' success, we had to weather several crises, including twice almost going broke and missing payroll. I felt tremendous stress, particularly because we had hired scientists from around the world and some of them had young children. One of these near-bankruptcy episodes was so stressful that some of my hair stopped growing, and I had to receive cortisone shots to revive the follicles.

Similarly, a low-risk investing strategy is likely to be stressful. One has to anticipate being pressed to one's limit. With near certainty, there will be times when everything appears rosy. At such times, our tendency to be envious will make us want to jump on the risk bandwagon. Such emotional points, we have learned, are likely to be terrible moments to change strategy.

If productivity stays significantly above historical levels, and financial risk continues to be rewarded, we will all gain. Even those of us who have a conservative financial plan. The benefits we will receive in a rosy world are direct and indirect. Most important, our opportunities will be vastly expanded, wages will rise, and the assets we own will increase in value.

In addition, even conservative investors will gain from national prosperity. Current projections show that the retirement of the baby boomers will put serious pressure on the U.S. budget. The annual budget deficit that currently stands at half a trillion dollars could soar to several trillion. In such an environment, it is inevitable that taxes will rise and benefits such as social security will fall.

Productivity and prosperity can save us from the baby boom retirement disaster. If they do, our taxes will be lower, our government benefits higher, and our opportunities far greater. Thus, even those who own no risky assets will earn a handsome return if the financial markets continue to rise.

Unfortunately, envy seems to be an integral part of human nature. In fact, the tenth commandment says, "You shall not covet your neighbor's house; you shall not covet your neighbor's wife, or his manservant, or his maidservant, or his ox, or his ass, or anything that is your neighbor's." The need to include this prohibition in the Bible reinforces the idea that envy and covetousness are part of human nature.

One technique to suppress human urges including envy is to construct a "frame," or a way of viewing investments. In this manner, I suggest viewing lower-risk investments as insurance. No one is unhappy when a car insurance policy is not used. We don't get mad if we pay money and then get through the year without an accident.

If we take out insurance in the form of a low-risk investment strategy we should similarly rejoice when that insurance is not used. Thus, we should think of our low-risk investments as a guarantee against an unpleasant world, or "dry powder" for those moments when prices become irrationally low. Such framing is useful, but the problem of decreasing risk is not so easily solved because our lizard brains create fundamental, psychological barriers.

The Barrier to Low-Risk Investing

Near the end of his career, a group of students allegedly played a joke on the famous behaviorist, Professor B.F. Skinner. During a lecture the students agreed upon the following secret plan. Every time Professor Skinner moved to his left, the students would smile at him. In contrast, whenever he took a step to his right, the students would frown and look at their notes.

By the end of the lecture, Professor Skinner was standing at the side of the room with his left arm essentially pinned against the wall. He had been induced to move to his left by the subtle signals sent by the students.

A central view of Professor Skinner's approach is that all animals, including people, learn to repeat pleasurable acts and to avoid those that are painful. Human brains are built with a "stimulus-response" mechanism that helps us navigate through the world.

I'm reminded of my own stimulus-response behavior whenever I drive to the Boston airport. As I enter the tunnel that leads under the harbor, my mind invariably flashes to the state trooper who pulled me over at that spot for speeding. As I recall the unpleasant memory of turning the corner and seeing him with a radar gun, I slow down. I may get ticketed for speeding again in my life, but never in the same spot as this previous ticket.

Professor Skinner's students played a trick on him. Stimulus-response behavior modification can be more subtle than a state trooper with a siren or a burned hand on a hot stove. Humans are social creatures, and we get pleasure and pain from our interactions with each other. With their facial expressions, Skinner's students "rewarded" him for his moves to the left and "punished" him for moves to the right. Unconsciously, he began to do more of the rewarded behavior and less of the punished, thus leading him to be pinned against the wall.

Professor Skinner was extreme in focusing on the conditioning effects of rewards and punishments, and ignoring the mental processes driving behavior. Even though the world now has a more nuanced and better understanding of behavior than Professor Skinner, no one denies the importance of stimulus-response. We humans share with other animals the brain machinery that teaches us to do again that which rewarded us in the past.

Our human stimulus-reward system can produce destructive behavior. A reformed crack addict whom I chatted with described his previous lifestyle as follows: A typical night begins with a group of friends all carrying as much money as they can scrounge up. The group drives (at least in California) to a crack house and smokes some drug.

The evening alternates between bouts of consuming crack and down time. The group generally travels between crack houses. The journey only ends when every penny has been spent. Almost every crack house includes women who will trade sex for drugs. Early in the night, when money is relatively easy, crack plus sex is better than crack without sex and worth the expenditure. Later in the night, when money is tight, the extra pleasure of sex is not worth the cost. The binge ends when everyone is broke, and the addicts find someplace to sleep. When they wake, they seek money to begin the process again.

One night after dropping off his buddies by car, my source told me that he chanced upon a big "rock" of crack that had somehow been left in the backseat. He couldn't believe his good fortune and enjoyed this unexpected final high for the night. For years afterwards, he would always look in the same spot when he got out of his car. In a manner that would have made Professor Skinner smile, this addict's brain had been altered by a potent reward.

Like a crack addict, we are built to look for rewards in the places (both literally and metaphorically) of our past joys. Presumably this stimulus-reward system was adaptive for our ancestors who lived in their natural environment. For rats in cages, and for humans in industrialized societies, the quest for dopamine can get us into serious trouble.

In *Austin Powers,* our hero, the international man of mystery, says, "Only two things scare me, and one of them is nuclear war." Similarly two things scare me about our human stimulus-response system, and one of them is drug addiction. While some people's lives are destroyed by the maladaptive activation of the stimulus-response system by drugs, almost all of us lose money because of its effects on our finances.

We are built to seek the dopamine high that comes from successes. For our ancestors, this system led them toward useful behaviors. In the financial world, however, this system is almost perfectly designed to create poverty. Investing is a changing game where the best strategy today is almost never the best strategy of yesterday. So our brains are built to replicate successful behaviors, but the financial markets punish such behavior.

Those who invest by stimulus-response will tend to do that which has worked, not that which will work. For example, after the huge stock market gains in the 1990s, investors ploughed a record $309 billion into stock mutual funds in 2000, just in time for the stock market bubble to burst. Over the two years of 2001 and 2002, investors invested a total of just $4 billion into stock funds, again timed perfectly to miss the huge stock market rally in 2003. In 2003, investors ploughed over $150 billion into equity funds.[4] To date, stocks have lost ground in 2004 (through mid-July). The backward-looking, stimulus-response system of investing is not profitable.

On a far grander scale, we have been rewarded for taking financial risk for a generation. The lizard brain is built to continue this behavior. This presents a significant barrier to taking a low-risk financial strategy.

How Little Risk Can You Stand?

My Harvard retirement money is deposited with a large investment company (chosen by Harvard). On their website, the company provides investment advice that is tailored to each individual. The investor answers a set of questions including attitudes toward risk and time until retirement. From these answers, a computer program suggests how much money to invest in stocks, bonds, and risk-free cash.

The computer advisor suggests that I invest 80% of my retirement money into stocks! I completely disagree with this recommendation, but I answered every question honestly. Why the disagreement?

Standard investing advice (and my firm is no different from most others) is based on two key premises. First, markets are efficient. Second, because markets are efficient, investors who want to make a lot of money, have to take a lot of risk. *Because stocks are risky, they must be profitable.* (I'm not making this bizarre logic up.)

So, this mainstream view says stocks provide the highest return, with two caveats. Investors must be in the game for the long run, and they must be able to take the ups and downs of the stock market. Thus, standard investing advice asks two main types of questions. Is the investor in the game for the long run? And can the investor take the bumps along the road? If so, back up the truck and buy stocks.

If markets were efficient, what should I do? I'm definitely in the investing game for the long run. Furthermore, I love volatility. The thrill of the ups and downs is so powerful for me that I even understand the wacky views of compulsive gamblers.

In *Double Down,* for example, Frederick and Stephen Barthelme explain how they gambled away their $250,000 inheritance. They explain that winning was better than losing, but losing was better than quitting.[5] Although I don't gamble, I love risk enough to understand the Barthelme brothers' odd priorities.

So if markets were efficient, then a risk-loving guy like me with a long horizon ought to buy risky stocks. If markets are not efficient, however, it is possible to make high returns without taking risk. Academic studies have found significant time periods when low-risk investments have high returns. The *Mean Markets and Lizard Brains* conclusion is that we are living in one of these time periods.

If the *Mean Markets and Lizard Brains* conclusion is correct, then it is possible to get the highest returns along with the lowest risk. Thus, the investments that are the safest may also end up with the highest return.

Whenever somebody gives an opinion, I think of the economic concept of "revealed preference." It cautions us to observe behavior and not listen to words.

Some years ago, my father-in-law, Joel, learned about revealed preference. During the early declines following the stock market bubble, I suggested that he sell the stock that he owned through a money management firm. Joel notified the firm of his decision to sell. One of the firm's bosses called to ask why Joel was "getting out at the bottom." Joel asked where the boss had his personal money invested and was told, "I've been in cash for quite a while." Joel hung up the phone and cursed under his breath.

A similar lesson is found in *Swingers,* where heartbroken Mike (played by Jon Favreau) learns dating rituals from suave Trent (a.k.a. "Big-T," played by Vince Vaughn). Mike asks, "After I get a woman's phone number, how long do I wait to call?" Big-T says, "if you call too soon you might scare off a nice baby who's ready to party" and concludes, "three days is kind of money." Mike then asks the revealed preference question about the three-day rule: how long until Big-T will call his "baby"? Big-T answers, "six days."

So a fair question is whether I've taken my own advice. The answer is not completely. In spite of truly believing that the low-risk approach is the way to go, I still have 10% of my money invested in stocks, including some high-flying Internet stocks. Why? 10% in stocks is the lowest amount of risk that I can take emotionally at this time.

A small risky investment is my effort to calm the lizard brain. During my entire investing life, risky investments have paid the highest return. Thus, my lizard brain constantly goes back to those heady days when there was easy money to be made. Although I'm using my prefrontal cortex to restrain the lizard brain, 10% is the lowest amount of risk that I can stomach these days.

The acid test of an investment strategy is how one feels when the strategy isn't working. When the stock market is soaring, and my low-risk investments are earning close to zero, my lizard brain screams, you fool!

Buy stocks! On those days, I need to have some money invested in stocks or the lizard brain will break out of its cage and buy risk at precisely the wrong time.

Take as little risk as you can stand. This is precisely the opposite of the mainstream advice grounded in the view that markets are efficient. In the fantasy world of efficient markets, we should take as *much* risk as we can stand in order to get those high stock market returns. In the real world of today's mean markets, perhaps we should take as *little* risk as we can stand.

Profiting from Manias and Crashes

The *Mean Markets and Lizard Brains* analysis suggests that we are in the midst of a new sort of bubble. While stocks, bonds, and real estate do not appear to be in bubble mode individually, the bubble may be in risk-taking itself. A generation of reward for taking financial risk has pushed us to take too many costly gambles.

The *Mean Markets and Lizard Brains* conclusion is that most people should reduce their level of financial risk. Our lizard brains have extrapolated from a golden generation that rewarded risk, and pushed us toward the risky investments that worked so well for so long. Unless productivity from the information revolution saves us, these risky investments are likely to disappoint.

Thus, the *Mean Markets and Lizard Brains* prescription is to reduce financial risk in order to be prepared for future opportunities. This advice is, of course, tempered and customized by individual circumstance and tastes.

If humans were the rational, cool-headed robots of economic theory, then achieving our financial goals would be easy. Because we are exactly the opposite—emotional beings subject to bouts of irrational moods and crazy decisions—financial success is difficult. In particular, in several keys areas we need to lean into our human nature in order to profit from financial opportunity.

Four Keys to Profiting from Mean Markets

1. Be Different

A key to making money is to buy when others are selling and sell when others are buying. In other words, in order to make money we have to do the unpopular behavior that others aren't doing.

Running against the mob is difficult because we are built to want to do what others are doing—we want to be part of the group. One study found that social isolation creates pain. In the study, three people played a ball-tossing game on a computer screen while one sits inside a brain scanner. The person in the brain scanner is told that the two other players are real people, but they are actually fake people controlled by the experimenter.

The experiment looked at the brain in two conditions, being part of the group or being ostracized. In the first, the real person is part of the game and gets the virtual ball frequently. In the second, the two artificial players exclude the real person by passing the ball back and forth.

Social isolation produced pain in these people. In fact, the brain scan revealed the same electrical pattern as physical pain.[6] So when we act differently from others we have to overcome our human desire to be part of the group.

This same study showed another interesting pattern. Those people who employed their cognitive abilities more, felt less pain. To be precise, the people who had higher levels of brain activation in the prefrontal cortex had lower levels of activation in the pain centers. As is one of the main themes of this book, success requires using cognition to control the lizard brain.

2. Make the Investment Moves That Do Not Produce Dopamine

Another key to making money is buying investments that have not done well and selling those that have done well. As humans, we still share the "do-it-again" brain centers with other animals. As B.F. Skinner made famous, animals, including humans, tend to repeat behaviors that were rewarded. Thus, Skinner's stimulus-response system leads us to love the investments that have made us money and hate the investments that have lost us money.

Our brains are actually bathed in pleasure-causing dopamine when we take the actions that have worked before. Spencer Johnson and Kenneth Blanchard captured the essence of this in their bestseller *Who Moved My Cheese?* In a world without change, the best way to find cheese is to return to the location where it was found previously. In a world with change, however, the best way to find cheese is to look somewhere new.

Financial markets are the worst environments in which to use stimulus-response processes. Precisely because most people fall in love with past winners, they tend to buy the investments that have gone up, not the ones that will go up. Thus, to make the correct financial decisions, we need to do exactly the opposite of what has been giving us our emotional reward. To make money, we need to break the dopamine addiction (at least in this area of our lives), and use our cognitive ability to control our behavior.

Those who want to follow the *Mean Markets and Lizard Brains* advice to reduce financial risk will have to do precisely the opposite of what has worked well for a generation.

3. Make an Emotionally Realistic Financial Plan

A third key to making money is to understand our own limits and to make a financial plan that we can execute.

In Plato's *Apology of Socrates,* the oracle of Delphi says that Socrates is the "wisest of men." Socrates is aware of his own flaws and so asks, "How can this be?" After a conversation with a man widely deemed to be brilliant, Socrates concludes, "I do not suppose that either of us knows anything really beautiful and good, I am better off than he is, for he knows nothing, and thinks that he knows; I neither know nor think that I know."

Socrates is the wisest of men, Plato suggests, precisely because he is aware of his flaws. Similarly, successful investors must be aware of their own irrationality.

In some unusual circumstances, people sometimes execute the perfect financial plan. For example, in 1987, a Massachusetts man (who wishes to remain anonymous) bought 1,000 shares of EMC for $15.75 a share. He held on to the shares for 13 years, by which time they had become 48,000 shares (because of splits) each worth more than $100.00.[7]

For 13 years, this investor patiently rode his profits and converted $16,000 into almost $5 million. In contrast, most investors make the mistake of harvesting their profits too quickly and riding their losses.

Even great investors tend to sell their winners too soon and to never sell their losers. In the 1940 investment classic *Where are the Customers' Yachts?* Fred Schwed, Jr. writes, "When a great and sagacious financier dies, and the executors go through the strongbox, they usually find, tucked well away in the back, bundles of the most hopeless securities whose very names have been long since forgotten."[8]

So how did our EMC holder resist the temptation to take profits? He simply forgot that he owned the stock! He originally bought 3,000 shares and sold 2,000. He didn't know that he owned any shares until he was notified by a state agency about his "inactivity."

Unless we can similarly forget about our investments, we have to anticipate our weaknesses. A frequent problem is that an investor has a "perfect" plan, but then makes an emotional trade at precisely the wrong time. Thus, in my low-risk financial plan, I keep enough money invested in stocks to stave off the lizard brain. Each person has to craft a customized financial plan that anticipates and preempts moments of irrationality.

4. Be Tough Enough to Stick to a Plan

When I was in middle school, my friend Paul ran the 600-yard run (the longest event) in the school's annual athletic competition. Opposing him was Jimmy, one of the bullies and part of the in-crowd. My friends and I desperately wanted Paul to win, and we gathered round him minutes before the start.

Paul knew that the race had implications for all his friends and for the school's entire social order. He spoke to us in a serious and calm manner.

Here's what he said: "I don't want you to get nervous if I'm behind in the beginning, my strategy is to come from behind. Don't worry, I'm going to win."

The race was three laps and—as Paul had forewarned—after one lap he appeared hopelessly behind. Confident in his certain victory, Jimmy started celebrating and gesturing to his fellow bullies in the crowd. On the final lap, Paul accelerated and easily passed a tired Jimmy.

John Maynard Keynes remarked that markets tend to stay irrational for longer than an investor can stay solvent. Therefore the investor who seeks to profit from irrationality has to anticipate being behind in the race for a long time. The goal, of course, is to have more money in the long run, not to be in the "lead" for a while.

Even the legendary Warren Buffett had to endure scorn during the late 1990s because he refused to buy bubble stocks. Buffett avoided overpriced stocks, which became even more overpriced before the bubble popped. Accordingly, he missed out on the ephemeral gains and many claimed that Buffet had "lost his mojo." Buffet's exceptional mental toughness allowed him to persist and prosper. Unlike most people, he never deviated from his plan.

Tame the Lizard Brain and Convert Mean Markets into Opportunity

Taming the lizard brain by following the *Mean Markets and Lizard Brains* advice is not easy. Quite to the contrary, it is very hard. The fact that making money is difficult is precisely what makes it possible. If it were easy to make money from others' irrationality, then the opportunities would vanish.

Interestingly, financial success does not require fancy mathematical skills or genius level IQ. No, it requires something far more rare and difficult. To make money investors need what Dan Goleman labels emotional intelligence (EQ):

EQ is not destiny—emotional intelligence is a different way of being smart. It includes knowing your feelings and using them to make good decisions; managing your feelings well; motivating yourself with zeal and persistence; maintaining hope in the face of frustration; exhibiting empathy and compassion; interacting smoothly; and managing your relationships effectively.[9]

Goleman argues that attaining one's goals in life requires emotional intelligence more than IQ. Similarly, successful investing requires the extremely rare quality of EQ. To profit from market excesses requires self-knowledge, self-confidence, endurance, and mental toughness. The successful investor has to face ridicule and must live with underperformance for extended periods.

"Money won is twice as sweet as money earned," said Paul Newman to Tom Cruise in *The Color of Money.* Similarly, I find money gained through savvy investing to be far sweeter than wage income.

Markets are irrational, and our backward-looking, pattern-seeking lizard brains push us to lose money. Investors who let the lizard brain make financial decisions tend to buy at market tops and sell at market lows. Because our instincts are exactly out of sync with financial opportunity, markets can be mean.

However, it is the very irrationality of markets that provides the opportunity to make sweet profits. Financial success is based on using emotional intelligence to shackle the lizard brain. Fortunately EQ can be increased by diligence, introspection, and discipline. Therefore, any investor willing to work to understand and tame the lizard brain can transform mean markets into money and satisfaction.

Notes

Preface

1. Johns Manville, www.johnsmanville.com.

Chapter 1 Introduction

1. Personal communication. See Chapter 7.
2. Leading Wall St. Firms' Asset Allocation Recommendations (for 2004). Dow Jones Newswires, December 31, 2003.
3. Investment Company Institute, www.ici.org, 2004 fact book, 88.
4. Federal Reserve Survey of Consumer Finances, www.federalreserve.gov.
5. Berkow, R., *The Merck Manual of Medical Information: Home Edition* (New York: Pocket, 1999), 1303.
6. U.S. Food and Drug Administration. Aspirin for Reducing Your Risk of Heart Attack and Stroke: know the facts. www.fda.gov.

Chapter 2 Crazy People

1. Those interested in more detail can see: Glimcher, P. W., *Decisions, Uncertainty, and The Brain: The Science of Neuroeconomics* (Cambridge, Mass: MIT Press, 2003).
2. Medawar, P.B., *An Unsolved Problem of Biology* (London: H.K. Lewis, 1952), 3.
3. Harig, B., "Woods 'Uncomfortable' with His Game," ESPN.com, April 26, 2004.
4. Tversky, A. and D. Kahneman, "Extensional versus Intuition Reasoning: Conjunction Fallacy in Probability Judgment," *Psychological Review*, 90 (1983): 293–315.
5. Burrough, B. and J. Helyar, *Barbarians at the Gate* (New York: Harpercollins, 1990).
6. Burnham, T. and J. Phelan, *Mean Genes* (Cambridge: Perseus, 2000), 83–104.
7. Tversky, A. and D. Kahneman, "Evidential Impact of Base Rates," *Judgment under*

Uncertainty: Heuristics and Biases, D. Kahneman, P. Slovic, and A. Tversky, eds. (Cambridge: Cambridge University Press, 1982), 154.

8. Svenson, O., "Are We All Less Risky and More Skillful Than Our Fellow Drivers?" *Acta Psychologica* 47 (1981): 143–148.

9. Ross, M. and F. Sicoly, "Egocentric Biases and Availability and Attribution," *Journal of Personality and Social Psychology* 37 (1979): 322–336.

10. Peters, T.J., *In Search of Excellence* (New York: Harper & Row, 1982), 56.

11. Lichtenstein, S., B. Fischhoff, et al., "Calibration of Probabilities," *Judgment under Uncertainty: Heuristics and Biases,* D. Kahneman, P. Slovic, and A. Tversky, eds. (Cambridge: Cambridge University Press, 1982), 306–334.

12. Roth, G. and M. Wulliman, eds., *Brain Evolution and Cognition* (New York: Wiley, 2001), chapters 16 and 17.

13. Minsky, M.L., *The Society of Mind* (New York: Simon and Schuster, 1986).

14. Lech, R.B., *Broken Soldiers* (Urbana: University of Illinois Press, 2000).

15. Cialdini, R.B., *Influence: The Psychology of Persuasion,* rev. ed. (New York: Quill/William Morrow, 1993).

16. Gazzaniga, M., *The Mind's Past* (Berkeley: University of California Press, 1998).

17. McGurk, H. and J. MacDonald, "Hearing Lips and Seeing Voices," *Nature* 264 (1976): 746–748.

18. Harlow, J.M., *Recovery from the Passage of an Iron Bar through the Head* (Boston: David Clapp & Son, 1869).

19. Thaler, R.H., *The Winner's Curse: Paradoxes and Anomalies of Economic Life* (Princeton, NJ: Princeton University Press, 1992); Gilovich, T., D. Griffin, et al., eds., *Heuristics and Biases: The Psychology of Intuitive Judgment.* (Cambridge: Cambridge University Press, 2002).

20. Schwager, J., *Market Wizards: Interviews with Top Traders* (New York: Prentice Hall Press, 1989), 117–140.

21. Guth, W., R. Schmittberger, et al., "An Experimental Analysis of Ultimatum Bargaining," *Journal of Economic Behavior and Organization* 3, no. 4, (1982): 367–388.

22. Roth, A.E., "Bargaining Experiments," *Handbook of Experimental Economics,* J.H. Kagel and A.E. Roth, eds. (Princeton, NJ: Princeton University Press, 1995). Roth, A.E., V. Prasnikar, et al., "Bargaining and Market Behavior in Jerusalem, Ljubljana, Pittsburgh, and Tokyo: An Experimental Study," *American Economic Review* 81, no. 5, (1991): 1068–1095.

23. Hoffman, E., K. McCabe, et al., "On Expectations and the Monetary Stakes in Ultimatum Games," *International Journal of Game Theory* 25 (1996): 289–301.

24. Cameron, L., "Raising the Stakes in the Ultimatum Game: Experimental Evidence from Indonesia," *Economic Inquiry* 37, no. 1, (1999): 47–59.

25. Henrich, J., R. Boyd, et al., "In Search of *Homo economicus:* Behavioral Experiments in 15 Small-Scale Societies," *American Economic Review* 91, no. 2, (2001): 73–78.

26. Sanfey, A.G., J.K. Rilling, et al., "The Neural Basis of Economic Decision-Making in the Ultimatum Game," *Science* 300 (2003): 1755–1758.

27. Burnham, T.C., "Pride, Status and Hormones: Rejectors in an Ultimatum Game Have High Levels of Testosterone" manuscript, 2004.

28. Kahneman, D. and A. Tversky, "Choices, Values, and Frames," *American Psychologist* 39, no. 4, (1984): 341–50.

29. Leeson, N. with E. Whitley, *Rogue Trader: How I Brought down Barings Bank and Shook the Financial World* (Boston: Little Brown, 2000).

30. Skinner, B.F., "'Superstition' in the Pigeon," *Journal of Experimental Psychology* 38 (1947): 168–172.

31. Tversky, A. and D. Kahneman, "Judgment Under Uncertainty: Heuristics and Biases," *Science* 185 (1974): 1124–1131.

32. Laibson, D., "Golden Eggs and Hyperbolic Discounting," *The Quarterly Journal of Economics* 112, no. 2, (1997): 443–477.

Chapter 3 Crazy World

1. Smith, V.L., "An Experimental Study of Competitive Market Behavior," *The Journal of Political Economy* 70 (1962): 111–137.

2. Bachelier, L., *Théorie de la Spéculation* (Paris: Gauthier-Villars, 1900).

3. Bernstein, P., *Capital Ideas: The Improbable Origins of Modern Wall Street* (New York: Free Press, 1992).

4. Malkiel, B., *A Random Walk Down Wall Street* (New York: Norton, 1973).

5. Siegel, J.J., *Stocks for the Long Run,* 2nd ed. (New York: McGraw-Hill, 1998).

6. MacKay, C., *Memoirs of Extraordinary Popular Delusions* (London: R. Bentley, 1841).

7. Shiller, R., *Irrational Exuberance* (Princeton, NJ: Princeton University Press, 2000).

8. Shiller, R., "Investor Behavior in the 1987 Stock Market Crash: Survey Evidence," Cowles Foundation Discussion Papers (#853), 1987.

9. Siegel, J., "The Stock Market Crash of 1987: A Macro-Finance Perspective," Rodney L. White Center for Financial Research Working Papers (#24-88), 1988.

10. Smith, V.L., G.L. Suchanek, et al., "Bubbles, Crashes and Endogenous Expectations in Experimental Spot Asset Markets," *Econometrica* 56 (1988): 1119–1151.

11. Investment Company Institute, www.ici.org, 2004 fact book, 88.

12. "The Death of Equities: Why the Age of Equities May Be Over," *Business Week* (August 13, 1979).

13. Investment Company Institute, www.ici.org, 2004 fact book, 88.

14. Prechter, R., *Conquer the Crash: You Can Survive and Prosper in a Deflationary Depression* (Hoboken, New Jersey: John Wiley & Sons, 2002), Figure 7.1.

15. Odean, T., "Do Investors Trade Too Much?" *American Economic Review* 89 (1999): 1279–1298.

16. De Bondt, W. and R. Thaler, "Does the Stock Market Overreact?" *Journal of Finance* 40 (1985): 793–808.

17. Thaler, R., ed., *Advances in Behavioral Finance* (New York: Russell Sage Foundation, 1993).

18. Berkshire Hathaway annual report 2003, 2.

19. Fuller & Thaler Asset Management, www.fullerthaler.com.

20. Popper, K., *The Logic of Scientific Discovery* (London: Hutchinson, 1959).

21. Tobias, A., *Money Angles* (New York: Linden Press, 1984).

22. Asch, S., "Studies of Independence and Conformity: 1. A Minority of One against a Unanimous Majority," *Psychological Monographs* 70 (1956): 1–70.

23. Profet, M., "The Evolution of Pregnancy Sickness as Protection to the Embryo against Pleistocene Teratogens," *Evolutionary Theory* 8 (1988): 177–190.

24. Lo, A., and D. Repin, "The Psychophysiology of Real-Time Financial Risk Processing," *Journal of Cognitive Neuroscience* 14 (2002): 323–339.

Chapter 4 U.S. Economic Snapshot

1. Keynes, J.M., "Economic Possibilities of Our Grandchildren," *Essays in Persuasion* (London: Macmillan, 1972).

2. Federal Reserve, www.federalreserve.gov.

3. Bureau of Economic Analysis, www.bea.gov, Table 2.1.

4. Bureau of Labor Statistics, www.bls.gov, Foreign Labor Statistics.

5. Schwarzenegger Press Conference, August 20, 2003.

6. Office of Management and Budget, Congressional Budget Office, see Figure 7.4 of this book.

7. Bureau of Labor Statistics, www.bls.gov.

8. Office of Management and Budget, Congressional Budget Office, see Figure 7.3 of this book.

9. Darwin, C., *On the Origin of Species by Means of Natural Selection, or the Preservation of Favoured Races in the Struggle for Life* (London: John Murray, 1859), Chapter 3.

10. Diener, E., "Cross-Cultural Correlates of Life Satisfaction and Self-esteem," *Journal of Personality and Social Psychology* 68, no. 4 (1995): 653–664. Diener, E., E. Sandvik, et al., "The Relationship Between Income and Subjective Well-being: Relative or Absolute?" *Social Indicators Research* 28, no. 3 (1993): 195–224.

Chapter 5 Inflation

1. Friedman, M., and A.J. Schwartz, *A Monetary History of The United States: 1867–1960* (Cambridge: National Bureau of Economic Research, 1963), 695.
2. Roth, A.E., and X. Xing, "Turnaround Time and Bottlenecks in Market Clearing: Decentralized Matching in the Market for Clinical Psychologists," *Journal of Political Economy* 105 (1997): 284–329.
3. Friedman, M., and A.J. Schwartz, *A Monetary History of The United States: 1867–1960* (National Bureau of Economic Research, 1963), 696.
4. Quiggin, A., *A Survey of Primitive Money; The Beginning of Currency* (London: Methuen, 1907), 250.
5. Einzig, P., *Primitive Money in Its Ethnological, Historical, and Economic Aspects,* 2nd ed. (New York: Pergamon Press, 1966), 310.
6. Angell, N., *The Story of Money* (Garden City, NY: Garden City Publishing Company, 1929), 88–89.
7. Mankiw, N.G., *Macroeconomics,* 5th ed., (New York: Worth Publishers, 2003), 79.
8. Connolly, B., and R. Anderson, *First Contact. New Guinea's Highlanders Encounter the Outside World* (New York: Viking Penguin, 1987).
9. Ringer, F., *The German Inflation of 1923* (London: Oxford University Press, 1969).
10. Bopp, K., "Hjalmar Schacht: Central Banker," *The University of Missouri Studies* xiv, no. 1 (1939): 13.
11. Bresciani-Turroni, C., *The Economics of Inflation; A Study of Currency Depreciation in Post-War Germany* (New York: A. M. Kelley, 1968).
12. Tyran, J., and E. Fehr, "Limited Rationality and Strategic Interaction—The Impact of the Strategic Environment on Nominal Inertia," University of St. Gallen Department of Economics working paper series, 2002.
13. Bernanke, B.S., and K. Carey, "Nominal Wage Stickiness and Aggregate Supply in the Great Depression," *Quarterly Journal of Economics* 111 (1996): 853–883. Bordo, M.D., C.J. Erceg, et al., "Money, Sticky Wages and the Great Depression," *American Economic Review* 90 (2000): 1447–1463.
14. Fischer, S., "Why Are Central Banks Pursuing Long-Run Price Stability?" in *Achieving Price Stability* (a symposium sponsored by the Federal Reserve Bank of Kansas City, 1996), 7–34.
15. Summers, L., "Commentary: Why Are Central Banks Pursuing Long-Run Price Stability?" in *Achieving Price Stability* (a symposium sponsored by the Federal Reserve Bank of Kansas City, 1996), 35–43.
16. Wincott Memorial Lecture, London, September 16, 1970.
17. Federal Reserve, www.federalreserve.gov; see Figures 6.3 and 6.4 of this book.

Chapter 6 Deficits and Dollars

1. Grabbe, O., "The Rise and Fall of Bretton Woods," Chapter 1 in *International Financial Markets,* 3rd ed. (Englewood Cliffs, New Jersey: Prentice-Hall, 1996).
2. International inflation rates from the International Monetary Fund, country information, www.imf.org.
3. Bresciani-Turroni, C., *The Economics of Inflation; A Study of Currency Depreciation in Post-War Germany* (New York: A. M. Kelley, 1968).
4. Powell, J., *A History of the Canadian Dollar* (Ottawa: Bank of Canada, 1999).
5. The value of the Canadian dollar over time: Federal Reserve, www.federalreserve. gov, see foreign exchange rates, historical data.
6. Statistics Canada, national income and expenditure accounts. Catalogue no. 13-001-PPB, Fourth Quarter 2000.
7. Statistics Canada, www.statcan.ca.
8. The value of the Mexican peso over time: Federal Reserve, www.federalreserve.gov, see foreign exchange rates, historical data.
9. Federal Reserve, dollar indexes, historical data, www.federalreserve.gov.
10. International Monetary Fund, www.imf.org.
11. "The End of the Affair?" *The Economist* (February 18, 2004).
12. Mr. Norfield and Ms. Foley are quoted in the same article: Litterick, D., "Euro Below 85 Cents after Duisenberg U-Turn Over Intervention," telegraph.co.uk, October 17, 2000.
13. "Big Mac Index," *The Economist* (May 27, 2004).

Chapter 7 Bonds

1. Mehra, R., and E.C. Prescott, "The Equity Premium: A Puzzle," *Journal of Monetary Economics* 15 (1985): 145–162.
2. Siegel, J.J., *Stocks for the Long Run,* 2nd ed. (New York: McGraw-Hill, 1998), and related Table 8.1 in this book.
3. Tobin, J., "How to Think About the Deficit," *New York Review of Books* 33, no. 14 (September, 25, 1986).
4. Presidential debate, Boston, MA October 3, 2000.
5. Federal Reserve Chairman Alan Greenspan's prepared remarks at the Conference on Bank Structure and Competition, sponsored by the Federal Reserve Bank of Chicago, Chicago, Illinois, May 6, 2004.
6. Burnham, T.C., "Limits on Liability Actually Are What Invite the LBOs," the *Wall Street Journal,* February 1, 1989.

7. Orphanides, A., "Monetary Policy in Deflation: The Liquidity Trap in History and Practice," Federal Reserve Publication, 2003.

8. Investment Company Institute, www.ici.org, 2004 fact book, 122.

Chapter 8 Stocks

1. All data in this section from Siegel, J.J., *Stocks for the Long Run,* 2nd ed. (New York: McGraw-Hill, 1998).

2. Dow Jones, www.djindexes.com.

3. Dimson, E., P. Marsh, et al., *Triumph of the Optimists: 101 Years of Global Investment Returns* (Princeton, NJ: Princeton University Press, 2002), 34–38.

4. Arnott, R. and P. Bernstein, "What Risk Premium Is 'Normal'?" *Financial Analysts Journal* 58 (2002): 64–85.

5. Hawking, S., *A Brief History of Time,* 10th anniversary edition (New York: Bantam, 1988), 129.

6. Ibid, 128.

7. Ibid, 129.

8. Chomsky, N., "Confronting the Empire," *Z Magazine* 16, no. 3 (January 27, 2003).

9. Taleb, N.N., *Fooled by Randomness: The Hidden Role of Chance in the Markets and in Life* (New York: Texere, 2001). Taleb, N.N., *The Black Swan* (New York: Random House, 2005).

10. Galbraith, J.K., *The Great Crash 1929* (New York: Houghton Mifflin, 1979).

11. The *Wall Street Journal.*

12. Microsoft conference call, July 22, 2004.

13. The *Wall Street Journal.*

14. The *Wall Street Journal;* see Table 3.1 of this book.

15. Dow Jones, www.djindexes.com.

16. "Bearish Merrill Strategist under Fire," Cnnfn, November 22, 2003.

17. Leading Wall St. Firms' Asset Allocation Recommendations (for 2004), Dow Jones Newswires, December 31, 2003.

18. Federal Reserve, see Figures 6.3 and 6.4 of this book.

19. Siegel, J.J., *Stocks for the Long Run,* 3rd ed. (New York: McGraw-Hill, 2002), 361.

Chapter 9 Real Estate

1. The Japan Real Estate Institute, Urban Land Price Index (Nationwide), www.reinet.or.jp.

2. Ricardo, D., *On the Principles of Political Economy and Taxation* (London: John Murray, 1817).

3. Mankiw, N.G., *Principles of Economics,* 2nd ed. (Fort Worth, TX: Harcourt College Publishers, 2001).

4. Fallows, J., "The Passionless Presidency: The Trouble with Jimmy Carter's Administration," *The Atlantic Monthly* (May 1979).

5. Office of Federal Housing Enterprise Oversight and Federal Reserve; see also Figure 7.1 of this book.

6. Mankiw, N.G., and D.N. Weil, "The Baby Boom, the Baby Bust, and the Housing Market," *Regional Science and Urban Economics* 19 (1989): 235–258.

7. S&P 500 (July 2004) 1101, Earnings estimate for S&P $61.50 for 2004 (Goldman, Sachs & Co.).

8. Dow Jones, www.djindexes.com.

9. Krainer, J., "House Price Bubbles," Federal Reserve Bank of San Francisco Economic Letter (#2003-06), 2003.

10. MacKay, C., *Memoirs of Extraordinary Popular Delusions* (London: R. Bentley, 1841).

11. Marx, G., *Groucho and Me* (Classics of Modern American Humor Series). (New York: AMS Press, 1991).

12. Securities and Exchange Commission, www.sec.gov.

13. Federal Reserve, Consumer Credit, www.federalreserve.gov.

14. Mortgage Bankers Association, www.mbaa.org.

15. Jacobs, B., *Capital Ideas and Market Realities: Option Replication, Investor Behavior, and Stock Market Crashes* (Oxford: Blackwell, 1999).

16. Dow Jones, www.djindexes.com.

17. Mortgage Bankers Association, www.mbaa.org.

18. "Killing Hope—The Imminent Execution of Sean Sellers," Amnesty International, December 1, AMR 51/108/1998, 1998.

19. Federal Reserve Chairman Alan Greenspan's prepared remarks at the Credit Union National Association 2004 Governmental Affairs Conference, Washington, D.C., February 23, 2004.

Chapter 10 Timeless Advice

1. Bowlby, J., *Attachment and Loss. Vol. I: Attachment* (New York: Basic Books, 1969). Bowlby, J., *Attachment and Loss. Vol. II: Separation, Anxiety, and Anger* (New York: Basic Books, 1973). Wilson, E.O., *Sociobiology: The New Synthesis* (Cambridge, Mass.: Belknap Press of Harvard University Press, 1975). Wilson, E.O., *On Human Nature* (Cambridge: Harvard University Press, 1978). Tooby, J., and L. Cosmides, "Evolutionary Psychology and the Generation of Culture: I. Theoretical Considerations," *Ethology & Sociobiology* 10 (1989): 29–49. Barkow, J.H., L. Cosmides, et al.,

The Adapted Mind: Evolutionary Psychology and the Generation of Culture (New York: Oxford University Press, 1992). Irons, W., "Adaptively Relevant Environments Versus the Environment of Evolutionary Adaptedness," *Evolutionary Anthropology* 6, no. 6 (1998): 194–204.

2. Irons, W., "Adaptively Relevant Environments Versus the Environment of Evolutionary Adaptedness," *Evolutionary Anthropology* 6, no. 6 (1998): 194–204.

3. Tooby, J., and L. Cosmides, "The Past Explains the Present: Emotional Adaptations and the Structure of Ancestral Environments," *Ethology & Sociobiology* 11 (1990): 375–424.

4. Gigerenzer, G., "The Bounded Rationality of Probabilistic Mental Modules," *Rationality.* K.I. Manktelow and D.E. Over, eds. (London and New York: Routledge, 1993), 284–313.

5. Gigerenzer, G., "Ecological Intelligence: An Adaptation for Frequencies," *The Evolution of Mind,* D. Cummins and C. Allen, eds. (Oxford: Oxford University Press, 1998), 107–125.

6. Personal communication.

7. Kahneman, D., and A. Tversky, "Variants of Uncertainty," *Judgment under Uncertainty: Heuristics and biases,* D. Kahneman, P. Slovic, and A. Tversky, eds. (Cambridge: Cambridge University Press, 1982), 512.

8. Shostak, M., *Nisa, the Life and Words of a !Kung Woman* (Cambridge, Mass: Harvard University Press, 1981). Hill, K., and M. Hurtado, *Ache Life History: The Ecology and Demography of a Foraging People* (New York: Aline De Gruyter, 1996). Chagnon, N., *Yanomamo,* 4th ed. (New York: Harcourt Brace Jovanovich, 1992).

9. Lee, R., *The Dobe Ju/'hoansi* (New York: Harcourt Brace, 1993), 42.

10. Barkow, J.H., L. Cosmides, et al., *The Adapted Mind: Evolutionary Psychology and the Generation of Culture* (New York: Oxford University Press, 1992).

11. Silverman, I., and M. Eals, "Sex Differences in Spatial Abilities: Evolutionary Theory and Data," *The Adapted Mind: Evolutionary Psychology and the Generation of Culture.* J.H. Barkow, L. Cosmides, and J. Tooby, eds. (New York: Oxford University Press, 1992), 573.

12. Barber, B.M., and T. Odean, "Boys Will Be Boys: Gender, Overconfidence, and Common Stock Investment," *Quarterly Journal of Economics* 116, no. 1 (2001): 261–292.

13. Lefèvre, E., *Reminiscences of a Stock Operator* (New York: G.H. Doran, 1923).

14. Morton, F., *The Rothschilds: Portrait of a Dynasty* (reprint edition) (New York: Kodansha International, 1998), 48–50.

15. Tversky, A., and D. Kahneman, "Judgment under Uncertainty: Heuristics and Biases," *Science* 185 (1974): 1124–1131.

16. Thaler, R., A. Tversky, et al., "The Effect of Myopia and Loss Aversion on Risk Taking: An Experimental Test," *Quarterly Journal of Economics* 112, no. 2 (1997): 647–661.

17. Thaler, R., "Mental Accounting and Consumer Choice," *Marketing Science* 4, no. 3 (1985): 199–214.

18. Homer, *The Odyssey,* book XII.

19. U.S. Supreme Court, Jacobellis v. Ohio, 378 U.S. 184 (1964).

Chapter 11 Timely Advice

1. Gross, B., "Dow 5,000," *PIMCO Investment Outlook* (September 2002).

2. Prechter, R., *Conquer the Crash: You Can Survive and Prosper in a Deflationary Depression* (Hoboken, NJ: John Wiley & Sons, 2002), 79.

3. Diners Club, www.dinersclub.com.

4. Investment Company Institute, www.ici.org, 2004 Fact Book, table 13, 122.

5. Barthelme, F., and S. Barthelme, *Double Down: Reflections on Gambling and Loss* (New York: Houghton Mifflin, 1999).

6. Eisenberger, N., M. Lieberman, et al., "Does Rejection Hurt? An fMRI Study of Social Exclusion," *Science* 302 (2003): 290–292.

7. Flaherty, J., "'Buy and Forget' Pays Off Big," *New York Times,* December 3, 2000.

8. Schweb, F., *Where Are the Customers' Yachts? or, A Good Hard Look at Wall Street* (New York: Simon & Schuster, 1940), 26.

9. Goleman, D., *Emotional Intelligence: Why It Can Matter More Than IQ* (New York: Bantam Books, 1995).

Index

A

Adjustable rate mortgages, 216–219, 221–223
Advances in Behavioral Finance, 49
The Adventure of the Silver Blaze, 269
Aggregate financial position, 255–257
Allen, Woody, 11, 34
Altria, 176
American Dream (documentary), 98
Ancestral traits, 5–6, 234–237, 240–241, 267
Anchoring effect, 254
Anna Karenina, 262
Annie Hall (movie), 11
Anthropic principle, 168
Apology of Socrates (Plato), 284
Argentina loan default, 128–129
Arkhipov, Vasily, 169–170
Asch, Solomon, 57
As Good As It Gets (movie), 221
Asimov, Isaac, 271–272
AT&T Wireless, 247
Austin Powers (movie), 252, 267, 279
Averaging losers, 249

B

"The Baby Boom, the Baby Bust, and the Housing Market" (Mankiw and Weil), 196–197
Baby boom retirement, 276
Bachelier, Louis, 39–40
Back to the Future (movie), 169, 187
Bacteria, 178
Baker, George, 12, 128
Barbarians at the Gate, 16
Barber, Brad, 245
Barings Bank, 30
Barter economy, 90, 97
Battle of Little Big Horn, 78
Behavioral economics, 15, 25–29, 33–34
Behavioral finance, 49, 51
Bernstein, Richard, 183–184
Berra, Yogi, 101
The Black Swan (Taleb), 170
Blazing Saddles (movie), 261
Blood viscosity, 5–6
Bonds. *See also* Treasury bonds
  bull market in, 154–157
  default on, 149–150
  fixed-rate debt, 157
  government bonds, 140–142, 162, 171

Bonds *(Continued)*
  inflation and, 110–112, 150, 151, 200, 201
  inflation-protected bonds, 111, 112, 270
  interest rates and, 141–142, 143, 154–155
  investment characteristics of, 200–202
  investment in, 58, 139–140
  losing money with, 149–153
  maturity terms, 158, 270
  monetary growth and, 108
  non-U.S. bonds, 134–135, 271
  opportunity cost, 150–153
  profitable investing in, 157–158
  Reagan bonds, 143, 156
  return on, 142–144, 171, 266
  short-term bonds, 158, 270
  taxes and, 200, 201
  value of, 140–142
Borish, Peter, 25, 159, 160, 191
Borrowing money. *See also* Loans
  Cheapskate, 115–116
  current account deficits, 117–119
  inflation effects on, 97
  interest rates and, 158
Boys will be boys study, 245–246
Brain:
  activity during ultimatum game, 28
  corpus callosum, 22
  lizard brain *(see* Lizard brain(s))
  McGurk effect, 23–24
  parts of, 20–22
  prefrontal cortex, 11–12, 20, 21, 23–24, 34, 283
  split-brain studies, 22–23
  subconscious, power of, 21–22
Braniff Airlines, 163
Brecheen, Robert, 219
Bretton Woods agreement, 93, 118
A Brief History of Time (Hawking), 167–168
British pound, value of, 133
Bubbles and crashes, 44–45, 52, 282
  Great Depression, 118, 163, 216

  housing bubble, 203–210
  1987 stock market crash, 42–44, 181, 182, 217
Buffett, Warren, 49–50, 286
Bush, George W., 146
Business investment, idle production capacity and, 74–75

C
Calculations, problem completing, 15–17
Canadian economy, 122–124, 125
Carnegie, Dale, 22
Carter, Jimmy, 86, 195
Cheapskate, 115–116
Chicago Bulls, 230–231
Chimpanzees, 232–234
Chinese baby problem, 16, 17
Chinese economy, 76, 133
Chinese treatment of Korean War P.O.W.s, 21–22
Chomsky, Noam, 169–170
Churchill, Winston, 24
Cisco, 43–44, 75, 210
Cohen, Abby Joseph, 184
Coin flips, 32, 36, 50–51, 239
The Color of Money (movie), 287
The Coming Crash in the Housing Market, 203
Communist markets, 166
Comparative advantage, 194–196
Completion bond company, 165
Compound interest, 80–81
Conformity needs, 56–58, 283
Conjunction fallacy, 14–15, 236–237
Conquer the Crash (Prechter), 273
Consumer Price Index, 162, 171
Consumer spending, 71, 72–74
Corporate profits:
  growth of, 177–180
  stock prices and, 180–183
Corpus callosum, 22
Cosmides, Leda, 235–236
Cosmology, 167–169
Crack addiction, 278–279
Crashes. *See* Bubbles and crashes

Credit card debt, 273
Cripps, Richard, 184
Critical self-examination, 12–14
Cuban Missile Crisis, 169
Currency prices. *See also* Dollar(s)
 devaluation, 119–120, 122–125
 inflation and, 121–122
 investment return and, 134–135
 loan default and, 129–130
 nominal exchange rate, 121–122
 real exchange rate, 121
 setting of, 117–118
 stocks and, 185–186
Current account:
 of Canada, 123–124, 125
 deficit in, 116–119, 120, 125–127
 defined, 116
 imbalances, 116–119
 of Mexico, 124–125
 surplus, 119

D
Darwin, Charles, 80–81
Davis, Gray, 76
"Death of Equities" (*BusinessWeek*),
 45–46
Death or Glory (DoG), 257
DeBondt, Werner, 48–49
Debt:
 government (*see* Government debt)
 personal, 271, 273–274
Decision-making skills, 4, 14–15
Deficit spending, 69–70, 71, 77
Deflation, 98–99, 106, 112–113
Detroit Pistons, 230–231
Devaluation of money, 119–120,
 122–125
DeVore, Irven, 240
Dickson, Chip, 184
Dirksen, Everett, 144
Dollar-cost averaging, 250–252
Dollar(s). *See also* Money
 creation of, 129–130
 value against Chinese currency, 133
 value against euro, 130–132

value against Japanese yen, 133
value linked to gold, 93–94
value of, 119–120, 122–125, 133–135,
 186
Dopamine, 279, 284
Double Down (Barthelme and
 Barthelme), 280
Dow Jones Industrial Average:
 before 1987 crash, 181, 182
 decline of, 273
 Great Depression, 163
 1987 stock market crash, 42
 over time, 45–46
Dow Jones Newswire, 184
Drug addiction, 278–279
Dutch tulipmania, 41–42, 52

E
Eals, Marion, 241
East German stock investments, 165–166,
 171
"The Economic Possibilities of Our
 Grandchildren" (Keynes), 66, 82,
 83
Economic growth:
 compared to stock revenues, 179–182
 consumer spending, 71, 72–74
 deficit spending, 69–70, 71, 77
 exported goods, 75–76
 Federal Reserve monetary policy,
 70–71
 government spending, 71–72, 76–77
 key to, 83–84
 longer-term trends, 77–79
 productivity of U.S. companies, 79–84
 savings rate, personal, 71, 73–74
Economic wealth, 82–83
Efficient market hypothesis, 38–40,
 47–48
 contradictions to, 49–50
 dogma of, 51–52
 luck of investors' performance, 50–51
 stock prices, 40
 winner and loser study, 48–49
Eisenhower, Dwight, 170

Elasticity, concept of, 205–206
EMC, 43, 54–55, 285
Emotional intelligence (EQ), 286–287
Emotion and investing:
    emotional mood swings, 175–176
    emotional response control, 58–60,
        243–246, 284–285
    self-control issues, 33–34, 259–262
    sentiment as predictor of future returns,
        45–46
Employment rates, 187–189
Envy, 275–277
Equity-risk premium, 139–140
Etoys, 56, 58, 246–247, 251
Euro, 119–120, 130–132
Exchange rates. *See* currency prices
Exported goods, 75–76

F
Fallows, James, 195
Favale, Vinnie, 28–29
Federal Reserve, 70–71, 103–105
Fed model, 171–174, 176–177
Fehr, Ernst, 100
Fei, 92–93
Ferrigno, Lou, 177
Fiat money, 93–94
Financial mast-strapping, 260–262
Financial news and information, 252–254
Financial plans, 285–286
Financial risk, 268. *See also* Low-risk
        investments
    amount of risk, choosing, 279–282
    productivity as cure, 273–275
    risk-reduction, 269–271, 282
    stocks and, 279–282
First Contact (movie), 94
Fisher, Irving, 153, 154
Fixed-rate loans, 110, 221–223, 271
Foley, Jan, 131
Fooled by Randomness (Taleb), 170,
        255
Foraging societies, 240–241
Ford, Gerald, 20, 86

Foreign investments, 134–135, 271
Foundation series, 271
Four new horsemen of the NASDAQ, 43
Freud, Anna, 21
Freud, Sigmund, 20, 21
Friedman, Milton, 87, 91, 101–102
Fuller, Russell, 51
Full Metal Jacket (movie), 238

G
Gage, Phineas, 24–25
Galbraith, John Kenneth, 176
Galbraith, Steve, 184
German economy:
    growth of, 75
    inflation, 96–97, 102, 106
German unemployment rate, 75
Gigerenzer, Gerd, 236–237
Glengarry Glen Ross (movie), 246–247
The Godfather: Part II, 55
"Goes to eleven," 156–157
Gold, 92
    dollar value linked to, 93–94
    investment in, 256–257
    prices, 54, 161–162
    return on investment, 171, 230
Goldilocks view of inflation, 97–100,
        108–109, 113
Goleman, Dan, 286–287
Gore, Al, 146
Government bonds. *See* Bonds
Government debt, 78–79, 126–128
    interest rates and, 146–149
    problems with, 127–130
    productivity and, 274–275
    projection of, 144–146, 276
    saving money and, 145
    social security fund and, 146
    trends in, 268
    U.S. economy and, 146–148
    U.S. overseas assets, 126
Government spending, 71–72, 76–77
The Graduate (movie), 229
The Great Crash (Galbraith), 176

Great Depression, 118, 163, 216
Greenspan, Alan, 42, 71, 106, 149,
    222
Gross, Bill, 273
Gross domestic product (GDP),
    146–148
Guth, Werner, 27

H
Hare, Brian, 233
Hawking, Stephen, 167–168
Helman, Bill, 184
Heuristics and Biases (Kahneman,
    Gilovich, and Griffin), 25
HIV problem, 17
Home equity, 216
Hoop Dreams (documentary), 164–165,
    168–169
Hormel Foods, 98–99
Housing loans, 128
"Housing Price Bubbles" (Krainer),
    209
*How to Profit from the Coming Real
    Estate Bust,* 203

I
Iliad, 13
Income growth, 73
Incredible Shrinking Man, 60
Individual irrationality, 14–15
    ancestral traits, 5–6, 234–237,
        240–241, 267
    conformity needs, 56–58, 283
    critical self-examination, 12–14
    emotional response control, 58–60,
        243–246
    environment and, 231, 237
    loss aversion, 29–30, 249–250
    mathematical calculations, 15–17
    overconfidence, 18–19
    understanding of, 56
Industrial Revolution, 66, 79
Inflation:
    in the 1970s, 85–86, 102–103

bonds and, 150, 151, 200, 201
causes of, 101–103
currency prices and, 121–122
deferred payment and, 96
defined, 95
deflation, 98–99, 106
effects of, 97
in Germany, 96–97, 102, 106
Goldilocks view of, 97–100, 108–109,
    113
hyperinflation, 96–97, 102
ideal rate of, 100
interest rates and, 150, 151
investment choices and, 200, 201
money illusion, 98–100
money supply and, 102–103,
    106–108
multiplication factor system, 96
predictions of, 105–106
protection against, 109–113
rates in U.S., 86–87
real estate and, 200, 201
seashell example of, 94–95
signs of building, 86–87
stocks and, 112–113, 185, 200, 201
wages and, 98–100
Influence (Cialdini), 21
Information technology revolution,
    79–80, 83–84, 272–273
Initial public offering (IPO), 246–247
Instinctual investors, 58–60, 244–245
Insurance companies, stock prices of,
    108–109
Interest, compound, 80–81
Interest rates:
    bonds and, 141–142, 143, 154–155
    borrowing money and, 158
    condition of, 78
    deficit spending, 77
    government debt and, 146–149
    inflation-adjusted, 211
    inflation and, 150, 151
    protecting investments from increases
        in, 157–158

Interest rates *(Continued)*:
    real estate and, 211–213
    saving money and, 158
    trends in, 268
In Triumph of the Optimists (Dimson,
    Marsh, and Staunton), 167
Investment choices. *See also* Profitable
    investing
    analysis of decisions, 19–20
    bonds (*see* Bonds)
    cash, 3
    conventional approaches to, 1–2, 10,
        159–164, 266
    currency prices and, 134–135
    foreign investments, 134–135
    mutual funds, 3
    rational thought and, 4–5
    real estate (*see* Real estate)
    stocks (*see* Stock(s))
    Treasury bonds (*see* Treasury bonds)
Invisible hand, 38
IPO (initial public offering), 246–247
I Really Didn't Say Everything I Said
    (Berra), 101
Irons, William, 235
Irrational Exuberance (Shiller), 42

J
Japanese economy, 66–67
    currency value, 133
    deflation, 98, 106
    growth of, 75–76
Japanese Nikkei, 251
The Jetsons, 47–48
Johnson, Ross, 16
Jones, Paul Tudor, II, 25–26, 28, 244–245,
    275
Jordan, Michael, 230
Jordan Rules, 230–231
Jubilee year, 97

K
Kahneman, Daniel:
    decision-making research, 4–5, 14–15
    Heuristics and Biases, 25

individual irrationality, 33
    loss aversion, 29–30, 249
    United Nations experiment, 253–254
Karate Kid (movie), 3–4, 7
Keller, Mark, 184
Kennedy, John F., 169
Keynes, John Maynard, 66, 81, 82, 96,
    129, 183, 273, 286
Kidney transplantation, 87–90
Kill the messenger tendency, 13
King Kong, 196
Korean War P.O.W.s, 21–22
Krainer, John, 209
Kumar, Subodh, 184
!Kung San, 239–240, 241, 242

L
Leahy, Dan, 95
Lee, Richard, 240, 241
Leeson, Nick, 30
Leno, Jay, 182
Leverage, 213–216
Linda-the-bank-teller question, 14–15,
    236
Liu, Ken, 184
Livermore, Jesse, 247
Lizard brain(s):
    ancestral traits, 5–6, 234–237,
        240–241, 267
    control of, 283, 286–287
    defined, 2
    environment and, 231, 237, 239–241
    financial blind spot of, 7, 55–56, 61,
        231, 237, 287
    history of term, 11–12
    influence on behavior, 23, 24
    interest rate overconfidence, 157
    patterns in random behavior, 30–33,
        238–239, 268
    role in financial decisions, 5–7, 10, 12,
        242–243
    self-control issues, 33–34
    stubbornness, 25–29
    testosterone levels, 28–29
Lo, Andrew, 60

Loans:
  adjustable rate mortgages, 216–219,
    221–223
  default on, 128–130
  fixed-rate loans, 110, 221–223,
    271
  housing loans, 128
Loan shark(s), 128
Lombardi, Vince, 79
Losers average losers, 248–250
Loss aversion, 29–30, 249–250
Low-risk investments:
  barriers to, 277–279
  as insurance, 276–277
  pain of, 275–277
  risk of, 271–275
  steps to, 270–271
  stress of, 275–276

M
MacBeth, 52
MacDonald, John, 23
Macroeconomics (Mankiw), 92
Malkiel, Burton, 40
Mandy (grandfather), 21
Mankiw, Gregory, 2, 92, 139, 142, 194,
    196, 199
"Man with the Golden Brain" (Daudet),
    125–126
Margin calls, 215–216
Market irrationality, 36–38
  bubbles and crashes (*see* Bubbles and
    crashes)
  debate on, 42
  examples of, 41–42
  1987 stock market crash, 42–44
  profiting from, 49–50, 51–53
  sentiment as predictor of future returns,
    45–49
Market(s):
  communist markets, 166
  condition of, 78, 279
  economic conditions and, 187–189
  efficient market hypothesis (*see* Effi-
    cient market hypothesis)

mean, defined, 35
mean, profiting from, 219, 230, 268,
    283–286
in other countries, 165–166, 168–169,
    170
rational, 35–36
trends in, 268
Market Wizards (Schwager), 25
Marx, Groucho, 215
Mast-strapping, 260–262
Mathematical calculations, 15–17
McGraw, Phil, 182
McGurk, Harry, 23
McGurk effect, 23–24
McManus, Tom, 184
Mean Genes (Burnham and Phelan), 16,
    17
Mean market(s):
  defined, 35
  profiting from, 219, 230, 268,
    283–286
Medewar, Sir Peter, 12
Melo, Fatima, 196, 197, 198, 214
Mental accounting, 255–257
Mexican economy, 124–125
Microsoft:
  analysis of, 171–173
  growth of, 175, 179, 183
  price to earnings ratio (P/E), 199
  value of dollar and, 186
The Mind's Past (Gazziniga), 22
Mini bar(s), 259–260
Minsky, Marvin, 20–21, 247
*A Monetary History of the United States,
    1867–1960* (Friedman and Schwarz),
    87
Money. *See also* Dollar(s)
  devaluation of, 119–120, 122–125
  fiat money, 93–94
  government control of, 93–94, 103–105
  inflation and supply of, 102–103,
    106–108
  mystery behind, 87
  storage options for, 155
  supply, growth of, 105, 107–108

Money forms:
cheese, 92
fei, 92–93
gold, 92
paper, 87, 91, 113
rice and grains, 92
seashells, 94–95, 102
Money illusion, 98–100
Monty Python cheese shop game, 34
Mortgage debt, 216. *See also* Loans
Motley Fool, 191, 250–251
Motorcycle purchase, 103–104
Motorcycle ride through game park,
224–225
Multiplication factor system, 96
Mutual funds, 3, 45

N
NASDAQ, 43
1987 stock market crash, 42–44, 181, 182,
217
Nixon, Richard, 93, 118
Nominal exchange rate, 121–122
No-red zone system, 262–264
Norfield, Tony, 131
Nortel, 59
Nuclear war, 169–170, 171

O
Object location memory, 241
Odean, Terrance, 47, 48, 245
The Odyssey, 260
Opportunity cost, 150–153
Oracle, 43
Organ-swapping arrangements, 88–90
Origin of Species (Darwin), 80
The Out of Towners (movie), 122
Overconfidence, 18–19

P
The Paper Chase, 163
Papua New Guinea, 94–95, 102
"The Past Explains the Present" (Tooby
and Cosmides), 235–236

Patterns in random behavior, 30–33,
238–239, 268
Paycheck security, 98–100, 188–189,
271
P/E. *See* Price to earnings ratio (P/E)
Personal debt, 271, 273–274
Personal savings rate, 71, 73–74
Pigeon experiment, 30–32
Pitch Black (movie), 6
Poker, 258–259
The Pope of Greenwich Village, 128
Popper, Karl, 52
Portfolio insurance, 217–218
Prechter, Robert, 273
Precious metal prices, 53–54
Predictions, making, 153–154
Prefrontal cortex, 11–12, 20, 21, 23–24,
34, 283
Pregnant women study, 58–59
Price to earnings ratio (P/E):
Cisco, 210
of houses or property, 199–202, 204
Microsoft, 199
S&P 500, 200
stocks, 19, 199
Treasury bonds, 200
Probability problems, 237
Productivity of U.S. companies:
business investment, 74–75
consumer spending, 72–74
economic growth, 79–84
economic wealth, 82–83
government debt and, 274–275
growth of, 80, 273–275, 276
idle capacity, 74–75
purchasers of, 71–77
Profet, Margie, 58
Profitable investing, 55–56, 268
aggregate financial position, 255–257
anticipating future events, 242–243
in bonds, 157–158
buy what is unloved, 53–55, 58
challenging conventional wisdom,
53–55, 279–282, 283–284

conservative investment position, 258–259
dollar-cost averaging, 250–252
emotional intelligence (EQ), 286–287
emotional response control, 58–60, 243–246, 284–285
financial reserve, maintaining a, 258–259
ignoring information, 252–254
key to, 230, 231, 283–286
loss aversion, 29–30, 249–250
low-risk investments, 270–271, 282
mast-strapping, 260–262
own a smaller house, 220–221
plan, sticking to a, 285–286
productivity and, 273–275, 276
real estate, 223–225
red zone, don't trade in, 262–264
self-control issues, 259–262
stocks, 189–192
tips, 246–248
trades, frequency of, 245–246, 248, 261–262
Profit growth, limits on, 177–180
Progenics Pharmaceuticals, 150, 274, 275
Psychohistory, 272
Purchasing power parity (PPP), 132

Q
Queen Elizabeth Park (Uganda), 224–225

R
A Random Walk down Wall Street (Malkiel), 40
Rational market(s), 35–36
Reagan, Ronald, 86
Reagan bonds, 143, 156
Real estate:
adjustable rate mortgages, 216–219, 221–223
buying behavior, 208–209
comparative advantage, 195–196
economic conditions and value of, 187–189

fixed-rate loans, 221–223
housing bubble, 203–210
housing prices, 194, 196–199, 204, 209–210, 223
inflation and, 200, 201
interest rates and, 211–213
investment characteristics of, 200–202
investment in, 193–196
leverage, 213–216, 223–224
local conditions and, 202–203
own a smaller house, 220–221, 271
P/E of houses or property, 199–202, 204
rental vacancy rate, 207–208
return on, 220–221, 223–225, 265–266
supply and demand, 205–207
taxes and, 200, 201
win-win outcome, 220–221
Real exchange rate, 121
Red zone, don't trade in, 262–264
Reminiscences of a Stock Operator, 247, 249
Rental rate(s), 200
Rental vacancy rate, 207–208
Repin, Dmitry, 60
Retirement, 90, 276
Revealed preference, 281
Ricardo, David, 194
RJR Nabisco, 16, 150–151
Roth, Al, 87–88, 90
Rothschild, Nathan Meyer, 253
Roulette wheel strategy, 238–239

S
S&P 500, 173, 200
Safety deposit box, 155
Samuelson, Paul, 194
Sanfey, Alan, 28
Saut, Jeffrey, 184
Saving money:
government debt and, 145
inflation effects on, 97

Saving money *(Continued)*:
  interest rates and, 158
  personal savings rate, 71, 73–74
Savings bonds I-series, 112, 270
Schwarz, Anna, 87
Schwarzenegger, Arnold, 76, 177
Science of irrationality, 2, 3–5. *See also*
  Individual irrationality
Seashells, 94–95, 102
Securities Act of 1934, 216
Self-control issues, 33–34, 259–262
Self-examination, critical, 12–14
Sentiment as predictor of future returns,
  45–49
Shakespeare in Love (movie), 190
Shiller, Robert, 42–43
Siegel, Jeremy, 40, 42–43, 160, 161–164,
  182, 190–191
Silverman, Irwin, 241
Silver prices, 53–54
The Simpsons, 144
Simultaneous exchange, 89–90
Skinner, B.F., 30–32, 277–278, 283–284
Slot machines, 48
Smith, Adam, 38
Smith, Vernon, 5
  bubbles and crashes, 44
  individual irrationality, 33
  supply and demand research, 38
  ultimatum game, 26, 27
Social isolation, 283
Social security fund, 71–72, 146
Society of Mind (Minsky), 20
Socratic method, 12–13
Soros, George, 133
Spin control, 255
Split-brain studies, 22–23
Squirrel(s), 155
Stampede(s), 36–38
Stern, Howard, 28–29
Stewart, Potter, 264
Stimulus-response behavior, 30–32,
  277–279, 283–284
Stock price(s):
  corporate profits and, 180–183

currency prices and, 185–186
efficient market hypothesis, 40
emotional mood swings, 175–176
number of shares, 20
price to earnings ratio (P/E), 19, 199
random component of, 32–33
slowdown in, 183
trends in, 268
valuation, fairness of, 174–177
Stock(s), 187–189
  analysis of, 171–174
  as average investments, 185–186
  buying on margin, 215–216
  commodity price change protection,
    109–110
  Fed model, 171–174, 176–177
  financial risk of, 279–282
  inflation and, 185, 200, 201
  as inflation or deflation protection,
    112–113
  investment characteristics of,
    200–202
  investment in, 1–3, 10, 159–164,
    189–192, 279
  love affair with, 189–191
  luck and, 170–171
  non-U.S. stocks, 134–135, 271
  optimistic view of, 46, 49, 174, 175,
    176–177, 183–185
  performance in other countries,
    165–166, 168–169, 170
  pessimistic view of, 45–46, 49,
    173–174, 176, 183–185
  portfolio insurance, 217–218
  reasons to own, 185–186
  return on, 161–164, 170–171, 186–189,
    265–266
  sentiment as predictor of future returns,
    45–49
  survivorship bias, 164–169
  tax deferment and, 186
  trades, frequency of, 245–246, 248,
    261–262
  U.S. economy, compared to, 179–182
  win-win outcome, 220

Stocks for the Long Run (Siegel), 40, 42, 160, 161–164, 182, 190–191
Stubbornness, 25–29
Subconscious, power of, 21–22
Summers, Larry, 100
Sun Microsystems, 42, 43, 180–181
Superstitious pigeons, 30–32
Supply and demand, 38, 205–207
Survivorship bias, 164–169
  analysis of, 167–169
  strong form of, 169–170
  weak form of, 168–169, 170
Swingers (movie), 281

T
A Tale of Two Cities (Dickens), 65–66
Taleb, Nassim Nicholas, 170, 255
Taxes:
  bonds and, 200, 201
  investment choices and, 200, 201
  real estate and, 200, 201
  social security taxes, 71–72
  stocks and, 186, 200, 201
Tecumseh, 51
Testosterone levels, 28–29
Thaler, Richard, 48–49, 51, 237, 255
This Is Spinal Tap, 156
Thurow, Lester, 68
Tip(s), 246–248
TIPS (Treasury Inflation Protected Securities), 111, 112, 270
Tobias, Andrew, 53–54, 55
Tobin, James, 144–145, 149
Tooby, John, 235–236
Top Gun (movie), 243–245
Toys R Us, 56, 58
Trades, frequency of, 245–246, 248, 261–262
Trahan, Francois, 184
Treasury bonds:
  Fed model, 171–172
  investment characteristics of, 200–202
  investment in, 58, 69–70
  monetary growth and, 108

price to earnings ratio (P/E), 200
  return on, 142–143, 175, 211–212
Treasury Inflation Protected Securities (TIPS), 111, 112, 270
Tulipmania, 41–42, 52
Tversky, Amos, 5, 14–15, 253–254
Tyran, Jean-Robert, 100

U
The Ultimate Weight Solution (McGraw), 182
Ultimate Frisbee, 257–258
Ultimatum game, 25–29
Unemployment rates, 78
United Nations experiment, 253–254
"An Unsolved Problem of Biology" (Medewar), 12
U.S. current account deficit, 116–117, 119, 125–127
U.S. dollars. *See* dollar(s)
U.S. economy:
  condition of, 68–69
  government debt and, 146–148
  growth of (*see* Economic growth)
U.S. Federal Reserve. *See* Federal Reserve
U.S. government. *See* government entries
U.S. overseas assets, 126
U.S savings bonds I-series, 112, 270
U.S. Treasury bonds. *See* Treasury bonds

V
Vitamin D supplements, 5
Volcker, Paul, 108

W
Wages, 98–100, 188–189, 271
Wall Street (movie), 253
Wal-Mart problem, 18, 19
Waterloo, battle of, 253
Waterworld (movie), 130
Wealth of U.S. families, 72–73, 109–113

Wedding toast, 152
Where are the Customers' Yachts (Schwed), 285
Whip Inflation Now (WIN), 86
Who Moved My Cheese (Johnson and Blanchard), 284
Wikipedia, 272
WIN. *See* Whip Inflation Now
Winner and loser study, 48–49
The Winner's Curse (Thaler), 25

Woods, Tiger, 13–14, 194
Wrangham, Richard, 103, 232

Y
Yap (Pacific island), 92–93
Yerkes Primate Center, 233

Z
Zambia inflation rate, 120–121
Zimbabwe inflation rate, 120–121